An Enquiry into the Nature and Causes of Poverty of Nations with Special Reference to Pakistan

Dr Tariq Riaz

To

My wife Shahin N Riaz

Who shares my passion for our birth country and whose
constant encouragement has helped in completing this book.

TABLE OF CONTENTS

PROLOGUE

This is winter of 2015 and I am on a visit to see my relatives in my birth country. I find here people restless, anxious and in a state of helplessness. Most of them live their lives on less than $2 a day.

The economy is in doldrum; unemployment is high, and almost 45% of young, age between 18 and 25, have no work. The electric supplies are off up to 16 hours a day. The gas trickle down the pipes in selected areas and the petrol pumps are shut as there is nothing to sell. The currency has hugely lost its value, and still, exports are not earning enough to pay for imports. In fact, the export earnings have been stagnant for the last 25 years because the export base is narrow, limited and shrinking. The industrial output has been stagnant, and its share of the GDP is on the decline. The energy shortages are killing the remaining industrial and agriculture processing units in the country. The majority of the population still depend on agriculture for a living. They are struggling to survive against the onslaught of energy shortages, increasing prices of agriculture input (i.e. fertilisers, pesticides, and water pumping) and ever-increasing inflation. The agriculture input and output prices are controlled to shift resources from agriculture to monopoly or semi-monopoly industries or commerce and then to foreign lands for safe keeping and to secure future for the rich and their partner in crime i.e. the political elite.

The country is devoid of any public services. Almost 85% of the population have no clean drinking water or sewage system. Almost 13% of the population practice open defecation that causes contamination of water and spread diseases. Millions of children have no schooling. The public health service is beyond a joke, and life security has no meaning. Human life is cheap here. The privatisation of violence and failure to provide public goods are a symptom of a failing State.

Pakistan Finance Ministers have gone begging to IMF 13 times over the last 25 years. Each time the country was granted expensive loans with attached conditions of structural reforms. The current Finance Minister, who is on record to accept money laundering acts, has been raising large foreign loans at high interest rates from the international lending agencies when interest rates are virtually zero in most of the western countries. The foreign loans mostly disappear without a trace under various Ponzi projects.

There is ever increasing 'gap' between the tax income and the national expenditures. Taxes are mostly indirect and collected from the poor. The rich and politically powerful do not pay any taxes. The national business organisations are on their last breath headed by politically appointed CEO's who are there to serve their masters interests. First, these organisations are turned into loss-making, then privatised and sold at nominal prices to the politician's partners or friends. After a short period, suddenly some of the privatised businesses become profitable; the others simply fold up and sold off as real estate to reap large profits.

There is no transparency and no accountability. The country seems to be surviving and escaping bankruptcy on foreign remittance of Pakistani working in different parts of the world. No one seems to have ever thought of using these remittances for productive purposes. There are endless stories of corruptions, stolen elections, crimes, and dysfunctional public institutions. The political parties are the personal property of few families and have no mass organisation. Their members are all feudal or new industrialists. The political workers or minor leaders have no courage or moral conviction to raise any voice against the owner of these parties. The political leaders not only control the parties they also control the vast areas of agriculture land and industries which are either monopolies or semi-monopolies. Some of the politicians have relatives in the civil service, judiciary, and armed services to provide them favours and receive favours in turn. The Politicians appoint and promote top positions and the appointees returns the favours and serve politicians interests.

The media is directly or indirectly owned by the ruling elite. A large number of TV channels show foreign shows, mindless films and dramas, and futile political discussions. There is no information or entertainment value anywhere. A few journalists who are intelligent and are not ready to sell their soul are doing their best to expose reality, but they are simply laughed at. The press is full of foreign copied stories and is devoid of any originality. The same can be said of all the experts who regularly appear on TV to flog their second rate borrowed ideas. In short, the ruling elites have become heavily focused on maintaining a monopoly on power; law and order institutions have become more advantageous to elites, and penalties for the general public have become more Draconian. The middle class has evaporated and the 'misery index' reflects on increasing rates of homicide, suicide, illness, homelessness, and drug abuse. There is a resurgence of fundamentalist religion, as once golden period stories are brought back to counter decay and decline. The sense of betrayal, desperation and despair has grown in the population. The effective reforms of the system seem impossible because the system is controlled by the corrupt.

I know corruption is only a symptom of poverty. It is legally and morally wrong, but except for two specific cases, it is not a factor in retarding economic growth or causing poverty. In most cases, corruption money is simply transferred from one account to another, and it has no impact on income or employment level. However, if corruption money ends up in conspicuous consumption or flies out of the country, in such cases, both investment and growth rates suffer. Similarly, election rigging and vote buying were a common practice among the rich countries such as UK and USA in the past when public life was quite corrupt. Unfortunately for Pakistan, most of its looted money is taken out of the country, which reduces national savings and investment and, in turn, retards economic development.

The prevailing political system is a British- style parliamentary democracy, which has become a mean of corruption and a way to fragment the society. The relation between economic development and democracy is quite complicated and in my view, democracy is not a causal factor in economic development. It may even have a negative effect on economic development in poor countries such as Pakistan. The Army has taken control of the defence and foreign affairs to fight against the terrorists and has set up courts to deliver quick justice and bring some stability. The civil administration is happy to relinquish responsibilities to the Army as it diverts attention from their poor performance and give them an opportunity to blame someone else for any failures. Both sides are happy, but the people of Pakistan have lost all hope for a better future. They know there will be no fair elections or accountability of the ruling elite'.

Besides poverty, Pakistan faces extreme inequality. At present eight large family businesses, namely Dawood, Saigol, Adamjee, Jalil, Colony, Habib, Nishat and Valika, own two-third of industrial assets, 80% of banking and 79% of insurance. The combined large businesses contribute 80% of GDP. Such inequality is harmful to economic development because surpluses are owned by few and do not show up in effective demand. In Pakistan, the rich take money out of the country and the level of savings and investment remains low or declines. The neoliberals claim that markets can deal with inequality through labour wages but in a country, with huge unemployment, the real wages never go up, and inequality keeps increasing. The rich do not pay taxes, and an ineffective State does not capture monopoly profits.

On cold dark days, I sit hoping, the sun will show its face and provide light and warmth to the decaying body of my birth country, and I start to think, a country which started with so much promise how come it has reached such a critical stage where her survival is at stake?

The poverty engulfs majority of people. The average Pakistani has a per capita income level of around 5% of the average American, and his life expectancy is at least 15 to 20 years less compared with an average American. Why is Pakistan so much poorer compared with the rich countries of the Europe or even Asia? Can she bridge this gap? Other Asian countries have become rich, and some have narrowed the poverty gap and raised the living standards of their citizen. Why has Pakistan failed?

Most Pakistani believes their country is rich in natural and human resources, but it has lost its way because of visionless and corrupt leadership. They explain their poverty by pointing out corruption, rigged political system, lack of education, law and order, accountability and justice. They believe Pakistan's economic problems stem from the way the political power is exercised and monopolised by a select narrow visionless ruling elites who put a priority on self-interest. Some academic economists sing the mantra of competition and globalisation and how it can overcome poverty. They all agree that Pakistan needs a change of direction. But they are not sure who will deliver that desired change? In the last few months of 2014, one political party was drawing huge crowds to their meetings. It is not a revolutionary or a leftist but a right of the centre party and is headed by a leader who is known, to be honest. His main message seems to be that political corruption is leading the country to destruction, and elections of 2013 were rigged. Therefore, the elected party has no mandate to rule the country. In December when the protests were getting serious, and there was a possibility that the government may fold under pressure, a major terrorist attack on a school completely changed the political scene in the country.

This study is about the differences in the poverty and riches of nations. It is about the differences in per capita incomes and living standards across the nations. Adam Smith published his classic work *'An Investigation into the Nature and Causes of the Wealth of Nations' in 1776*. It formalised economics as a subject and provided a formal explanation of the nature and causes of riches of nations. Smith observed that *'Consumption is the sole purpose of production.* James Mill (88) described consumption as the purpose behind economic activities consisting of production, exchange, and distribution. Thus, consumption is an ultimate criterion of economic success in the classical and the neoclassical economics. All pioneer thinkers of my subject such as Smith, Ricardo, Marx, Schumpeter, List, Veblen, Keynes, Hayek, and several contemporary economists have spent a lifetime to understand and explain the process of economic prosperity in order to improve the well-being of human race. The causes of prevailing economic conditions in various nations have been investigated to draw policy inferences. I believe it is important to know the hidden interconnections underlying the increasing prosperity of rich nations. How come some nation-states such as European and North American have achieved great prosperity whereas others such as Asian and African, have mostly remained poor? With information and communication revolution of late 20th century, the questions about the varying rate of development of the nation-states have taken a sharper edge, and voices have become louder against this disparity. The process of early human progression can provide an understanding of the fundamental process of economic growth. There is an obvious link between economic development and human welfare. The classical economists had established this link through the utility theory. This study makes an effort to provide an insight to the poverty problem and its relationship to human welfare.

If one is born in a poor country then fewer problems are more important or interesting than the rates at which development had proceeded in successive generations in different countries of the world. The differing rates of economic growth have led to inequality between people and across nations. The sea of unemployed semi-starved people makes you question this inequality across the globe.

I start this study by summarising the ideas of great economists and observe similarities and differences and how their ideas have matured in present-day theories and policies. I learn from historical ideas how the subject of the political economy got converted into a science of economics based on false human nature and unrealistic assumptions. Indeed, far-reaching claims have been made for the superiority of mainstream economics and its mathematical modelling and quantitative estimations. At present times, these claims are being subjected to critical reviews and revisions. The scope and validity of assumed human nature are found narrow and even inhuman. The far-reaching assumptions underlying the elegant mathematical models are unreal and lack any empirical support. The estimation methods are make believe methods. Can one define randomness with probability? If we do, then it is to recognise that probabilities do not exist without a specific system-context. Thus, the judgements are made on the basis of observations that are actually never made. Infinitely repeated trials or samplings never take place in the real world. It means it is not possible to show that the economic data does not satisfy all the conditions of the distribution of the deviations corresponding to a normal curve and therefore the statistical inferences used, lack sound foundations. Besides, all estimated models miss out some variables. The error term included in the estimation cannot be independent of missing variables or their combined effect. The mean value of error term cannot be assumed as zero. Thus, most of the results that economists present with their econometrics models depend to a substantial part on the use of mostly unfounded 'technical' assumptions.

History tells us that economic policies had not been based on mainstream economic theories in the economic development process of any rich country. The dominant neoclassical economic theories of free markets and free foreign trade which provide a framework for efficient allocation of resources have never been used as policies to achieve prosperity either in Smith time or later in history. This fact was known to a German economist, Von Justi in 1750, who had stated that *all countries that have been forced into raw materials production would come to understand that they are being kept poor intentionally.* He did not know that a British economist called Ricardo was going to challenge his observations with the theory of comparative cost advantage to promote free international trade. They claimed that the colonies had a comparative advantage in the production of raw materials and therefore it would be a grave mistake if they developed manufacturing capacities. Adam Smith had provided a market framework in 1776 and had argued that a natural harmony or equilibrium will come to prevail if the markets were given a free reign. Other classical economists contributed to the Smith work to complete the deductive model of market equilibrium. The neoclassical economists refined the classical thinking and turned free markets, free trade into a general equilibrium model and an accepted methodology.

After the collapse of Russian socialism in 1989, the free markets and free foreign trade policies were reinvented and imposed on the poor nations through the structural adjustment reforms of the international lending agencies. The collapse of socialism was famously coined as 'the End of History' by Fukuyama (34), a Japanese–American scholar. The neoliberals' paradigm has refined the neoclassical general equilibrium model to present it in precise policies such as free markets, free trade, free capital movements, deregulation, privatisation, democracy, and an independent central bank. They claim that adoption of their paradigm would ensure that poor countries will become rich.

The enforcement of these policies started a new phase of imperialism which claimed that the free markets, the free foreign trade will unleash forces that would level out any difference in wages among rich and poor countries and will result in economic progress and harmony in the world. But the implementation of the neoliberals' paradigm has proved brutal and harmful to the poor nations and their poverty has not ended.

I follow German and European economic traditions not to accept neoclassical or neoliberals' paradigm at its face value. The markets have inherent tendency not to achieve harmony or equilibrium and waiting for the markets to deliver economic growth could span over centuries. The state intervention in stagnating economies becomes essential to increase effective demand to deal with unemployment and poverty. The European nation-states had not favoured free markets or free trade policies in the aftermath of the industrial revolution or at the end of WWII. For economic development to happen, a particular form of long-term economic structure has to be constructed, matched by a political and social structure to break out of 'vicious circle' of poverty. The poor countries domestic policies (i.e. industrial, trade, and technology) either adopted in ignorance or imposed by others, have directly contributed to their poverty.

Plan of the Book

Part 1 looks at the early history of political economy and provides a brief description of human evolution and the constant struggle to improve living conditions or in other words economic development. Then a brief history of economic ideas is presented and a brief debate compares individualism and state role in economic development.

Part 2 defines some basic concepts such as economic development, productive capabilities and relationship between economic development and welfare. It looks at the process of structural transformation of the economy as economic development proceeds. The historical evidence of how rich achieved prosperity is detailed by looking the economic history of some rich countries.

Part 3 presents a summary of the Washington Consensus Policies based on the neoliberals ideology. These policies are subjected to a critical review to show defective reasoning and dark side effects for the poor countries. Under attach the neoliberals' have come up with new theories of poverty which are detailed and subjected to critical review.

Parts 4 provide details of the historical development of four Asian countries and compare their progress over time. Pakistan comes at the bottom of the class. The successful countries policies and practices are compared to identify causes of Pakistan failures.

Part 5 venture into normative economic and suggests policies and measures which, if implemented, could transform Pakistan economy and turn Jinnah's dream of a welfare state into a reality.

Book's readership

This book is intended for those who are interested in poverty problem and wish to do something. It is also intended for the thinking People of Pakistan who care about their country's future and future of their coming generations. It might interest politicians, policy makers and administrative classes and can help academics to understand why mainstream economics has become obsolete and why they need to explore new ideas.

PART 1

HUMAN EVOLUTION AND ECONOMIC IDEAS PROGRESSION

The past becomes present and the present, in turn, shapes future. The current conditions reflect on the interactions of existing capabilities and factors which were shaped by the past decisions and policies. Therefore, the present conditions provide an incomplete view and to gain real insight one must comprehend the past as well.

A careful study of the causes and nature of poverty of nations can open up possibilities for the future prosperity. Economic activities have become more complex with time. Each society had to construct specific institutions to deal with increasing complexity of economic life. The economic transformation process of rich societies can provide an insight into the process of economic development. The past economists have investigated the nature and causes of the wealth of the nations by observing the changing economic conditions. I summarise some of the pioneer contributions to gain insight into the process of economic growth. I also highlight their differences.

1

HUMAN SOCIAL PROGRESSION

Modern economic life represents a complex system which consists of millions of activities and decisions. It is facilitated by numerous institutions that interact to perform production, exchange, and distribution functions to satisfy human consumption. The individuals' decisions and activities take place within markets regulated by a state and its constitution. The markets which define human living cannot function without an enforcement mechanism and even then, fail to provide public goods. The consumption, production and work organisation chart out the material standard of livings that reflect the differences between rich and poor countries.

It has taken thousands of years to reach current stage of economic development. Over time, humans learned by doing and adopted new institutions and technologies to make them more productive. In the pre-historic period, they evolved as hunter-gatherers, man and woman bondage began, and union of families took place. Some families started to live together, discovered benefits of exchange and settled in village-like settlements.

Agriculture followed hunting and spread rapidly across plains and along rivers everywhere. The animals and crops became domesticated. The irrigation system got developed and the settlements started to grow. The material and social life moved on from custom and traditions to a powerful new force of a central

"

authority. The King States political and social organisation lasted a long time and covered the period up to the 18th century. The King owned everything and his interests took priority over everyone. He appointed loyal friends as governors, allocating them different parts of his country to rule in his name and provide him with revenue and soldiers. The ordinary people cultivated land to feed them and pay an agreed amount to the Landlord, who had the ownership rights at the pleasure of the King. Throughout the rule command period, the land rights rested with the King. When he died, his authority passed on to his son or a successor.

The agriculture-based societies established institutions such as law and order, property rights, public marketplaces, depository institutions, risk covering and business organisation. These institutions, in turn, contributed to the co-evolution of economic, social and political systems and encouraged technological inventions and innovations. During this phase of evolution, the decisions such as what, how and for whom to produce were custom and society based and could hardly be called decisions. The life followed a set pattern; different crops grew in different seasons and the amount produced was affected by the weather conditions. The distribution was as per the society's rules. At some stage in time, the distinction between public and private goods started to emerge. The provisions of law and order, defence and highways sharpen this distinction. The power structure in the rule-command period was coined as feudalism. The King and his loyal friends i.e. feudal owned land and became rent seekers. The distribution of property was the result of conquest and violence, which gave an advantage to some and purposely fostered inequalities and prevented fairness.

Islam spread over vast areas of the world between 609 and 1700. The Islamic ruler considered himself as a shadow of God on earth to provide justice and security to the citizen. The new religion provided a strong code of human conduct and clearly defined rights and obligations of individuals and the authority regarding property, inheritance, trade and religious matters. It stressed the importance of social justice ensuring the security of life and equality in law. The individual rights and social justice created a favourable economic environment where individual efforts got rewarded and in consequence, the societies became prosperous. The Islamic State collected taxes from the rich to distribute these to the poor, a first step in the creation of a welfare state. The prosperity allowed people to develop arts, literature, and sciences. The Islamic State in Spain had established a fair harmonious and prosperous society through cotton looms industry where knowledge and arts took root. The society had a social harmony where all faith co-existed with mutual tolerance and respect. The Islamic and Jewish scholars excelled in extending new thinking and knowledge. Spain and India under Islamic rule were probably the richest countries in the world. The Islamic influence and knowledge had reached parts of Italy, Spain and France.

China had established and managed a great empire and civilisation starting in 200BC. She had already made some progress in developing technology and agriculture techniques around 1700. Adam Smith observed that '*China has been long one of the richest, and one of most fertile, best cultivated, most industrious and most populous countries in the world.*' The Chinese and Islamic civilisations had existed before the European civilisation and had developed individuals' rights, business rules, knowledge, arts, architecture, and literature.

In the 14th century, Islamic scholars had been advancing knowledge in various branches of arts and sciences. Early on they had completed the translation of Greek, Chinese and Indian knowledge into Arabic which had provided a base for further research and thinking in every field of knowledge. An Arab Scholar by the name of Ibn Khaldun had started to re-write history by questioning the previous methodology of transmitting knowledge without question. He analysed the credibility of the sources prior to accepting the narrative. He suggested that the narrative must be checked in the context of 'Human Social Organisation' to determine the truth from falsehood. Daniel Olah (106a) has described the contributions of Ibn Khaldum to the subject of economics. He states that it is misleading to identify the roots of modern economic theories with either mercantilists, Physiocrats or Adam Smith. Ibn Khaldun was probably the pioneer who looked at the human social organisation as a yardstick to analyse society and laid down a scientific method to make a distinction between true and fake historical information. He identified 'division of labour' as a basis for a civilised society. It is 'division of labour' which creates surplus value and economic growth. Khaldun used carvings of doors and chairs to illustrate the division of labour and creation of surplus value. The division of labour occurs in both manufacturing and professions. The markets had evolved to accommodate division of labour and the forces of supply and demand operate in a simple didactic manner similar to Marshall Market's interaction. The market price includes wages, profit and taxes. A good produced without any labour input carried a zero price. Thus, Khaldun had laid down foundations for the labour theory of values. He made a distinction between labour and land markets and built a dynamic growth model in which the State plays a crucial role by collecting taxes and spending money on infrastructure and human welfare. The full details of Khaldun (59a) can be found in his work.

It seems that the English and European economists have formed economic history to justify their originality. Khaldun ideas are found in Smith, List, Marx, Ricardo work which appeared in the 19th century. Khaldun public spending is just like Keynes public spending and his ideas were written almost five centuries before the subject of economics is supposed to take shape.

Up to 1500, Europe was fragment into small non-significant states, but human development had been taking place, and some kingdoms with flexible borders had come into existence. The European States had started to emerge from their laggard status around 1700. It was a slow process which displaced medieval traditions and feudal commands and then laid down the foundations for a new Europe. The word 'State' in its modern sense was used by Machiavelli in the 16th century in Europe. Frederick II of Prussia was the first European ruler to make a distinction between the monarch and the State. He called himself the first servant of the State which conveyed the message that the State was even more important than the monarch. *The State is not there for the monarchy; the monarch is there to serve the State.'* This concept represented a fundamental break with the past and established the State as a separate entity to be served by the governing authority which acts as an agent to promote the interests of the people over and above his own interests.

An important part of European story relates to how it emulated technology, knowledge, and skills from other civilisations. This learning process started in the Norman King Frank time. All sort of knowledge was translated from Arabic sources into European languages.

The installation of the first blast-furnace in Britain in 1709 and the inventions of flying shuttle, spinning frame and the steam engine led to large-scale production and laid foundations of the industrial revolution in Britain, which eventually changed the economic, political, social and technological structure of all European societies. The farm workers became the industrial worker who started to earn weekly wages. The labour force worked in large mills which led to factory laws to harmonise the workplace. The business organisations got transformed from sole traders to partnerships and the limited liability Corporations. The large-scale production for exchange was an institutional innovation which happened as individuals became more autonomous and family oriented. The exchange process encouraged manufacturing of tools and other technical innovations and started personal decision-making with consequences. The resource ownership started to change. The individuals became the owner of machines and factories. The accumulated heritage grew, as each generation added its quota of new knowledge, factories, tools and techniques to the wealth of the past. The increase in knowledge and technology increased human productivity with astonishing rapidity.

This co-evolution of economic, social and political institutions over the recorded history has shaped resource allocation issue. The effectiveness of economic system determines the well-being of the State and its citizen and has been of great interest. Is there a particular economic system that is more efficient in allocating resources, produces maximum output and welfare of people living under that system? In spite of various claims about the superiority of the free market mechanism to achieve optimal allocation and efficiency, no one has bought the idea that markets could replace a central authority. The State enforces laws and implements policies within which markets function, and it has a scope which encompasses the welfare of society.

The transformation of economies led to new economic, social and political order which required a new mode of classification and was dubbed as capitalism. The means of organising material life came to be known as an economy, and its explanation system is called economics which explains the forces of change that have taken the humanity to the present stage of existence.

The excesses of the capitalism, in turn, gave birth to the ideas of the socialist system which overcame the abuses of property ownership and excessive power of a class. The poverty became a topic of debate among thinking classes. Some thought poor were to remain poor as it was their lot. The other thought poverty was essential to increase a nation's wealth. A few considered it evil. Strong nations with naval power had colonised vast areas of the world and had subjugated people to serve their interests. International trade had brought its rules for harmonious conduct.

The changing economic structure brought prosperity in different parts of Europe. City-states such as Venice and Amsterdam were first to achieve relative prosperity for their citizens through manufacturing and international trade. These cities had become meeting places for culture and goods exchange. Dutch invented a double entry accounting system to facilitate trade. France, Germany, England and USA, all followed city states, to develop industries and trade for prosperity.

The Mercantilists movement in Europe thought that national power was the natural object of economic endeavour. The gold possession made the nations strong and it could be acquired through trade. Thomas Hobbes (50), an English philosopher, agreed with the Mercantilists on national power concept and stated that a strong State is essential to prevent human beings falling into solitary, poor, nasty, brutish and short lives. The foreign trade became a central source of acquiring gold and a nation's prosperity. Thomas Munn, another Englishman, developed a theory of trade balance. In 1621, he published his book, '*A Discourse of Trade, from England unto East Indies.*' He suggested that national gold reserves indicate the power of a nation-state and a nation increases its wealth and treasure by trade.

Mercantilist thinking (from 16th to the 18th century) promoted strong public role in the regulation of national economy, protectionist trade policy, strong naval power, manufacturing, and closed colonial markets. They claimed that favourable trade (i.e. excess of exports over imports) brings gold and silver to the country, maintains high employment and larger output at home. Thames Munn of England, Jean Baptiste Colbert of France and Antonio Serra of Italy, are representative figures of this ideology. Jean-Baptiste Colbert, born in 1619, transformed French economy and turned France into one of the strongest nations in Europe. He adopted protectionist trade policy, developed national infrastructure, shipping, and naval force. He promoted public industrialisation, modernised taxation system, imported skilled manpower and encouraged arts and sciences in the country. Antonio Serra (125) published his book called *'Breve Trattato'* in 1613. He observed that Naples economy was based on natural resources whereas Venice economy was based on manufacturing as it had no natural resources of its own. Naples had remained poor where Venice had prospered. He concluded that Venetians had become rich because they had harnessed the power of increasing returns and scale economies in manufacturing activities. He goes on to say that to achieve development it was essential to have many activities with increasing returns which are the main ingredient of economic development. Serra's suggested enlightened policies to promote increasing returns activities, a division of labour and state ban on landed class to play any role in economic or political affairs. A Genovesi, another Italian, revived the concept of increasing returns to create wealth around 1740 and claimed that free *trade does not exist in any country on earth and especially in the countries that best understand the trade.*

The physiocrats, European thinkers, were concerned about human welfare around 1764 and suggested free trade can increase human welfare. This view was in clear contrast to the Mercantilism. Quesnay published his ideas titled as *'Physiocratie, du Gouvernement le plus avant-ageux au Genre Humain'* in 1765. He compared circulation of income in society to the circulation of blood in a human body *and suggested* that wealth of a nation depends on the production of goods and services. He promoted free trade in goods and ideas to increase economic prosperity. Quesnay's second book *'Despotism in China'* published in 1769, had promoted the role of the State in economic development by citing how the benevolent ruler, supported and advised by the intellectuals, could use 'reason-based policies' to promote the welfare of people. He had praised Chinese rulers for the Chinese prosperity. He differed from English economist on freedom of choice based on self-interest.

The practice of political economy had evolved by the second millennium, and it was the State authority that exercised it. The officials and administrators wrote about public administration, agriculture, manufactures, commerce, and navigation issues but did not present any analysis. They focused on how each job created wealth and how individuals went on to gain at the expense of each other. This tradition of experience based economics goes back to Tudor policy of trade protection and industrial development in England. Other European countries started to practise similar policies such as Italy around 1588-1613, France around 1597-1651 and Germany around 1684. The Economists time had arrived.

2

PROGRESSION OF ECONOMIC IDEAS

The Classical Analysis

The industrial revolution transformed the British economy and created a new social and political structure. Her national output, at the time, consisted of only two types of goods (i.e. agriculture and manufactured). The landowning aristocracy governed but an urban manufacturing society had started to emerge and to claim political participation. The industrial transformation was restructuring economic and social relationships. The observation on changing production and distribution of output laid down the foundations for the subject of political economy in Britain. The investment level and distribution of income could significantly affect economic growth. In observing politico-economic changing conditions, the classical economists claimed to have discovered a new scientific knowledge with indispensable laws for human improvement. Their observations were based on logical deduction to ensure maximisation of national physical output, consumption and well-being. Their allocation rules maximised national output **and** their utility theory explained how individual choices could lead to maximum output, consumption and human happiness. The allocation framework also provided a way to distribute national output. Their emphasis on individual choice as the final criterion of happiness was unique in the history of social philosophy, but it did not deny the utility of paternalism which might become necessary from time to time.

All classical economists are towering figures. Adam Smith and his 'invisible hand' remains the most celebrated economist of all times. Ricardo's theories of rent and comparative cost advantage have dominated economic thinking ever since. Malthus dismal science has survived over time. The theory of population growth and contributions to the law of diminishing returns has remained a part of economics. Hume and Bentham utility theory provided objectivity to the classical thinking. Mill refined utility theory and then went on to discuss liberty, individualism and democracy

Adam Smith (1723-1790)

Adam Smith's book *'The Theory of Moral Sentiments'* had discussed moral approbation and disapproval. He formalised the subject of economics in his second book *'The Nature and Causes of the Wealth of* Nation' in 1776. He observed that man is selfish but capable of forming a moral judgement and an impartial observer to assess the merits of a case. Humans have a sense of right and wrong, follow established norms enforced by punishment and are interested in their reputation as much as their monetary income. Humans respond primarily to their immediate concerns, but their preferences could not be collapsed into a single generic concept of self-interest. He did not say *'the man was entirely self-interested'*. This observation of human nature has played a pivotal role in the development of economic ideas.

Smith extended 'doctrine of natural law' to economics by arguing that *'nature has provided a set of rules of justice and morality, which possess an authority superior to commands of human sovereigns, and customary legal and moral regulations. His doctrine of natural law* laid down a rationale for freedom of choice for consumers and producers to allocate their resources in impersonal markets to maximise their profit or satisfaction. Given a minimum state intervention (i.e. law and order and essential public services), the object of economic activity (*maximum happiness*) would be served by a system of spontaneous cooperation between consumers and producers in the marketplace. The consumers would be free to buy what gives them most happiness or satisfaction and the producers would be free to use their labour and property to produce goods and services which in their judgement would bring them the maximum reward in money or satisfaction. The impersonal mechanism of the markets would harmonise divergent interests and *individuals' seeking their gain would be led by an invisible hand to promote an end (i.e. maximum welfare of society) which was not a part of their intention.* The application of such a just legal system will create a harmonious, beneficial economic order. He drew an inference that freedom of choice in the marketplace should be free of obstacles to achieve spontaneous cooperation and efficiency. Hume and Bentham both rejected Smith idea of natural laws. They claimed all laws and rights are man-made.

Smith's second profound borrowed idea is *'division of labour'* and how it increases the efficacy of the production system and economic growth. The 'division of labour' or specialisation provides production time savings, helps in inventing better and more efficient machines and increases labour dexterity and productivity which drives and accelerates economic growth. The capital accumulation and size of the market, however, put limits on the division of labour and specialisation. Smith's trade theory follows physiocrats universal doctrine of laissez-faire. The exchange takes place when both parties benefit from it and free trade maximises the benefits of exchange by extending markets for a nation and humanity.

Smith uses two factors (i.e. capital and labour) to explain economic growth. The capital accumulation leads to more businesses, higher demand and higher wages for labour. Labour creates value in production which depends on human skills and quality of machines used in the production process. The capital accumulation and the size of the market open up the possibilities for the division of labour which leads to an increase in labour productivity and economic growth. The universal free trade expands the scope and size of the markets for the prosperity greater of a nation. The increased prosperity, in turn, increases population which widen the market and increases national savings and greater national wealth. The external economies create efficiencies through interdependence and complementarity of various sectors of the economy. When one sector grows, it stimulates other sectors not only by increasing demands but also by decreasing costs. The population growth rate can be a limiting factor to the economic growth. The first limit comes from the wages, an increase in population can reduce wage rate, reduce national demand and the level of output. The relative bargaining strengths of the workers and the Capitalists determine wage rates. The employers have all the advantage to keep wages at the subsistence level. However, when capital accumulation is increasing rapidly, it increases labour demand and wage rates which encourage population growth and that in time reduces wage rate back to subsistence level. The difference between the rate of capital accumulation and the rate of the population growth affects wage rate, profit share and economic development. The profits, the share of the capitalist in national income, decline with an increase in capital accumulation and an increase in wage rates. At the start, the limited capital stock and large labour supplies push up profit rate, but an increase in the rate of capital accumulation increases wage rate and reduces the profit share in national output. A high rate of accumulation keeps wage rates at a high level. Finally, as the population grows, the capital stock becomes very large, and economy attains, *'that full complement of riches which by nature of its soil and climate, and its situation in other countries, allow it to acquire'*. At that stage, capital accumulation slackens, wage rates decline, and the economy becomes stationary. The process of capital accumulation and economic development ceases. But the rents levels stay at a higher level compared with the earlier stages of development. Smith seems to imply that landlords greatly benefit from growth in national product.

Smith's development process is a gradual, self-perpetuating and driven by the capital accumulation of profit-seeking capitalists and limited by the population growth rate. In a growing economy, the prices of industrial goods fall and the prices of agriculture goods rise. When capital accumulation stops in a stationary economy, the profit and wage rates usually fall but the rent level remains high. Thus, landlords benefit at the expense of labour and the capitalist.

Thomas Robert Malthus (1766-1834)

Malthus book *entitled 'Principles of Population as it Affects the Future Improvements of Society'* **was** published in 1798. It explained that food intake and sexual urges are natural requirements of humans and given sufficient food, humans tend to double in numbers in 20 years. The land cannot be multiplied in the same way although it can be added laboriously and slowly. Hence, a fixed amount of land and a growing population would result in diminishing productivity and individuals would end up constantly living at subsistence level and would suffer from malnourishment. The gap between population growth and the food supplies had to be bridged to avoid hunger and starvation. The preventative measures such as a voluntary limitation on population can avoid food shortages but when these fail, the positive checks in the form of infanticide, war, famine, disease and above all poverty will control population to close the mismatch between availability of land resources and the level of population. Any technological breakthrough in agriculture will only produce a temporary relief and in the long-run, the population will outgrow the food growth.

Malthus like Smith, explains economic growth and income distribution by the size and growth rate of the population against the availability of other resources. He opposed income or wealth redistribution as it simply increases population growth rate and damages the social and political structure of England. Similarly, any increase in manufacturing output compared with an increase in agriculture output will attract labour supplies to the manufacturing and increase agriculture wages and output prices. Any increase in wage rates will increase population and labour supplies to lower wage rates back to the subsistence level. The rate of economic growth could not exceed the rate of population growth and, therefore, humanity was doomed.

Adam Smith and Ricardo's accept population theory in their work but observed that free trade could generate high profits for long periods and alleviate the pressure on scarce resources and checks on the population growth. Similarly, some voluntary means were quite feasible such as education and birth control measures to slow down the population growth rate. Given these possibilities, the population should not become a hurdle in the development process. Malthus did not foresee technological changes, birth control measures popularity, declining fertility rates and large migration and hence his dire prediction has not materialised. Could it be that the unforeseen factors have merely postponed the widening gap between population and food supplies? Malthus prognoses are almost correct in the context of most poor countries.

Malthus published another book titled *'Principles of Political Economy'* in 1820 and used it to rebuttal Ricardo' theory of rent and raised two serious issues i.e. glut of goods in the marketplace and excessive savings level. The excessive savings in the economy was later on adopted by Keynes to develop his idea of effective demand. But Say's law *'supply creates its demand'* provided a suitable counter argument against market glut at the time.

Malthus dismal science has stayed in human conscience ever since and in most recent times the neoliberals have used population levels as a cause of poverty. His theory on the glut of goods was correct, but this glut was dumped on the colonial markets to destroy potential industrialisation.

David Ricardo (1772-1823)

Ricardo's book *'Principles of Political Economy and Taxation'* appeared in 1817. It claimed that agriculture was the most important sector of the economy and it was subject to the laws of diminishing returns which could cause shortages of food for an expanding population.

Ricardo's universe contains undifferentiated workers, capitalists, and Landlords. The workers are addicted to *'the delights of domestic society'*, that increases their number with every rise in wage rates and forces them to live on subsistence living. The capitalists direct the production of goods and services (hires land, labour, buy machines and raw materials), and plays a key role in the economy. But their entire purpose on earth is to accumulate profit for reinvestment and hire more workers. *They perform two functions: seek profit opportunities and initiate the process of economic development.* By continually searching for the most profitable employment opportunities for their capital, they equalise the rates of profit by fixing wages among various branches of manufacturing and agriculture leading to an efficient allocation of resources at any particular period. The process of economic development gets underway when the capitalists reinvest their profits income to increase the rate of capital accumulation which ignites a series of reactions that result in the growth of national income. The workers work to earn a wage, capitalists run the show and earn his profit but landlords benefit from the power of the soil and his income i.e. rent is not controlled either by competition or by the power of the population. When population and output grows, the land becomes relatively scarce, and its price i.e. rent rises. Thus, landlords are a unique beneficiary in the organisation of the society. The term rent has special meanings it is not the payment for the use of land but the difference in the productivity of an existing Farm compared with the marginal farm. The economic surplus is defined as the difference between gross revenue and net revenue. Where Gross Revenue is the market value of the final goods produced during a particular period, and the net revenue is the value of goods needed just to sustain the labour force that produces that output. It is this economic surplus that is re-invested to drive economic development. Once profits decline the economic surplus disappears and economic growth ceases. Thus, income distribution plays a crucial role in the development process. Only capitalists save and without them, development will cease.

Ricardo's extended Adam Smith labour theory of value in explaining price determination. ' *the ratios at which reproducible commodities exchange for each other, in the long run, and in a purely competitive market, depend on the comparative quantities of labour increased in producing them.'* Labour is the sole provider of value, and its work hours determine the cost of production. Ricardo might have been aware of theory's many shortcomings such as the assumed quality of labour input, lack of factors substitution, the durability of capital employed in different production processes, and constant money prices of goods with constant labour requirement. In spite of this awareness, he used labour theory of value to compare exchange relationships among commodities that were physically dissimilar and formulated the comparative cost theory of universal trade. Ricardo economy always reached equilibrium as income is fully spent in buying goods and services.

According to Ricardo's theory of income distribution landlords claim a growing share of national income in a growing economy and given the share of rent in the output, the labour and capital are both paid as per their marginal contribution to the marginal output. But wages play a more active role as Profit rate depends on the level of wage rate and nothing else. The wage rate is equal to the size of wage fund divided by the number of workers. The natural price of labour is equal to money price that is necessary to sustain a real subsistence wage rate. The rate of profit tends to fall as the population grows and capital accumulates. The positive profit rates lead to an increase in capital accumulation and an increase in wage fund and wage rate. The higher wages are spent on agriculture and non-agriculture goods. This additional effective demand will impact in an uneven way. Over time population demon takes over, and more babies are born, this, in turn, shifts more spending on agriculture goods and increases their prices but increased agriculture revenue goes into higher rent. Whereas manufacturing output and wages increase but non-agriculture goods prices will fall. Thus, profit share will fall in national income. As long as the rate of capital accumulation remains higher than the rate of population growth, the wage rates will remain above the subsistence level. The economy, however, becomes stationary when the rate of profit does not cover the cost involved in additional capital formation. In such a state capital accumulation and population both cease to grow. Ricardo's economy is dynamic and explains how major variables of capital accumulation, population, profits, wages, and rent interact in a dynamic framework. *The international trade and the capitalist desire to accumulate and reinvest are two drivers of economic growth.* Ricardo rejects the distribution of income and wealth by taxation as it encourages overpopulation and discourages incentives which can slow down economic growth.

Ricardo's main contributions such as the laws of rent have been accepted and applied to fixed supply factors. The theory of comparative cost advantage has become the main component of the free market economy and the capitalist system. He analysed international trade emphasising differences in the capabilities of different countries and explained how Portugal and Britain could have a mutually beneficial trade. He used two countries, two goods single period restrictive model with the following unrealistic assumptions:

a. Both countries are operating at full employment

b. Goods cost consists of only labour input hours

c. All production takes place under constant returns to scale

d. Perfect mobility of factors of production within each country and across the borders

e. Total specialisation of production

f. There are no trade costs

g. No barriers to trade such as tariffs and perfect knowledge, so the trading parties are aware of the cheapest source of desired goods internationally.

Under these simplifying assumptions, he allows Portugal to be more efficient in the production of both cloth and wine and shows that the trade can still be beneficial to both countries if each country was to specialise in the production of a good where it was relatively more efficient. None of the assumptions are satisfied if one looks at the operations of international trade across nations. Most importantly the intrinsic capabilities or comparative advantages and specialisations are the results of past national decisions. The changing employment conditions change the input costs of output and the time factor changes the capabilities of the countries.

Frank Graham (45) has shown how Ricardo's trade theory enslave countries into their starting comparative advantage. An industrial country would keep its specialisation in the production of manufactured products, and the agriculture country would keep producing agriculture goods, and this scheme of things will make the industrial country rich and an agricultural country a poor one forever. E S Reinert has explained that the comparative advantage in raw materials production can lead to a spiral of diminishing returns and rising cost of production. Whereas the comparative advantage in manufacturing ends up with increasing returns, higher productivity and falling average unit costs in production. He makes an additional point that the comparative advantage theory uses labour theory of value as a sole source of production cost. The world trade is, therefore, a bartering of the labour hours which are identical and have no skills or other characteristics. However, uses of capital and knowledge in the production have serious implications for the production cost.

Ricardo prediction that land rent would remain high for an extended period proved wrong. The value of *farmland* has declined with the shrinking share of agriculture in the national income. However, Ricardo's insight into the price of a scarce factor has remained valid, and it would be a serious mistake to neglect its importance. But his free trade theory has been heavily criticised as it does not lead to prosperity or equality for all trading nations. It simply reduces freedom of choice for poor countries for investing. The short-term gains from trade cannot offset the cost of long-run capabilities loss.

Jeremy Bentham (1748-1832)

Bentham was born in 1748 and trained as a lawyer but devoted his life to moral and political philosophy. He is best known as the founding father of an ethical system called utilitarianism although Hume had already discussed its core idea in his work. Utilitarianism is only a subset of a broader theory called consequentialism, which explains that an action is declared morally right or wrong by its consequences alone and nothing else.

Bentham (9) explains that two sovereign forces of pain and pleasure motivate and direct mankind. A man is busy in arranging his life to maximise his pleasure from the consumption of goods and services. Utility measures individual's happiness which he aims to maximise. The maximisation of utility function provides a rationale to the market-based allocation system. Bentham, however, is not promoting selfishness; to him, everyone's happiness is to count equally, and society should aim to promote the greatest happiness of the greatest numbers, which should act as a criterion for morals, legislation, and all economic activities. He devised a formula to determine a morally right course of action in any given circumstances. The intensity and duration of particular pleasures and pains played a role in the calculation of happiness. A long and intense pleasure counts more than a short and feeble one. The total sum of pleasures can be affected by the intensity and duration, of pleasure or pain and how many people experience it. Mill differed from Bentham when he made a distinction between higher and lower level of pleasures.

Bentham considered equality or maintaining equality as a disaster and regarded proposals for the abolition of property as an action against security, incentives, and hurdle to prosperity. He rejects the idea of public goods as it goes against the concept of utility and yet provides a surprisingly long list of duties that a state needs to perform for a stable society. Utility theory has been the most dominant, ethical justice theory for a long time and it has dominated the traditional welfare and public policy economics. The critics reject the idea that human value pleasure above everything else in life. They point out that people have certain rights such as the right to live and the right to justice which may take preference over pleasure seeking. There are further issues related to the interpersonal comparison of utility and difficulties of formulating a common utility function.

John Stuart Mill (1806-1873)

Mill was a most remarkable man who ever lived. By the age of 11, he had already mastered Greek, Latin, philosophy, Geometry, Algebra, Calculus, and Roman History. By the age of 13, he had learned logic and work of Hobbes and had completed a survey of political economy. In 1848, he published two long volumes of *'The Principles of Political Economy'*. Where he reviewed Adam Smith, Ricardo and Malthus work and stated that the production was the central issue and not the distribution. He claimed that the economic laws of production were nature based, and human behaviour guided by self- interest was as impersonal and as absolute as the laws of the expansion of gases or the interaction of chemical substances. Mill's work was probably the first effort to place economics on foundation comparable to physics.

Mill, not only rejected distribution as the central issue, he stated that the existing distribution of property was unfair and the protection of 'property rights' was over stressed. In his words *'the distribution of property is based on conquest and violence and not by industry. The laws of property have never yet conformed to the principles on which the justification of private property rests. They have not held the balance fairly between human beings, but have heaped impediments upon some, to give an advantage to others; they have purposely fostered inequalities and prevented all from starting fair in the race. That all should indeed start on perfectly equal terms is inconsistent with any laws of private property'*. On the distribution of production, he states that *once the output has been produced humanity individually or collectively can do with it as they please'*. The distribution of income and wealth, therefore, depended on the laws and customs of society which were determined by the opinions and feelings of the ruling portion of the society at any time. The implication was simple, that if a society wished, it could change the distribution according to its wishes. The market allocation is biassed and perpetuates a class interest.

Mill's idea of separating production from distribution came under attack from both conservatives and radicals. They stated that distribution would change the production process and output level. Thus, production and distribution cannot be separated and especially in a feudal society where the mode of payment is usually embedded in the mode of production. In spite of this criticism, it would be wrong to undermine Mill's insight as present-day Scandinavian welfare economies are a direct expression of Mill's vision.

Mill differed with other classical economists on the gains from the universal free trade. He explained the manner in which demand and supply conditions determine the equilibrium ratio of the exchange of one country's commodities for another's. A larger output of raw material causes prices to decline which put raw material producers in great disadvantage and the benefits of trade mostly end up with manufacturing nations. Mill argued a case for protection of 'infant industry' as such: '*The only case in which, on mere principles of political economy, protecting duties can be defended, is when they are imposed temporarily (especially in a young and rising nation) in hopes of neutralising a foreign industry. The superiority of one country over another in a branch of production often arises only from having begun sooner. There may be no inherent advantage on one part or disadvantage on another, but only a present superiority of acquired skill and experience. A protecting duty continued for a reasonable time, might sometimes be the least convenient mode in which the nation can tax itself for support of such an experiment. But it is essential that the protection should confine to cases in which there is good ground of assurance that the industry, which it fosters will after a time be able to dispense with it; nor should the domestic producers ever be allowed to expect that it will continue beyond the time necessary for a fair trial of what they are capable of accomplishing*'.

Mill's model of a capitalist system aims to maximise output to maximise human welfare. In his system profit, can get eroded by rising wages but wages do not decline from population pressure as the workers can educate and change their reproductive instincts. He rejects Malthus and Ricardo's idea of population changes resulting from wage changes and the persistence of subsistence wages at the stationary stage of economic activities. He also rejects the idea of universal gains resulting from the international trade and makes a case for the protection of 'infant industries'. To him, the society through higher output and just distribution can end up at a higher stage of economic development where humanity would spend its energies in the pursuit of liberty and justice and not just economic growth. Mill's greatest work is in the field of politics and is entitled 'On Liberty'. His other work consists of *'Logic' 'Contribution on Representative Government' and 'Utilitarianism'*.

Classical Economic Policies

The classical economists had claimed to establish a body knowledge of political economy which was logical and their predictions were based on comprehensive analysis of the complete economic system. The producers and consumers led by self-interest interact in the neutral marketplace to produce and consume optimal output, harmony and well- being. From this theoretical framework, they drew inferences for economic policies such as free competitive markets, free internal and cross-border trade, free movement of factors of production, minimum taxes and limited state role in the management of the economy. They opposed redistribution of income and wealth by the state as it distorted the allocation process. There were differences among the classical on different components of their system. Others objected to the unrealistic assumption underlying their logic such as human nature, freedom of choice, perfect markets, state role, failures of the markets to provide public goods and exploitative nature of free trade. The critics also claimed that the individuals' preferences could not be summed up into a single generic function and emphasis on individual choice as the final judge of happiness makes individualism, a mean and an end. The classical economist's persistent failure to recognise 'uncertainty' in the economy which leaves very little scope for successful maximisation. It was said that the classical had fixed the end (i.e. maximum human happiness) and constructed their scientific apparatus around it which made it difficult to argue against it. In summary, history has been kind to the classical thinking, and most of the present-day economics, one way or other, still hinges on their work.

Marxian Analysis

Karl Marx (1818-1883) observed economic transformation process in Europe. The ongoing industrialisation had led to a vast exodus of population from rural areas to urban slums. The increased agriculture productivity had reduced demand for the labour force. The expanding industrial sector was opening new employment opportunities. The increase in population and rural migration had created urban slums. The misery of human life in slums helped Marx and Engels to write the Communist Manifesto in 1848. It **contained** a philosophy of history which predicted the collapse of capitalism and the victory of the communist revolution by stating that the history follows certain discoverable laws and produces ever-changing, ever-new forms of social organisation and it is the social existence of man that determines his consciousness and evolutionary causes of all social life.

Marx's key to human behaviour rests with the 'mode of production' and each 'mode of production' has an appropriate social system with a set of property relations and society's class structure of a dominant, directing class and a toiling oppressed class. The economic and social (super) structures are bonded together by laws, supervised by a government and inspired by religion and philosophy. The thoughts and ideas of the superstructure are the product of environment but may aim to change that environment. Evolution in society occurs mainly from changes in the material forces of production (i.e., the elements that constitute the mode of production) or some independent forces. this can transform society from a feudal to a capitalist society with new social classes of merchants and proletariat and with conflicting interests and desire to change existing distribution of wealth. The economic transformation rapidly transforms the entire 'superstructure' of noneconomic activities, ideas, and institutions. A hunting community could not have the superstructure created by the complex industrial society. All history follows this cycle of progressive revolution. Marx and Engels discern four social systems in history: (1) primitive communism, (2) ancient slave state, (3) feudalism and (4) capitalism.

Marx sets himself to discover the intrinsic tendencies of the capitalistic system and its inner laws of motion in *Das Kapital* published in four volumes in 1883, 1885, 1894 and 1910. The work presents a model of an ideal capitalist system and shows how it will collapse in time. Then it goes on to predict that the actual capitalist system will follow the same path of destruction as outlined in his model.

Marx's theory of surplus-value provides the framework on which he hangs his analysis of economic development under capitalism. His system consists of two classes, the capitalists, owner of all means of production and the workers, who have only their labour to sell. The ideal model of capitalism has no unions or special advantages. Every commodity sells at its exact proper price that is its value which is the amount of labour input embedded in it. Marx has borrowed this idea from the classical economists who might have borrowed it from Ibn Khaldun. If it takes twice the amount of labour to produce X compared with product Y, then X will sell for twice the price of Y. The labour input can be direct or indirect. The labour used in making a machine is an indirect labour. But no matter what its form, everything is eventually reducible to labour input. Capitalist strives to accumulate capital and wealth in a competitive environment, and labour force enters the market to sell labour at the highest wage and is no longer a slave to reproductive urges. If everything is priced at its exact labour input value, then profit cannot exist. However, a worker takes up employment at subsistence wage to survive. *The working hours of contracted employment are mostly higher than hours required to provide him subsistence wage and in consequence, he creates more value in production then he takes out as a wage. The difference is surplus or profit.* The capitalist can gain surplus (profit) by selling the product at its true labour value, and his monopoly over means of production ensures him surplus or profit. He can simply refuse to provide work unless there is a discrepancy between actual work and subsistence wage hours.

The competition among Capitalist and their desire to accumulate push wages up reducing profit level. Adam Smith and Ricardo at this juncture had assumed that wages would fall with rising population. But Marx like Mill rules out this possibility. He says that Capitalist will introduce labour saving machines and create surplus unemployed labour (industrial reserve army) that would bring wages back to the subsistence level. But by doing so, he has substituted non-productive factor for a productive one because he had paid the full value of labour gone in making that machine. He can only gain from the unpaid hours of labour working time. Thus, the substitution of labour saving machines will result in reducing his profit base. The competition put further pressure on profit level which gets smaller and smaller. With increasing unemployment, effective demand declines and goods remain unsold, this results in some firms going bankrupt. The new situation, however, create new opportunities, the unemployed workers accept lower subsistence wage; the dumped machines get sold at a fraction of their true value, and the surplus value reappears in the marketplace. Each boom creates its bust and in each bust some larger firms take over smaller firms and become a bigger industrial monster which eventually goes down, leaving bigger wreckage. The system breaks down and leads to the creation of a classless society without property ownership.

Marx ideal model assumes that technological improvements happen at a rapid speed. Whereas Ricardo had assumed that technological changes were fairly insignificant. Marx's perceives that the enticement of ever-improving technology will lead the capitalist class to its eventual demise. Technology has a strong tendency to improve the quantity and quality of machines in operations leading to higher capital-man ratio, higher labour productivity and a surplus valve which in turn generate higher savings and higher capital accumulation. The introduction of efficient machine lowers unit cost and gives a temporary advantage to the pioneer capitalist and an opportunity to gain extra profits before his competitors introduce latest and most productive technology in their production operations. Thus, each capitalist tries to get the jump on his competitors or, failing this, introduces new machinery merely to hold his relative position in the industry. Marx assumes that the aim of each capitalist is to *accumulate*. Which allows him to predict an apocalyptic end to capitalism; either the rate of return on capital would steadily diminish, or capitalist's share of national income would increase indefinitely and, in either case, no stable socioeconomic or political order was possible.

Marx theory of development combines many parts. The labour works for the capitalists who exploit them by the centralization of capital. The increasing inequality of income and wealth leads to revolt by the working-class helped by production organisation, education, and unity of interests. The centralization of capital and the socialisation of labour ultimately reach a point where they become incompatible and during one such crisis the final revolution or overthrow of capitalism is likely to take place.

Marx makes a distinction between two types of business cycles, i.e., short-term and long- term. The long–term analysis contains surplus labour, lower profit, and concentration of capital. The maximisation of surplus value (profit) increases power, control, and living standards of the capitalist. The profit and capital accumulation have two-way correlations. With constant technology, the combination of expanding capital accumulation and labour force can lead to greater profitability and the rising labour demand can increase wages which can cut down both profit and capital accumulation and creates surplus labour. The wages, in the long run, do not fall and are maintained at a level which supports the existing population levels and even encourages population growth.

With improving technology, the expanding capital accumulation increases labour productivity, profit and further capital accumulation. The capitalist can expand surplus value (profit) by introducing labour-saving machines. But there are inbuilt forces which offset this advantage. When all capitalists in an industry, introduce new technology, the price of the product declines to reflect the smaller labour input. But if one capitalist introduces new technology before others, he can increase labour productivity and profit without causing a price fall, since his output is only a small fraction of total market production. Other capitalists will follow but some of them will go bankrupt or taken over. The higher concentration of capital will reduce the number of capitalists and the technological advance will produce a surplus army of labour substituted by machines. The excessive labour supplies put downward pressures on the wage rates. The size of surplus value increases but the rate of profit may decline because of vigorous competition. The number of capitalists will reduce further to provide stability, but this stability can vanish if decreasing profits result in reducing capital accumulation itself. The eventual stagnation can endanger the existence of the capitalism.

The short-term business cycles are caused by falling rates of profit, underconsumption, and disproportionality of production lines. At full employment, any rise in wages will reduce profit and slackens capital accumulation which starts stagnation process. The speculative ventures pursued to avoid the fall in profit rate hasten decline and once a crisis gets going, it can destroy the credit system and the confidence in the economy. Marx contends that the consuming power of the capitalist class is restricted by the 'tendency to accumulate' surplus value. The larger accumulation increases the size of working class which drives wage rates to near subsistence level. This situation creates a contradiction between larger productive power and a narrow consumption base. The resulting overproduction manifests itself in periodic crises and economic stagnation and the disproportionality of production result from the errors and blunders on the part of capitalists in estimating the market conditions. Poor information can create surpluses and shortages that can precipitate general crises.

Marx and his followers highlight the vicious nature of international capitalism by stating that early colonial expansion played a major role in the development of the capitalist system. *'the discovery of gold and silver in America, enslavement and entombment in mines of the aboriginal population, the beginning of the conquest and looting of the East Indies, the turning of Africa into a warren for the commercial hunting of black-skins.' Such exploitation* led to primitive accumulation and expansion of markets for the colonists surplus manufacturing. The 'universal trade' provided opportunities to the colonial capitalists to take advantage of the larger markets for their manufactured goods, cheaper raw materials and foodstuff. The control over trade forcefully imposed, benefited the so-called mother countries, which controlled expanded markets. The concentration and centralization of capital gradually eliminated most areas of free competition and at that stage imperialism emerged allowing division of the world among international trusts and division of territories among great capitalist powers. This enabled the export of capital to backwards areas where profits were high to maintain the vitality of the Capitalism and avoid stagnation. The capital move to the poor countries led to an increase in differences in the rate of development of world economies instead of decreasing them'. The contradictions of the capitalist system started to emerge. After the world domination, rich countries turned on each other to solve their economic problems by extending their spheres of influence. The wars among rich nations were fought to dominate and to exploit resources. At the same time, class conflict grew and nationalism increased.

It is not difficult to see the appeal of the Marxian process of economic development. Marx does not see markets as a self-correcting mechanism, and his view of the capitalist system differs from the classical. Smith saw the capitalist climb upward into the future. Ricardo saw the upward climb of the capitalist being halted by the climbing Landlords rent. Mills saw future assuring as the society could distribute its products as it wished regardless of the classical economic laws. Marx did not buy Mill assurance because he saw the State as an organ of capitalist ruling elites. Marx did not agree with Say's 'law' that supply creates own demand, and did not have to wrestle with the principle of diminishing returns. Marx promoted the universal welfare and collective ownership of resources and a central authority to allocate national resources to avoid wastage, to achieve efficiency and provide for each according to his needs. He explained the causal relation between the economic structure and socio-political structure of the society. If one was to accept this linkage then it is easy to claim that the present- day imposition of the western superstructure of the political and legal framework on poor agrarian nations is misplaced. The free foreign trade can turn into a source of exploitation. The technically advanced countries can destroy all local productive capacity by dumping or cheaper goods. The free flow of capital destroys financial stability of poor.

Marx view of history has been criticised being simple, lacking past influences, being a rigid cycle of change, and a two-class society that does not match the complex real world. The theory of increasing labour misery and inequality was dampened down in the last quarter of the 20th century but has re-emerged in the aftermath of financial crises in 2007. Marx had predicted that capitalist system has a propensity to the crisis. The crisis results from the greed and need of the capitalist to grow. The formation of giant corporations eliminates small-scale craftsmen, artisans, and export capital to poorer areas to destroy local industries and competition. The system leads to wars to redraw new boundary lines. Most of Marx predictions except for the collapse of the system have come true. His explanation of business cycles and especially the role of effective demand are unsatisfactory. But the theory of imperialism is being played out at present. The globalisation, enforcement of free trade and free capital flow, the constant ongoing proxy wars conducted in various parts of the world by imperial powers makes his predictions a reality.

The Neoclassical Economics

Around 1870, just about 100 hundred years after the publication of Adam Smith's '*The Wealth of Nations...,*' European nations had prospered. Each had vast colonial markets at their disposal. The technology advances had opened up opportunities that were previously hard to imagine. Real wages had risen well beyond the subsistence level. The profit rates were high, and the rent did not constitute a major share of the national income. The fear of stagnation had disappeared, and the long-term growth was expected to continue well into the future because the economies were nowhere near the full employment. The problems of economic development had faded away. The classical economists' concerns regarding population explosion, diminishing returns, subsistence wage rates and capital formation had become minor issues with emerging economic prosperity. The link between the distribution of income and size of saving in the economy got de-linked, as wages were no longer at subsistence level. Economic development depended on capital stock, technology and labour force. The independent variables were exogenously determined which could be increased and substituted with each other in the production process. The development process was a slow, gradual, harmonious process which could continue without restriction into future. The inventions and innovations were slow, gradual and autonomous. Therefore, the economy automatic mechanism could sort out unemployment and stagnation problems. The neoclassical economists with their assumptions of individual rationality, utility maximisation and supply and demand tools continued to explore and refine economic relations. They kept general equilibrium framework and used a variety of ad hoc modifications reflecting on seemingly empirical regularities to show how both individual behaviour and markets depart from the optimal situation. However, they kept uncertainty at bay. So, economic development would be sorted out once the resource allocation efficiency was achieved.

A perfectly competitive equilibrium would achieve allocation efficiency. The deductive reasoning did not need any empirical proof. With given factors supplies, it was possible to show, that under perfectly competitive market, if the market forces allocated resources, the level of national output would be greater compared with any alternative allocation scheme. International trade mainly extended markets and the free trade based on the comparative cost would benefit both parties. The capital transfer did not create any serious balance of payment difficulties as net difference between imports and exports were rectified by the long-run capital movements. The development of utility theory by Jeremy Bentham and its refinement by Mill had opened the way for greater mathematical elegance to general equilibrium model. Leon Walras took over the task to provide a mathematical representation of general equilibrium which could provide a mathematical demonstration of the invisible hand. He succeeded in providing a mathematical proof of this possibility, but only by making a lot of unrealistic assumptions.

Francis Ysidro Edgeworth (1845-1926)

Francis Ysidro Edgeworth published a book entitled *'Mathematical Physics'* in 1881. He translated economic relations into mathematics and by doing so he opened up a way for economics to delink itself from the political economy and declare it a science. The mathematical formulation provided a neat precision and exactness; however, such precision was achieved at the cost of reality and simplicity, and underlying assumptions which had no relation to the real world.

Edgeworth borrowed utility theory from Bentham and formulated his model assuming individuals as utility maximisers. He believed that aggregate human actions do tend to show some statistical regularity and the constrained maximisation problem could be solved using differential calculus. Under perfect markets, each utility maximiser and the society would achieve the highest amount of utility that could be achieved with given amount of resources. His mathematical formulation was so neat and beguiling that its success was immediate. Edgeworth had brushed away problems posed by human nature, interpersonal comparison, uncertainty, the initial distribution of income and wealth, and the imperfection of the marketplace. He stated that these would be taken care of in the long-run. Edgeworth and Walras's work commanded enormous prestige because it represented the idea that economics can be comparable to the science of classical physics.

A new school of mathematical economics emerged within no time. Von Thunen (158) of Germany developed a formula to determine just wage of labour. Leon Walras of France showed how a mathematical model would work out exact prices that would clear the markets of any shortages or surpluses. W Stanley Jevons of Manchester University explained how the humans struggle for existence is '*mere a calculus of pain and pleasure.*' His theory was pure mathematics, and it ignored every aspect of human life that was not suited to the precision of mathematics. Since then numerous economists have indulged in modelling economic relations within the framework of the market's equilibrium. The idea of market equilibrium took a central place, and it described directions of markets movement when random decisions of utility maximisers interact in time and space. This tradition of the mathematical disposition of economic has become the dominant way to deal and develop economic ideas since 1881.

Alfred Marshall (1842-1924) and Others

Marshall published his book entitled '*Principles of Economics*' in 1890. He was primarily interested in self-adjusting, self-correcting nature of the economy. He combined mathematical precision with a discursive style and homely examples to explain economic concepts. His greatest insight to economics lies in his repeated attention to the importance of time in the equilibrium process. *The* slow, gradual adjustment process allowed him to justify his partial equilibrium analysis. Marshall (76) observed '*Nature does not willingly take a jump...is especially applicable to economic development.*' In Marshall words, ''*While the part which nature plays in production shows a tendency to diminishing returns, the part which man plays shows a tendency to increasing returns*'', which cancel each other out and the economy operates under constant returns to scale.

Marshall pointed out that the meaning of equilibrium changes with the time scale. The short-run equilibrium was reached by changes in prices with fixed quantities of goods and services. Therefore, the price indicated the utility of goods reflected in its demand. In the long-run, the supply of goods can change with changing demand, the cost of production becomes important and forces of supply and demand interact to determine the price.

In dealing with short-term business cycles, Marshall looks at the economic life of individuals and explains how prices are determined. By doing so he is explaining the behaviour of a group of individuals, each seeking to maximise his or her utility. But he ignores the social order of power and obedience that provide a structure to all stratified societies. Economic causes do not operate in a socioeconomic vacuum and have to be set in a contextual structure to be able to operate. His main contribution rests with time-related market equilibrium. In the second half of 19th century, the imperialism and colonialism had changed the face of earth planet. The neoclassical simply ignores the fate of poor countries and colonial people, and their economics is mainly related to rich countries.

Since Marshell, there have been numerous neoclassical economists who have essentially refined the subject using rigorous mathematical tools or have applied mainstream subject to various applications. The essence of Neoclassical economics focuses on a deductive methodology without any evidence to justify its relevance. A number of new schools have been formed such as monetarism, supply-siders and neo-Keynesian. Almost all of them have relied on mathematics to make economics a science.

Deductive models and methods are hopelessly disconnected from reality. These cannot predict, explain or understand real-world economic systems. The real world does not conform to the closed-system structure of the neoclassical models which tend to function as substitutes for empirical evidence. A gadget is just a gadget and even silly simple models like IS-LM cannot help us in working out the fundamental issues of modern economies. Even brilliantly complicated models such as calibrated DSGE or RBC are no help in dealing with the real issues of the modern economies. These models assume that macroeconomic aggregates are caused by imaginary shocks, instead of actions that people take. This is what is implied in real business cycle model (RBC) by Kydland and Prescott (47). The critics doubt about the value of so-called calibration work of Lucas, Prescott, Sargent and Kydlandn, which plug consumer choice model into an empirically concordant aggregate model which does not have any justification. Human behaviour is based on conditional expectation based the assumption of the world being stationary but unanticipated events occur which cannot be predicted. This makes prediction impossible. The calibration ignores error probabilities (future probabilities will be different than the past) and provides no way to assess the reliability of inference. How useful is such an exercise in futility? Lucas and co have turned rational expectation into an irrefutable proposition like a religious conviction which needs no testing or challenge. Romer (129a) criticism is truly remarkable on the subject. He believes *that reducing macroeconomics to Walrasian general equilibrium is like committing a murder*. Leontief, in a recent blog, states that 'uncritical enthusiasm for mathematical formulation tends often to conceal the ephemeral substantive content of the argument behind the formidable front of algebraic signs. The attention is on step by step derivation of its formal properties. By the time it comes to interpretation of the substantive conclusions, the assumptions on which the model has been based are easily forgotten. But it is precisely the empirical validity of these assumptions on which the usefulness of the entire exercise depends'.

The neoclassical theory is based on a false conception of human nature. Humans are not entirely self-interested. They have a sense of right and wrong. They are interested in reputation as much as their monetary income. The single assumption of self-regarding preferences banishes a large fraction of real-world preferences from the magical mathematical kingdom. Neoclassical man can think like Einstein, store more memory than computers and exercise the willpower beyond human capability. He is a rational thinker and acts in his own self-interest at all times, never learning from or considering others. People do not behave the same way. Their decisions reflect sensitivity to both the average outcome and variation around the average. But neoclassical economists use only average expected cardinal value but not its distribution.

Milton Friedman in 1970 mounted an attack on Keynesian economics by declaring that government policies to maintain full employment were misguided and opened a way for the market-fundamentalist revolution. This revolution was based on intellectual fallacies such as markets are always rational and efficient; that central bank's main concern was inflation and not unemployment of financial stability; that the fiscal policy should balance the budget and forget about economic growth. These fallacies were blown away by the financial crisis of 2007.

The neoclassical approach to economic development tends to minimise the significance of changes in political conditions, habits and customs of society, individuals' tastes and level of human capital in the development process. Economic activities are not influenced by the social and political structures of the society and yet take place within the social, economic and political framework of a society interacting with other societies. The social life by its very nature is eco-political and as economics aims to maximise human happiness which shapes human destiny and diminishes destructive forces of greed and social indifference, therefore, it cannot be separated from the social, political structure of society. Human habits, customs, culture and motivation are formed and change over time with changing production systems. Economics deals with ever changing and subtle forces of human nature and is nothing like physical sciences; which the neoclassical economists have spent all their mental energies to turn it.

According to neoclassical economists, the long-run development problem can be resolved by increasing independent variables such as labour, capital, and technology. The capitalistic seeking profit will ensure that there is a continuous increase in capital and new technology to increase prosperity for all. The assumption of the slow, gradual development process assumes the existence of an economic environment of certainty that creates stable prices, interest rates and practice of rational calculation. The free market forces provide a framework for eventual full employment general equilibrium of maximum output and social harmony. Mostly economy is not at full employment, but any intervention by the state would have adverse implications for the economy.

The mathematical formulation of general equilibrium model had shifted the central concern of economics to market equilibrium, and 'political economy' was turned into economics. The growth process became slow, gradual, harmonious and everlasting march towards long-run equilibrium. There is a need to ask questions whether the equilibrium or the markets at rest depict any reality or fundamental reality of any social universe or system. Adam Smith, Ricardo, Mill and Marx, all had believed that the central force (self-interest) of an economic system had an inbuilt tendency towards some sort of balance. The psychological force of greed has come under attack as a motivating force in recent times. The greed can bring about destruction and not harmony. The financial crisis of 2007 had pushed the economies to the destruction and not harmonious growth. None of the noble prize winners saw this crisis coming. Most were blind even to the possibility of such a catastrophic collapse. In modern times currencies are totally based on fiat and a state cannot run out of money. Spending is the prime mover in stagnation and budget deficits are not a major problem. The money multiplier assumes that the central bank controls the money supply by setting the required reserve ratio but this one big fallacy. In the real-world bank's first, extend credits and then look for reserves. At a deep fundamental level, the supply of money is endogenous. The mainstream monetary economic belongs to a dustbin.

European thinkers were not impressed with the classical framework of markets equilibrium or by the elegant mathematical world of neoclassical that had no relation or relevance to the real world or impacted on the policy makers and their policies. The policy makers had continued to practice restrictive international trade and strong state policies. Henry George, an American, in 1879, had claimed in his work entitled *'progress and poverty'* that *'the political economy has been degraded, shackled, gagged and her truths have been distorted, and protests about wrong have been turned into an endorsement of injustice. The new economics of mathematical models of equilibrium has blinded itself to see what had been clearly laid out, the remedy to the endemic poverty. Mathematical models based on simplistic assumptions and devoid of reality are hardly fit to unlock these dilemmas. There are paradoxes of the public and private interests and their potential collision, the feasibility of automatic mechanism of market forces to correct its failures and suppliers of public goods. More importantly, can the market forces automatically prevent the perverted interests of the political structure it has created? The answer is a resounding no.'*

In summary, neoclassical mathematical economic models have very little relation to the real world but content with proving things about the imaginary world. Empirical evidence plays hardly any role whereas models largely function as substitutes for empirical evidence. To them, mathematical deductive modelling is the only scientific activity worthy of pursuing.

John Maynard Keynes (1883-1962)

JM Keynes was born in 1883, became a Cambridge University **don**, and probably an unrivalled economic thinker of all times. His first book was on *mathematical probability*, and Bertrand Russell declared it impossible to praise too highly. His second book *'Indian Currency and Finance'* appeared in 1913 and led to a membership of Royal Commission on Indian Currency problems in 1916.

At the end of WW1, disillusioned with the peace treaty, he expressed his views in a treaty titled '*The Economic Consequences of Peace*' in October 1919, which proposed re-industrialization of Germany to achieve prosperity and long-term peace. He was opposed by France that wanted a complete destruction of Germany through the acquisition of territory and penalties. The Dawes plan, to which Keynes had contributed, appeared in 1924, to repair the harm done by the 1919 treaty. It provides Keynes insight into the economic development process of nations. He recommends *Mercantilism to promote industrialisation* in defeated nations because without increasing returns activities, they would have no chance to grow and if they remained poor there would be a price which Europe would have to pay in the form of disharmony, war and destruction.

Time has moved on and the WW1 had become history. The world had already forgotten that millions of lives were lost for economic gains. The USA had become new leader and super power of the world. It is now 1929, and the world economies (especially the rich economies) are in free fall. In two months of October and November, the American financial markets have lost almost 80% of their value. The spectres of unemployment are haunting nations. The dream of ending poverty has gone in the smoke and along with it the automatic adjustment model of the market economy. The inequality of the income distribution in rich countries had created an ugly picture. The depression seemed endless. Keynes had discussed trade cycles problem in his treatise on money in 1933. He had observed that national income is a flow of goods and services and not a static stock of wealth. The income flows from one person to another. Each time we buy we transfer a part of our income to someone else and every bit of our income (be it wage, rent, interest, or profit) comes from someone else purchases. The economy can be vitalized from our buying and selling. Our spending habits are fairly consistent with other habits. A part of our income is spent consistently on consumption goods and a part becomes saving. The saving part is either directly invested in securities or ends up with businesses via banks to be invested. In each case, the saving enters into circulation and turns up as someone income. However, if the saving part of our income does not get spent and remains hoarded; it reduces the flow of income and results in a cumulative fall in everyone's money income. The flow reduces as less and less of aggregate saving is returned to the circular flow and the economy goes into depression. A thrifty society always saves a part of its income but the businesses may or may not wish to invest this amount. *The saving does not turn into investment automatically.* The investment only takes place when there is profit-making opportunities and uncertainty about future is low. When businesses confidence is low and internal cash flows limited, the businesses are unlikely to invest. The un-invested aggregate saving can lead to a decline in the national income. The same result will occur if the country decides to hoard and not invest it. The difference in the magnitude of aggregate saving and investment is the result of the businesses and individuals' decisions which have repercussion for the national income stream. The classical and neoclassical economists had claimed that saving and investment difference goes through an automatic correction through the flexibility of interest rate i.e. the cost of saving and investment. Keynes said that the automatic correction fails at times when the interest rates are extremely low or even zero or businesses are pessimistic about the future. The great depression of 1929 witnessed this breakdown, and the financial crisis of 2007 has witnessed another such breakdown.

Keynes masterwork that has changed the world forever and has led to a new major branch of economics (i.e. Macroeconomics) appeared as '*The General Theory of Employment, Interest, and Money*' in 1936. Keynes explains that classical automatic correction does not work in a stagnating economy and blows away the myth by stating that *'economy was like an elevator that was going up or down or could be just standing at the base.'* The economy could remain stagnant at base indefinitely. Could cheap money (resulting in zero interest rate) not solve the problem? The answer was no then and it is no now. Depression will dry up personal saving as well as the demand for consumption goods. The cheap money supply by the central bank would not solve the problem as businesses will not find profitable opportunities to invest. The animal spirit gets dampened down or goes missing altogether. Here we have an economy which is stagnant and in equilibrium with unemployed labour and closed factories. There will be no full employment equilibrium of mathematical economists which reflects on the paradox of poverty amidst plenty. But the stagnant economy can have contracting investment resulting from the uncertainty that would lead to further decline. *Keynes declares we can deal with the problem, by the deliberate undertaking of government spending and cutting taxes to stimulate the economy. If cheap money did not encourage investment, the higher consumption expenditures will surely increase effective demand for goods and services and will provide further incentives for the investment to take place.* Keynes believes that over the business cycle life, the State must act as a counterweight to the behaviour of the private sector and should engage in deficit spending during the economic downturn and aim for a budget surplus during an economic boom. Keynes policy worked all right, but it was ideologically upsetting to others. However, he has come back to haunt his critics. The USA had adopted Keynesian policies in the aftermath of 'dot.com' bubble, during budget deficits periods of 2003 and 2004 and again in the aftermath of the financial meltdown in 2007.

Keynes accepts Individual and state as two separate entities which can differ in rational behaviour. For instance, in a contracting economy, firms cut wages when the demand for products fall and labour force becomes fearful of job security. An individual acting prudently will reduce spending which will cut aggregate effective demand, thus, increasing the possibility of bankruptcies and redundancies. Whereas a state responsible for the management of the economy should increase spending to counter the tendency of the private sector and increase aggregate effective demand to expand economy and employment opportunities. Keynes suggests that public policies can deal with the problems of unemployment and inflation. In doing so, he rejects neoclassical economics idea of an automatic adjustment process in the economy by stating *'we are all dead in the long run.'*

Keynes policy recommendations of the State role contain his thinking on long run economic development. He accepts existing social and political structures of the society and recommends that national policy should be used to safeguard against stagnating economy and resulting political disorder. His suggestions make a perfect recipe for poor countries to deal with budget deficits in the medium and long-run as resulting debt is sustainable but it is opposed by the neoliberal using 'crowding in and out' or inflation argument in recent times. Keynes deals with inflation problem as effectively as with the problem of unemployment. The excessive demand for investment and consumption causes inflation. The cut in public spending and higher taxes on expenditures and incomes will increase saving and cut down aggregate demand to normalise prices in the marketplace.

When WWII came, Keynes had already written another book entitled *'How to pay for the War'* which proposes a deferred saving plan to finance war efforts. The state would take a portion of every wage packet and automatically invest in government bonds that will only mature after the war and at that time, it could be cashed in to boost effective demand in the economy. Keynes thought his deferred saving plan might help in the redistribution of wealth. Keynes final major contribution was in helping to establish International Monetary Fund and International Bank. His death came in 1946.

Keynes is not a revolutionary; he wishes to protect the sick capitalist system. He has proposed policy changes to deal with problems of inflation, unemployment and poverty and has advocated a limited role for the government to correct undesirable features of the capitalist system. He answers those, who believe that the automatic mechanism of the market forces will end the stagnation in the end; by saying 'we are all dead in the long run.' Keynes backing of industrialisation to achieve economic growth makes him unique among the English economist. Keynes general theory on employment remained dominant till 1980. Then it was subjected to scrutiny first by those who wanted a conciliation between micro and macro aspect, then by the monetarists in the treatment of inflation and then by the least government preachers. The Chicago school economists namely Friedman (33), Lucas (80), and Hayek will have their say. Friedman in the wake of stagflation, created by a hike in oil price, would claim that the trade cycles are better explained by permanent income hypothesis and money supply. Hayek would talk about the tyranny of power and loss of human liberty if the government (state) were to intervene in the market system and yet he accepted as much that Keynes policy of dealing with unemployment might be acceptable. He talked about long-run equilibrium though accepting it may not be a full employment one. Lucas applies stable preferences, rational behaviour and market equilibrium to macro economic issues of unemployment and inflation without any justification for the assumptions and in the light of positive proof that macro economic was not just an aggregate of micro. In real business cycle theory, unemployment becomes voluntary and leisure induced rather than real. The trade cycle is explained in term of lack of information based on just an assumption. Chicago school has been cultivating the view that scientific theories have nothing to do with truth. All three of them won a noble prize for condemning correct knowledge and spreading false assumptions and make believe economic explanations.

In recent times, some economists have started to call themselves 'New-Keynesians', though they have nothing much common with Keynes. The apologetics like Krugman, Mankiw and wren-Lewis build models using neoclassical paradigm which is flagrantly at odds with reality and does not contribute in any significant way to macroeconomic policy making. I end this section by quoting Keynes. *'It is better to be vaguely right than precisely wrong'*.

F Hayek (1899-1984)

Hayek was born in a Jewish family in Vienna in 1899, spent two years in the US as a research assistant and got a lecturing position at LSE in 1933 to compete against Keynes influence in policy making and to counter Keynesian ideas. Although a European, he is a neoclassical economist and father of neo-liberalism. Given this background, it is not difficult to understand his obsession against totalitarianism and his preference for individual freedom.

Hayek published his first book entitled *'Economics and Knowledge'* in 1936, which reassesses the notion of an economic equilibrium and question the existence of a perfect market but still rejects any intervention in the marketplace. He states that economic decisions are made under imperfect information and partial knowledge as only current conditions are known. The future information is no more than guesswork. Individual base their decisions on different information but when such divergent information combines, these form a picture of a market in operation. The prices reflect the communal wisdom of market situation and an outside intervention in the market such as price fixing would frustrate and curtail wishes, happiness, and liberties of individuals in whose interest the intervention has taken place. He accepts some minimum state intervention is essential to preserve health and capacity to work. He is aware but ignores the consequences of partial information and its implications for efficient allocation. His other book entitled *'The Pure Theory of Capital'* was published in 1941 and discusses pricing and production processes by making a distinction between short and long-run. The real cost of production determines prices in the long-run. Marshall had said the same thing. The money by nature constitutes a loose joint which impedes the self-correcting equilibrium apparatus of the price mechanism. The monetary policy is to improve the self- correcting forces of the price mechanism and help to avoid a more violent reaction. It is only of limited use in dealing with the business cycles.

Hayek's most important work 'The Road to Serfdom' was published in 1944 in Britain. In it, he conducts a debate between free market operations and a planned economy and points to twin evils of socialism and fascism that can come about through the central planning process. He sees the replacement of market operations with central planning as loss of individuals' liberty. But this loss of liberty in a democracy would be an agreed loss and society might not consider it a loss but an act to improve the welfare of society. However, a welfare state, which provides public goods and voluntarily redistributes wealth, goes against Hayekian way of thinking.

Hayek articulates his vision of individual freedom and rights as both an end and means to solve the poverty problem and by doing so, he champions human self-interest and impersonal markets framework to achieve allocation efficiency and prosperity. He is on record to say *'we must make the building of a free society once more an intellectual adventure' 'What we lack is a liberal Utopia.'* He was a committed free market believer, a member of Mont Pelerin Society, who made greed fashionable and left millions of people in dire straits. Hayek and Friedman are the founding fathers of 'Neoliberal' economics. To them, every problem was caused by the state and the solution, in every case, was the free market.

3

EUROPEAN ECONOMIC IDEAS

During the late 18th century, British economic thinking had diverged from the continental European ideas. Adam Smith defined economy as a 'commercial society' focused on buying and selling. Inventions and knowledge become exogenous and production and trade decisions were reduced to labour input cost. The classical and neoclassical economists had formulated their economic system using deductive methods of Physics. The resulting so-called science of economics gives an illusion of order and simplicity which is seductive but demand the heavy cost of giving up qualitative aspect of economic activities. The European rejected logic based deductive reasoning and used inductive methods of biological sciences which can incorporate qualitative differences and use historical patterns and observations to build economic theories. The traditions of deductive and inductive reasoning go back to 18th century. Both methods have existed side by side but the European theories based on inductive reasoning have remained neglected in the mainstream economics.

The law of increasing returns describes a production process when doubling of input leads to more than doubling of output and unit cost of production falls with output expansion. Serra of Italy had observed increasing returns in the production process in 1613 when he put it at the core of wealth creation. The German economist Ernst Ludwig Carl explained the same concept using a pin factory around 1710, *the same pin factory, that was used by Adam Smith later on to explain the division of labour, specialisation, and efficiency. The* classical and neoclassical economists concentrated on the laws of diminishing or constant returns to scale and ignored increasing returns in their work, but two German economists Friedrich List and Wilhelm Roscher put the law of increasing returns on the map by stressing its importance in economic growth in the second half of the 18th century. In 1923, the increasing returns idea was again revived by Frank Graham (45) of USA, but later on, it was abandoned as it was not compatible with the equilibrium model. In 1980, Krugman (69) reintroduced it in international trade but was dismissed by J Bhagwati (11) of India and the USA. More recently Romer (128) has dismissed all constant returns growth models on the ground that these are not capable of incorporating increasing returns concept which generates economic growth or value-added activities.

The industrial production with embedded improving technology generates productivity and produces cumulative causation or reaction to create structural changes and economic development. The Law of increasing returns to scale also play a crucial role in determining who gets benefits from the international trade. If all economic activities were increasing returns than the comparative cost advantage theory can be supported without much difficulty. But this is not the case because most industrial activities are increasing returns whereas all agricultural activities are diminishing returns. The trade benefits mostly go to the countries with increasing returns activities. The differences in the economic activities had provided Europeans economists' different prospectus to put a priority on industrialisation to achieve economic development. The globalisation policies have imprisoned poor countries with diminishing return activities and have closed doors on them to better themselves. Gunnar Myrdal (96), a Swedish economist, was of the view that world trade tends to increase existing differences in incomes between rich and poor countries. Samuelson (116) had claimed that free trade will lead to 'factor-price equalisation.' Maybe he had overlooked the distinction between economic activities. A recent study proves Myrdal point by concluding that the inequality between rich and poor in 2016 is higher compared with inequality just after the colonies had gained independence.

Friedrich List (80), Schumpeter (134,135,136), Veblen (160), Schmoller (133) and Keynes (61,62) all have contributed to this experience based economic policy debate. In the USA, this tradition was carried on by Hamilton (46), Raymond (117), and by Carey (15) in the formulation of industrial policies. In more recent time this tradition has helped such countries as Japan, Asian Tigers, China, and India to achieve economic development.

Friedrich List (1789-1846)

He was born in 1789 in Wurttemberg Germany and published his work entitled '*The national system of political economy*' in 1841. He criticised the classical thinking for lacking empirical base and based his growth and trade policies on historical patterns of the rich nations. He observed that an effective strong State must initiate and promote industrialisation and restrictive international trade policies for economic growth.

The fundamental ideas of Listian theory consist of: free imports of raw materials combined with an effective protection of national manufacturing against foreign competition as flourishing industries provide the most effective support for the agriculture sector. He supported his theory by drawing a clear distinction between 'cosmopolitan' economy of Adam Smith and political economy of a nation. He states that Smith had borrowed Quesnay's ideas to ignore the true political economy which represents a nation's economic interests. He identifies a nation as a separate entity for allocation decisions and makes a distinction between national, individuals and humanity based decisions. A national economy and an economy of individuals are not the same, and it is a nation-state that ensures how it maintains and improves economic conditions. The difference between current and future advantage of an allocation policy based on national interests is fundamental one and the restrictive trade policy plays a major role in the development of productive capabilities at the cost of current consumption. A free trade policy can only be justified once a nation has already established strong industrial and social cohesion.

List criticised Smith theory on its use of exchange value of goods and services and labour input as output cost which turns all economic activities qualitatively alike making actual output un-important. He argued that the classical Economists had ignored the differences between income and wealth and causes of wealth generation and their overwhelming influence on economic conditions of the nations. The stress on the comparative cost advantages makes them forgetful of the productive capabilities that can change the future comparative advantages. Similarly, the State and individual traders judge national benefits of the foreign trade differently. An individual trader judges trade solely according to the theory of values for a single period (i.e. profit related to a period or discounting future to present time). Whereas a State must take account of all conditions on which its present and future existence, prosperity, and power depend. A State must sacrifice some present advantages to ensure greater benefits in future. Labour is not a homogeneous input, and the quality of labour is of paramount importance. The labour force productive capabilities and employment determine the differences in the quality and levels of output. The money spent on education or health of youth, promotion of justice, and defence of the nation is to increase the future productive power of a nation-state. The human motivation and social structure make a difference to the productive power of a nation. He has argued that only an effective state can ensure the balanced development of productive capabilities by adopting policies for industrial, technology and human capital development. The power of producing wealth is infinitely more important than income, as income without the productive capabilities depletes quickly. *The prosperity of a nation is not greater in proportion in which it has amassed more income (i.e. values of exchange), but in the proportion in which it has developed its power of production.* Listian theory of production differs from Adam Smith's theory of values of exchange. The trade and protection are both means to an end, namely the greatest development of productive power or capabilities of a nation-state. The protective trade policy may increase the price of the goods in the short-run, but the future gains from the additional productive capabilities will more than offset this loss as goods will be produced more cheaply at home. This increase in productive capabilities, not only secures the nation an infinitely greater amount of material goods, but also industrial independence that will be so essential in case of any war with other countries. A nation must adjust its trade system according to the stage of development. The level of restrictions on trade will depend on the level of industrialisation of a nation. Having reached the highest degree of productive capabilities, a nation can adopt a free trade policy of unrestricted competition at home and abroad to gain from division of labour, and specialisation of other nations.

A protection policy provides protection for new industries to enhance productive power or capabilities in sectors of the economy in which a nation has available or required natural resources. The dumping practices of the industrial nation can be destructive for the poor economies. An agrarian nation with some indispensable industries fails to benefits from the division of labour and division of commercial operations among its citizens. The labour force productivity differs in different branches of agriculture and manufacturing. The labour productivity in agriculture depends on the exchange of agriculture and manufacturing outputs in the domestic markets. List criticised Smith's division of labour and uses division of commercial operation concept to explain productivity gains. Adam Smith's division of labour is subjective in the sense that several persons share in the production of a single object. Whereas the objective division of labour implies that the same person is doing several jobs. The division of labour and division of commercial operations collectively unify energies, intelligence, and power to increase productivity. The greater productivity results from the union of two divisions of operations. The most important division of occupations is between mental and material capabilities for a nation, and both are mutually dependent on each other.

In summary Listian model of the economic development, identifies a nation-State as a separate entity from individuals', which plays a dominant role in creating productive capabilities of a nation. The creation of productive capabilities takes priority over current consumption as well as over individuals' preferences in early stages of economic development. The restrictive trade policy is essential to protect infant industries and the human capital and technological development must go along with physical development. Otherwise, industrialisation process will face skills shortages of managers and technical experts. Once a country has attained a significant industrial, technical, and human capital base, it could start to relax foreign trade barriers, to take advantage of specialisation in the world.

Schumpeter (1883-1950)

Schumpeter, an Austrian, was born in 1883. He thought that capitalism was inherently dynamic, growth oriented, but prone to crisis and would not last in the long-run. He favoured public policy measures in the short-run to alleviate social distress during the depression but did not think there was any need for the State to adopt long-run policy measures in the economy.

Schumpeter's first book *'the nature of Economic Theorizing'* earned him a professorship in Austria and his second book *'the theory of Economic Development'* earned him a world reputation. He did not directly deal with poverty problem, but his explanation of the Capitalist system provides an insight into the growth process. Schumpeter main contributions rest with highlighting the role of invention and innovation and the entrepreneur leadership in the economic development and social order. His economic system is a dynamic imperfect competition where industries with increasing returns prosper, prices remain fairly stable, the workforce is skilled with sticky wages, and rising profit for the producers result from inventions and innovations. There are no diminishing returns, population explosion, unfair distribution of income, lack of investment opportunities and institutional rigidities to impact growth process. Capitalism can yield ever increasing levels of real income at the cost of nothing more than a temporary disruption in economic conditions and the stagnating economy is merely like taking a shower. The entrepreneur is the central figure in the economic development process that introduces innovation, disrupts equilibrium and creates economic growth. An entrepreneur may or may not be a capitalist or an inventor, but he is a risk taker, a leader, and exploiter of a continuous stream of innovations. His motivation for profits comes from his desire to have high consumption levels and to build a private dynasty. He makes decisions in uncertain and risky conditions, which can lead to uneven spurts in a dynamic world and create boom and bust conditions.

Schumpeter starts with an economy that is static with unchanging 'circular flow' of income. There is no capital accumulation to steer growth. The competition has already removed all excessive rewards, and factors of production only get what is their true value in the production process. The economy repeats economic activities as a routine. The new technological inventions or production organisations disrupt the circular flow. An innovating capitalist adopts new technology or production organisation to produce goods cheaply compared with his competitors. The lower unit cost allows extra profit and higher circular flow of income which is a direct result of innovator intelligence. The rush to bring new technology (or innovation) into operation starts the boom which gathers pace. Prices and money incomes rise and induce a secondary economic expansion. The new flow only creates a transient extra profit and misconceived expectations of higher future money incomes. The generalisation of invention/innovation removes extra profit. The size of investment gets much larger for the producer goods compared to consumer goods which start a creative destruction process. The old firms find their markets curtailed by the competing cheaper or new goods. In consequence, theses either go bankrupt or get reduced to a minor role in the industry. In short, a painful process of readjustment starts to absorb effects of the primary entrepreneurial activity. The deflationary forces set in, forcing prices and money incomes to lower levels. Which intensify downward adjustment process but does not cause a full-scale depression? The recessionary climate, however, changes soon, and economy once again becomes ripe for further entrepreneurial activities and new expansion take off.

Schumpeter book on *'Business Cycle'* makes a distinction between 3 different types of interactive Business cycles (i.e. short-run, long-run and a very long–run) and explains how bunching of innovations and swarming of business people can create swings in the economy. The long run cycle can run up to seven years, and a very long-run cycle can last up to 50 years and is usually caused by a major invention such as a steam engine or a transistor chip. All three cycles reach the lowest point simultaneously, and some external factors like war could also start a cycle. The break in the flow of inventions/innovations and foolish speculative decisions of competing speculating imitators could cause stagnation.

The royalties from inventions/innovations are reaped by the inventors, but the entrepreneurs lose their share of income in the declining economy. But soon a new entrepreneur can capture the market with new invention/innovation and bankrupt the established firms. *'It is the dream; joy and will to conquer that make Entrepreneur carry on with his work.'* All cycles eventually end. Each time economy regains equilibrium; its new starting point is higher than the one from which the growth began. National and per capita incomes in real term continually rise via a cyclical mechanism, and all income groups benefit from the economic development. Schumpeter growth analysis assumes rapid unrestricted innovations and their rapid introduction into the production process to lower unit cost of existing products and to bring new products to the market. The economy grows rapidly towards full employment. New investment in inventions/innovations bids up prices, and inflationary pressures can force saving up to become an important source of capital accumulation. The repayment of bank loans at the completion of projects curtails inflationary pressures. The credit system ability to expand credit facilities plays a crucial role in facilitating economic development. It is an enterprising producer who decides what new products to bring to the markets, opposite to the classical concept of consumer sovereignty.

Schumpeter' theory has been criticised as narrow and partial because it puts emphasis on only one player i.e. entrepreneur as an innovator. The inventions/innovations activities were undertaken either by the inventors or the entrepreneurs who buy use rights of inventions/ innovation. Nowadays the inventions or innovations are mostly carried out by large corporations in a routine manner and are merely a normal part of business activity. Research and development costs have become business expenses that yield a normal return in the form of new product or process. So, entrepreneurship has become an obsolete concept. But to others, the art of entrepreneurship (i.e. the risk taking) is alive and well and still plays an important role in small to medium size enterprises and economic development.

In summary, the key individuals in Schumpeter's theory of development are the entrepreneurs. They are the initiators of significant advances in national product. The inventions and innovations happen rapidly and capital is borrowed from the credit institutions. The development is uneven and cyclical swings are the cost of economic development under capitalism. The Capitalism does not live just on its economic success, it requires faith in its cause, values and virtues of civilisation that it produces and which in turn, reproduces it. Its economic success, however, does not guarantee that people will not lose faith in its cause and values. Schumpeter's discusses the future of capitalism in *'Capitalism, Socialism, and Democracy.'* And to answer the question, can capitalism survive? He first presents a picture of plausible capitalism that is successful in creating economic dynamics but fails to develop a sociologically successful ideological superstructure. The rationalist attitude evolved goes on the attack against the private property concept and the whole scheme of bourgeois values. Would or could a loss of belief overtake capitalism? Yes, but then he looks at an alternative system of central planning and observes that such a system first produces high growth then leads to inflationary pressures, mismanagement of resources, stagnation and finally a loss of faith that leads to its collapse such as witnessed in the case of Soviet Union.

As a final point, Schumpeter says history is a narrative of change and development, but history itself is a story of the impact of elites on the inert mass of society. In a different setting, the qualities needed to exercise influence, (military talent has its place in a feudal society and economic talent in a market economy), but the driving force of an elite of one kind or another is always there. Thus, the echelon of leaders constitutes a special group and it always assumes its rightful place at the apex of society. The leaders may change but not the leadership. The real leadership rests with only a tiny minority.

Thorstein Veblen (1857-1929)

Veblen, a Nordic migrant to the US, published his first book entitled *'The Theory of Leisure Class'* in 1899, which discusses nature of an economic man, evolution of a community and emergence of a leisure class. He breaks away from the mainstream economics to considers capitalism as an advanced system of piracy.

Veblen society is characterised by idle curiosity, parental urge, and 'cheating' man. These characteristics act as a force to determine long–run development and composition of national output. Thus, he differed from the classical economists who had assumed 'self-interest' as a guiding force in explaining human behaviour and urban settlements. The classical man had promoted his self-interest by forming families, exchanging goods, establishing settlements and societies. In a constant competitive struggle, some individuals rise to the top where others remain at the bottom, and those who prosper minimise their physical work to enjoy leisure as a reward. Veblen was unsure if 'self-interest' could be a binding force or if leisure was a preferred option in a society. He investigated some previous societies and found that they did not have any leisure class. Men competed to outperform each other as a matter of pride and worked without feeling demeaned by hard work. The concern about a future generation (parental bent) provided them with the drive to do their best. The abstinence from work was not condoned or respected. Veblen had researched pre-industrial Polynesian, Icelanders, and Japanese societies. All of these had well-defined leisure classes who *were not idlers but busiest, but their work was mainly predatory. They had seized wealth either by using force, cunning or by cheating and did not perform any physical work or took part in any production process.* The leisure class was supported and approved by the society as it was composed of strong and able individuals. The winning of wealth by force was admired, pure labour got tainted with indignity and an honourable way of life got degraded under the impact of predatory spirit. Veblen's modern man is only a shade removed from his forefathers and his new leisure class has refined the predatory approach and uses all means to seize, accumulate and display wealth lavishly to earn the envy and respect of others. Veblen society is bonded by attitudes and customs. Lower classes are not in conflict with the upper class because of intangible but steely bonds of common attitudes. The workers do not seek to displace their managers; they seek to emulate them. Indeed, workers themselves acquiesce in the general judgement that the work they do is somehow less dignified than the work of their managers, and their goal is not to rid themselves of the superior class but to climb to it. The theory of leisure class contains the kernel of a theory of social stability. Veblen and Marx come together on the concept of private property being theft, but Veblen does not see any class struggle or revolution against the exploiters. I find present day Pakistan's society almost a replica of the Veblen society of yesterday, where looter and cheater are admired and envied rather than condemned.

Veblen second book *'The Theory of Business Enterprise'* was published in 1904. It predicted that the machines will come to dominate societies, and economic development process will become mechanical in character to produce goods and services. Machines will need technicians and engineers, to make whatever adjustments were needed, to ensure the most efficient cooperation of factors in the production process. The society's superstructure would become mechanical, highly coordinated and specialised clockwork. A financier should have no real role in such a society but as a member of leisure class wishes to make and accumulate money and therefore conspires to achieve his objective by ensuring that the flows of output break down regularly, resulting in fluctuating values (prices). He capitalises on the changing conditions and confusion to make money. The regular boom and bust in national output (i.e. trade cycles) occur because credit and finance control production and constantly sways shifts. This opens up opportunities for profit-making. However, the society pays a high price for the unforeseen swings in the economy and inefficient use of economic resources. The financiers desire to create and end up creating business cycles. The new machines are the main instrument of economic activities which provide the financier's opportunities to exploit for their benefits. Veblen has given us a different society with different binding forces where a class through foul means acquires wealth and status and is admired and envied for doing so. Veblen had believed that machine expert engineers would win in the long run, and the financier will disappear. This prediction has failed and the financiers still rule the world. In rich countries, they control financial resources and make money through novel Ponzi schemes, credit manipulation and created trade cycles. Once they are in trouble, they are bailed out by the State as they have made their security as a precondition of economic system's security and viability. They control political class through media ownership and political funding. In poor countries, their wealth and control of credit institution give them political and economic power and hungry masses admired them.

Gunner Myrdal (1898-1987)

Myrdal was born in Sweden in 1898. He obtained his doctorate in economics by investigating the role of expectation in price formation and uncertainty in ex-ante and ex-post expectation in the economic processes. His first notable work appeared under the title of *'An American Dilemma: The Negro Problem and Modern Democracy'*. He highlighted that the majority rule ignores minorities' interests and in consequence, the high American ideals have got ignored in dealings with minorities in the USA. Myrdal other research work pinpointed the problems of using correlation as a causal explanation.

Myrdal classic work entitled *'Asian Drama'* follows Marx's ideas of interaction between political and economic structures and imperialistic nature of free trade. He narrates the story of exploitation and forceful destruction of ex-colonial countries and their resulting lack of human and physical capital, and primitive production system. When an individual does not know where the evening meal is going to come from then the political participation becomes insignificant and a source of exploitation. The ex- colonies have broken will and culture of obedience. There is no economic surplus or technology base. Under these conditions, who is going to save or invest or have the technical know-how to introduce new technologies overnight? He prefers economic improvements over political participation in the earlier stages of economic development and is convinced that without an authoritarian approach economic development efforts could not succeed in poor countries. He states that economic development takes place in a broad political and social framework. The free trade between the countries in different stages of development harms poor countries and the free flow of foreign capital exploits poor countries resources and damages their economies. He proposes a planning theory and an active role of the State to plan, initiate, drive, and support economic development efforts in poor ex-colonial countries. *The State should invest public funds to plan, initiate and promote industrialisation. In addition, it should impose various controls, inducements, restrictions, support measures to guide the private sector to initiate and establish industries to steer economic development.*

Myrdal finds 'natural forces' or automatic adjustment process to be ineffective in eradicating poverty or economic stagnation and believes that economic development in ex-colonies can only be initiated and accelerated by the State. The strategy for the development policies would emerge from a rational analysis of national conditions, facts, and a set of development goals.

Erik S Reinert

Reinert was born in Norway in 1949 and published his work entitled 'How Rich Countries Got Rich....' in 2007. He builds on European legacy and sets out an argument against neoliberal economic policies which have been imposed on poor in the guise of structural reforms and as default conditions for economic growth and welfare. *He suggests that only a particular form of economic structure based on increasing returns activities can transform a poor economy.* Like List, he details the industrialisation of rich nations and shows how every rich country had industrialised under protection from foreign competition. He concludes that no agrarian economy has ever become rich under free markets, free trade economic system.

Reinert universe is made up of humans who possess Schumpeterian wit and entrepreneurship and use inventions and innovations as moving force to transform the economy. Individuals' decisions are made on experience and under uncertainty. The mode of analysis is mostly qualitative. The entrepreneurs introduce inventions and innovations in the production, just as they did in Schumpeter or Veblen universe, to drive competition and growth and create demand for capital to gain from increasing returns of new technologies and knowledge. The production processes with embedded new technologies promote large-scale operations creating, monopolies or imperfect competition and economic growth. The State is an active and decisive player in the organisation and management of the economy. The protection of increasing returns manufacturing is an essential policy act to safeguard these activities at least in the early stages of development. The welfare and growth are activities specific, and the cumulative forces of productive capabilities are more important and rest at the core of the economic system. Reinert theory *'the other cannon'* is like the reincarnation of early European economic traditions. The state develops and protects productive capabilities against foreign predators. The market structure is imperfect competition which allows capital formation and the introduction of new technologies in production processes.

Concluding Remarks

Since 1980, the neoclassical economists and especially their neoliberal version, have subjected the State role in resource allocation to an avalanche of attacks. The idea of individuals' freedom has become an end as well as a mean to that end. Hayek's ideas of individual rights and liberty have become the primary objective. The State intervention has been attacked as it destroys freedom of choice, uses the imperfect information to allocate resources and impossibility of coordination in production. The fall of Berlin wall in 1989 led to the demise of socialism and made neoliberal paradigm supreme.

The economics ideas presented in the last two chapters reflect on the diverging thinking regarding the role of individuals and the central authority in the allocation and development process. The neoclassical economics assumes human selfish nature, individual freedom of choice, free trade and the neutral markets will achieve efficient allocation and prosperity. The inbuilt forces can correct unemployment, inflation and lead to long-run full employment equilibrium. The European economists reject the idea of automatic correction, agree on human social concerns, harms of free trade and advocate a strong role for the State to promote industrialisation in economic transformation.

Easterly (26,27) have claimed that *'history can help in finding the causes of poverty. Why some countries are rich, and other poor and this enable us to draw lessons accordingly for how to escape poverty'.* He claims that history of political rights of individuals in the West can be productive in learning about causes of poverty. He suggests that allowing political participation you can turn poor countries into rich. But he ignores history and causes of ex-colonial countries poverty and how individuals were denied rights and subjected to economic policies which have imprisoned them. He likes to forget that as individual freedom ideas were emerging the subjugation policies had denied these rights to the ex-colonies people. I agree with Hayek's saying that *further advance could not be expected along old lines.'* Easterly has used this quote to support individual freedom as a mean to remove poverty, but I use this quote to denounce the old colonial policies and the new neocon's policies of new imperialism.

4

INDIVIDUALS, STATE AND ECONOMIC DEVELOPMENT

The last three chapters have described civil progression and the emergence of divergent economic ideas. The nation-states have been formed to meet changing social and economic needs of humans who have accepted a central command and restriction on liberty in exchange for security and greater opportunities. The relationship between individuals and the State has gone through numerous changes over time. At present and in principle, State gets its legitimacy through the will of citizen and aims to secure the maximum welfare and internal and external security. The history of economic ideas shows a considerable divide in the practical and analytical aspects. The 'great divide' is based on human nature, individual choice, markets nature and scope, political systems, foreign trade, factors movement, inequality and the State role in the management of the economy. The mainstream economics accept and promote the capitalist system based on selfishness, individual choice, free markets and free foreign trade to achieve optimal allocation and steady growth. The individuals are motivated by self-interest and have freedom of choice to interact in the perfectly competitive markets to produce and consume the correct amounts and to utilise available economic resources, maximise output and welfare of the society. On the other side of the divide, some reject capitalism and free market mechanism and their assumptions and values. They claim that the neoclassical model is routinely based on assumptions of rational expectations, market clearing unique equilibrium, time invariance, homogeneity of input/outputs and technology, intertemporal optimising and representative agents with homothetic and identical preferences. These assumptions are hard to find in the real world. In addition, there are problems such as complexity, diversity, uncertainty, coordination, non-market clearing prices, real aggregation problems, and expectations formations. They reject false assumptions and conception of human nature. Thaler and Sunstein in their book *'Nudge: Improving Decisions about Health Wealth and Happiness' make a distinction between* 'Human' and 'Homo economicus'' and suggest that the theory and policy should be humans based.

At the time of writing this book, the great divide in the practical and analytical economics is between austerity–imposing Say's law and Keynesians fiscal-stimulus. While this divide is raging in the West, the poor are still forced to accept austerity policies cloaked under the structural reform programmes of the international lending agencies to deny the structural transformation of their economies which could eradicate poverty.

Are human selfish and greedy? What role individuals or a state play in the development process? Is it individuals' selfish choice and free markets mechanism which ensure efficient allocation and optimal output? Or an active State initiation, support, and guidance that transform agrarian into industrialised economies to promote collective welfare? These are not new questions and have been debated over the last few centuries, but more recently the powerful voices have put them on the back burner by declaring that economics is a science of resource allocation and the individuals' freedom in the marketplace achieves economic efficiency. They claim that defeat of socialism provides proof to their claims. The State intervention has no role in the management of the economy. However, the rapid growth of East Asian countries achieved by the active State role has provided proof to negate the neoliberal claims. Let us look at the debate on 'Individualism versus State' in a greater detail.

Individualism

The classical economists had laid down the foundation of the capitalist system based on individual's freedom and the markets neutrality. The consumers and producers had the freedom of choice, acted in self-interest to maximise satisfaction and profits. They interacted in the neutral markets to create allocation efficiency, market clearing prices and equilibrium output. They considered capital formation, population and technology as important factors in the development process. The classical economist's differed on human motives, population growth and the State role in the management of the economy. Smith did not believe that people were entirely self-interested because people have a genuine concern for others, care for reputation and have a sense of right and wrong that leads to the establishment of norms enforced by punishment. The States performed three functions: protection from invasion and internal violence, provision of justice to all and duty to erect and maintain public works and public institutions, as it can never be for the interest of any individual or a small number of individuals to undertake these. The man is also a moral being which implies that human behaviour is not always selfish. Bentham had developed utility theory and wanted minimum state intervention but listed a large number of state responsibilities. Mills did not agree with distribution based on marginal productivity and said that a society could distribute income and wealth as it wishes. But the neoliberal with their neoclassical economic model adopts Herbert Spencer (142) most extreme doctrine of individualism. Spencer theory is based on individual rights where a state has no authority beyond justice.

The neoclassical's have refined the classical economic system with an elegant mathematical model of general equilibrium. The objective function maximises a nation's level of output and welfare which is subject to the available resources and technological constraints. The maximisation is achieved under restrictive assumptions. The equilibrium between the supply and demand of goods and services (excluding public goods) determines a unique price for each good and factor which reflects social opportunity cost and maximum human welfare. Walras had provided a mathematical proof but no empirical backing for the model. He had claimed that individuals maximising their local concerns can organise into well-functioning economies and therefore top-down regulation by state leaders was unnecessary in the economy. The underlying assumption of the model is found to be unrealistic and require empirical backing which has not been established. The market system by nature concentrate wealth and at some point, wealth concentration strangles the flows of spending, production and income and the very market that create it. The minimum tax regimes mean that less money is transferred to the poor who spend a larger percentage of their incomes. When wealth concentration is extreme the poor end up with less income and wealth and economy stops growing. The minimum state policy also limits state activities such as redistribution, improvement of markets functions and provisions of public goods even with a clear comparative advantage such as national defence.

The neoclassical obsession with freedom of choice, free markets and allocation efficiency has diverted focus from economic development. The elegant mathematical general equilibrium model of competitive markets (domestic markets integrated with international markets) leads to an efficient allocation of resources and therefore poverty need not be a problem. The State role in the economy is restricted to the provision of infrastructure, few public goods and elimination of market distortions. *The Washington Consensus policies of liberalisation, privatisation, and fiscal discipline are based on the neoclassical model and incorporate extreme versions of Spencer, Carlyle, and Lassalle doctrine of individualism, limited state role and integrate a domestic economy more completely into the international economies.* Yet there is no empirical evidence to prove that resource allocation through the freedom of choice and neural markets can generate sustainable economic growth.

The neoclassical paradigm which has become dominant since 1989 has come under attack in recent time. The self-interest or greed ignores the human concerns for others. An individual on its own has no meaning. A recent survey by **the common cause** based on the response of 1000 people has found that 74% of them identify with unselfish values such as helpfulness, honesty, forgiveness, and justice than in money. Humans show empathy and concern for the welfare of others and have the ability to create moral norms to restrain their selfless tendencies. Individuals' decision to live in groups reflects on altruism. Humans are not like the 'Homo Economicus' of the neoclassical paradigm. The free international trade based on the comparative cost advantage has no empirical backing to show that it can benefit all trading parties. Moreover, it fails to explain why the comparative advantages are the way these are in the first place and why these cannot be changed with public policy? Krugman (68,70,71), a new Keynesians economist, has accepted that under conditions of increasing returns to scale and imperfect markets, the comparative advantage theory only serves the interests of rich states. Baumol (9) recent research has provided empirical proof of poor countries exploitation through free foreign trade. Fukuyama (36) has noted contradictions of neoliberal minimum state in developing countries and has argued that state should be supported and strengthened and not weakened in these countries, *'The Economists who promote liberalising economic reforms understood this perfectly well in theory. But the relative emphasis in this period lay very heavily on the reduction of state activity. Which could often be confused or deliberately misconstrued as an effort to cut back state capacity across the board?'* In addition, markets failures related to technology, labour skill training, small firms credit facilities, intellectual property rights, and infant industries are well known.

Williamson, the father of WCP, having witnessed the failure of his policies now accepts an active role for the state. However, his failed policies remain in business and are being carried out by the IMF, the World Bank and the WTO, which usually attack the size of 'government spending ratio' in poor countries without looking at its composition or its need. A weakened State loses its ability to enforce law and order or implement public policies. A weak State cannot effectively administer, control corruption or maintain a high level of transparency and accountability of institutions. A minimal State is not capable of providing comprehensive welfare provisions, intervention in the economy or proper control and management of the economy. Would people in rich countries give up their welfare provisions? I doubt it. Besides, the State and individuals 'productive capabilities' are interdependent, and any reduction in the State scope can harm individuals' capabilities.

The idea of unbounded 'individualism' is a bit odd and rather unsatisfying. An individual without others has no meaning and formation of society indicates that individuals gave up freedom for the sake of security and greater opportunities. An individual cannot defend against aggression, and his self-interest does not allow him to invest in public goods such as external and internal security, education or health. If he is forced to invest in public goods or national defence, it limits his private liberty. The neoclassical's support of individualism based on maximum output and welfare has no empirical validation and the political idea of human rights is bound with the common interests of the nation-states. Thus, selfishness is too narrow a motive for human beings.

State

There are many antagonists to the market efficiency. They point out numerous market failures and the positive role a State can play in managing the economy by adopting effective policies in the form of tariffs, subsidies, credit controls, manpower training, technology promotion, and direct ownership of industries for rapid industrialisation. They offer an alternative economic system where a State steers' economic transformation to achieve economic development and collective prosperity.

A State is much more than a total of individuals living in its territories. It has international boundaries, a capital city, and monopoly over the use of force and tax collection. It protects independence by its own power and resources, abides by the international laws, and sets a goal of national prosperity and fairness. People living within its territorial boundaries have a common national identity, consider them a nation, united by a thousand of ties and interests and differ from others in language, literature, history, manners, customs, laws and institutions. Peace among nations is a rarity, and strong nations have always subjugated weak and carry a great deal of influence over the world affairs. Each nation has its domestic currency, but only dominant states currency act as an international medium of exchange with tremendous advantage of borrowing in own currency and without much cost. It is a fact that the world is divided into nation-states, and each nation pursues her interests through foreign relations or wars. The recent wars and conflicts in the Middle East reflect on divergent economic interests of the strong nations.

The State as a constitutional entity clarifies differences among states, between agent and principal, state and citizens. Each State protects national interests to maintain internal and external security, provides public goods, regulates internal markets and is responsible for the citizen welfare. The multi-tier social hierarchy and unregulated pursuit of self-interest can undermine functional organisation of a State. In other words, what is good for an individual is not necessarily good for his family and what is good for a family is not necessarily good for a nation-state. What is good for a nation-state is not necessarily good for the global economy.

Each nation-state faces an agency problem i.e. the possible conflict between an agent and the common interests. The agent (i.e. the government) behaviour determines the performance and effectiveness of a State. A State becomes effective when an agent gives priority to the national interests or his own interests co-inside with the national interests. A divergence between an agent and principal's interests makes a state ineffective. In economic and political literature, the term government (agent) and state (Principal) are interchangeable, but a distinction between the two is most important. The powers of the State get exercised through its agent who may put personal interest over the interests of the State. In this context, the form and effectiveness of a government can pose a serious problem, and it is different from other social disorders because it carries an irreducible coercive authority.

A state has two distinct aspects, strength and scope. The first includes the ability to defend, enforce laws and policies. The second covers a range of functions and competencies of management and control of the economy. It is possible to have great strength and small scope or large scope and meagre strength. But both aspects of the state are interdependent and mutually complementary, and it is not possible to separate them without damaging the existence of the state.

The wealth of a nation-state is much more than the wealth of her individual members. A little reflection can make it obvious that the individual decisions are based on self-interest, aloof of internal and external security, environment pollution, intergenerational concerns, and thousands of other elements which may not serve the long-term interests of the state. A nation-state can and does print currency, but an individual does not have this ability or power to do so. In thousands of cases, the power of the State is forced to impose restrictions to change individuals' behaviour and her productive power is not synonymous with the aggregate productive powers of its citizen. Individuals productive power depend on social and political conditions, a division of labour and internal productive capabilities of the state. Therefore, an individual achieves his mental abilities, culture, productive capability, security, and prosperity within a nation-state. The productive capability of a nation-state will be restricted or may even decline if the buying decisions were based only on least-cost criterion. The cheapness of today might result in big losses in future. Thus, inter-generation decisions take on new priority compared with single generation decisions. The policy of 'buy cheap and sell dear' at a particular time may not always be the wisest national policy. The use of discounting does not capture the essence of future. The individuals and the State interests are not always in harmony. The national decisions could be opposite of individuals' decisions. The differences in personal preferences make the formulation of a consistent national objective extremely unlikely. Could a state exist if individual's goals take preference over national goal? The answer is an obvious no. The distinction between the present and future advantage from the national standpoint is a fundamental idea and the allocation of national resources requires long-term consideration.

In the 18th century, the European States had realised that no country could win a war without industrialisation and military power supports economic development through advantageous foreign trade, subjugation of foreign countries, internal security and political stability. Thus, industrialisation and military power became a national priority and each state rushed to industrialise under protection to maintain prosperity, freedom and international influence. Some States are super powers; others are merely rich, but all of them are industrialised and still have a desire to improve their ranking in the world. The State intervention supporters accept that the liberalisation of domestic markets may do some good but fear that an integration with the world economy before industrialisation can harm economic growth in the poor countries.

Concluding Remarks

Behind the efficiency claims of neoclassical model lurks the promotion of a loaded value system i.e. capitalism which promotes inequality among individuals and nations. The level of growth and alleviation of poverty are affected by the State intervention and its effectiveness in implementing appropriate social, political and economic policies. This fact cannot be allowed to get lost in either vague generalities or a unique version of the path to a utopia.

The question of market imperfection cannot be ignored because these could only be corrected in theory to improve efficiency. The market imperfections have not disappeared in the rich countries. There is no engine of growth or externalities in poor economies. The diminishing returns activities have no in-built automatic mechanism to turn them into increasing returns operations. The poor can rot in hell forever, and the western world can live lives of luxury, sip Champaign, put blinkers on their consciousness and send few pieces of silver to the poor to make them believe that the rich world cares about their poverty.

The neoliberal claim that capitalism could cure poverty problem as default conditions, but it did not solve the problem of unemployment in 1929 or since. Keynes had provided a solution to the stagnation problem by suggesting that the State must increase effective demand to overcome depressed investors' expectations. But the libertarians criticised Keynes with their imaginary theories to promote individualism at any cost. Can the poverty- stricken individuals emerge from their miserable existence without a state major role in the management of the economy? How is a free market system going to help a poor country to compete against the technologically advanced countries with selective walls to protect their markets? The answer to both these questions is a resounding no.

A perfectly competitive free market or centrally planned economy has never existed in the world. The benefits and failures of these opposing systems regarding efficiency and growth are known. Only mixed economies exist in the real world with shared allocation in public and private sectors. The State has to provide goods and services that the markets fail to provide such as defence, law and order, pollution remedies, and social services such as education, justice, and health. The freedom of speech, assembly and protest, property rights and enforcement institutions are all provided by the State. In short, it is a state responsibility to protect its borders and citizens and promote welfare and fairness. Only an effective state can achieve these objectives with allocation policies. Sen (138,139), a Nobel laureate, is aware of the unrivalled efficiency of the markets, but he is equally aware of the need for decisive state policies to direct growth. He has supported the idea of an active and decisive state, which should adopt vigorous policies to create productive capabilities for a nation to eradicate poverty. Individuals in poor countries are competing against other poor to overcome their poverty, and poor nation-states are competing against each other's as well as the rich nations to improve their nationals' lives. This struggle is almost like a war which the poor are not winning.

PART 2

ECONOMIC DEVELOPMENT AND HUMAN WELFARE

The last part has set the scene by providing historical development of economic ideas. The mainstream economics concerns itself with the efficiency of allocation to achieve economic growth and human well-being. The critics have suggested that the state intervention in resource allocation can be a positive force in steering economic development and to overcome market failures. The differences in the nature and objectivity of social structures, the role of individual and the state, markets efficiency, industrialisation and the foreign trade policy have been highlighted. Most people agree that 'more is better than less' but the relationship between welfare, output and allocation efficiency is only a tentative one.

This part provides some building blocks by defining terms and concepts such as economic development, development process, measurement and aggregation problems, income and wealth, productive capabilities, and economic ranking of the nation-states.

5

GROSS NATIONAL PRODUCT AND PRODUCTIVE CAPABILITIES

Human civilisation has evolved from hunter-gatherer to post-industrial phase passing through different stages of socio-economic development. However, different societies (or countries) have evolved at differing rates. Some societies have moved to the machine-based production with increasing productivity but others are still living with basic tools and agricultural activities. The development stage of each society is reflected in how it combines factors of production (capital, labour and technology) to produce goods and services. This, in turn, reflects the efficiency of the production process and the economic structure of the country. At each phase of development, different societies invented more efficient machines to increase their productivity and the differences in the productivity growth rates have turned into different levels of income and wealth. The quantity and quality of goods and services consumed and produced separate individuals and nations into rich and poor categories.

In the aftermath of WWII, colonialism folded and ex-colonies emerged as free nations and dirt poor. A new economic system termed as socialism started to become a role model for the poor and the rich nations suddenly developed a conscious of paying attention to the poverty problem. A large number of books on the causes and cures of poverty appeared in the market. All, claiming that lack of investment (capital) has caused poverty as labour was abundant and technology could be bought. Thus, financial aid, loans and encouragement for domestic savings can cure the shortage of investment funds to make poor rich. Economists from rich nations were dispatched with promises of aid and loans to act as advisors and to turn around poor countries.

Within a couple of decades, it became clear that growth recipe of neoclassical economics was not working, and the development programmes had nothing to show except some rotting import substitution machines and a flourishing 'rent-seeking' class in most poor countries. The blame for this failure was squarely put on the poor because their political elites could not care if their citizen had enough to eat or not.

The mainstream economists developed amnesia and turned their attention to making their subject a science of resource allocation. The production process went into shadows of supply and demand forces which interacted in the marketplace to create equilibrium. The neoclassical economists claimed that once institutional arrangements of markets were in place, self-interest will drive each economy to its maximum production potential to ensure an efficient allocation of resources. The 'invisible hand' will guide the free markets to the full employment equilibrium to take care of poverty problem. However, nothing like this happened, and some countries on the quite went on to adopt opposite of the neoclassical policy recommendations and got rich. The successes of State-directed economies became a direct challenge to the market orthodoxy.

In the mean times, poverty has remained the world greatest economic problem. Globalisation policies of the neoliberal economists have made the situation even worse. Poor want more than what they have and rich wish to maintain and add to their riches which lead us to the question of growth and fairness which is faced by each society on this planet. At present in some poor countries, citizens have less than $1.25 per day to spend on goods and services which represent an absolute poverty level and thus, per capita income becomes a measure of poverty. I need some definitions to make it simple and coherent to understand the nature, causes, and possible cure of poverty problem.

What is Economic Development?

Human survival and standard of living depend on consumption. A production process converts factors of production into goods and services. The investment in machines increases factors productivity to produce more output. The technology improves through inventions and innovations and its introduction in the production process increases productivity to produce more output using less and less input. Thus, the process to produce more goods and services for consumption and investment is called economic development

Some economists make a distinction between the terms economic development, economic growth, and secular change. But in essence, these terms are synonymous. Economic growth means an increase in national output; economic development means improvement in human conditions and secular change means both economic and social changes. Thus, the differences in terms are immaterial, as material changes take place in human lives with an increase in national output.

The term economic development gets defined in many ways, but no single definition seems to be entirely satisfactory. Some define it as an increase in gross national product (GDP) or real national income (RNI) over a year. The others define it as an increase in the per capita income over a year, which is the difference in the growth rates of real national income and population. The per capita income is equal to real national income (RNI) divided by the number of people in the country.

An economic structure can help to explain how changes in various variables determine the course of GDP or RNI. The changes in output are caused by the changes in factor supplies and demand in the production process. The factors supplies result from changes in national resources, capital accumulation, population growth, and changes in technology or organisation capabilities. Whereas the changes in factors demand take place with changes in size and age composition of the population, tastes, distribution of income, production organisation, and institutional changes.

Measurements of National Product

The production, exchange and distribution activities link earnings and work, production and revenue, consumption and expenditures. National accounting measures these aggregate, just as financial accounting provides information for business activities. Simon Kuznets (73,74, and 75) had come up with the idea of compiling the measurement of public and private sectors output aggregates into a single holistic indicator which he called gross domestic product (GDP) and since then it has turned into a de facto standard for measuring economic progress and development.

Gross Domestic Product (GDP) is total output of economic activities (i.e. agriculture, mining, manufacturing, utilities, construction, trade, transport & communication, public administration, education health & social work and others) conducted on the territory of a nation-state. Gross National Product (GNP) gets calculated by adjusting Gross Domestic Product for the overseas incomes from foreign assets of a State's residents.

The different measurement methodologies are used in different countries which create problems in comparing countries using their income levels. GNP does not account for unpaid work or environmental costs and does not include illegal activities such as drugs and prostitution. New measurement challenges have stemmed from an increasing share of digital products consumption which is delivered at a zero price or funded through advertising. These goods have value to the consumers, but these are excluded from GDP or GNP numbers. Similarly, transfer payments, intermediate goods, and some services such as defence are treated differently in different countries national accounts. The leisure has a value but it is not counted in GDP. The exclusion of these outputs or differing measurement methodologies means that the calculation may not be capturing the activities or growing share of an economic activity and therefore may not provide a complete or accurate information.

The per capita real income is an average number and does not provide any information on the distribution of income or wealth. Rich countries, however, have higher per capita income levels compared with poor and the per capita income of $1.25 is used to indicate absolute poverty level internationally.

International Ranking

Some economists measure economic development by Gross National Product (GNP) or Real National Income (RNI) and use it to compare different countries for their level of economic achievements. A foreign exchange converter is used to convert different currencies into a common international currency before any such comparison is performed, but currency rates fluctuate from day to day and pose a problem for measurement. Another measure of economic development is 'the Purchasing Power Parity (PPP) index' which measures the cost of maintaining a given standard of living across countries but again it suffers from the same conversion process. John Rawl (116) includes primary goods (*'rights, liberties and opportunities, income and wealth, and the social bases of self-respect'*) along with income for international comparison. However, these primary goods are nothing but general resources and once included in the comparison are subject to same limitations as income. Mahbub ul Haq of Pakistan purposed that *'actual living conditions' should be used for international comparison,* but the need for various commodities in different countries and their impact on living conditions becomes a matter of interest and even debate. Another comparison measure is a level of output per working hours, which measures productivity across the countries and is estimated using market exchange rates. But the market exchange rates, as stated before, are subject to daily fluctuations. To overcome this weakness productivity is also measured using purchasing power parity which provides a more stable measure. However, productivity as a measure also has certain weaknesses. It measures output per working hour without taking into account of capital input. A farmer in a poor country works with almost no capital equipment whereas a farmer in Europe or the USA has a great deal of capital input such as tractors, harvesters, etc. at his disposal. Therefore, the productivity of US worker may be indicating or including the productivity of capital and not just labour. With these shortcomings, the levels of income can only be a limited guide to compare economic development or quality of life. Hence, all measures of international comparisons are partial and could not be assumed as perfect.

Some economists have argued that GNP, in spite of imperfections, is still a valuable concept as it measures the number of goods and services that people enjoy and which determines their living standards. They say no one knows what the distribution of income should be? An equal income can kill incentives and an extreme inequality could lead to political unrest and instability. The public policies of subsidies and taxes may solve inequality problem over time. But both equality and inequality are likely to discourage economic growth. But can inequality be brushed away? The answer has to be no. The increasing productivity is mostly captured in profits and not wages. The stagnating wages affect aggregate demand with impact on employment and output levels.

Others economists have proposed alternatives or supplementary indicators to GDP to measure success in a way that can reflect performance in areas such as social welfare and progress. The Genuine Progress Indicator (GPI), the Index of Sustainable Economic Welfare (ISEW) and the Social Progress Index (SPI) are just a few of the possible contenders. The GPI uses 26 indicators to give a more accurate picture. The ISEW use GDP and indicators that GDP ignores, such as unpaid work, social costs, environmental damage and income distribution. Each factor is weighted equally. The SPI makes an attempt to understand the relationship between economic development and social progress and measures it independently. Some countries are making an effort to adopt SPI as a measure of economic performance. The debate on the measurement methods seems futile in the context of poor countries where deprivation and starvation are the real problems.

Present world Ranking

The last section has highlighted some of the difficulties faced in comparing countries national output or income levels. The World Bank has taken a lead to compile and develop a range of economic and social indicators to compare countries of the world. It provides estimates for The Gross National Income and Product for 208 countries to facilitate their ranking. The rich countries list include most of the European countries, North America (i.e. the USA and Canada), Australia, New Zealand, Japan, Singapore, South Korea, Taiwan, Israel, Saudi Arabia, Qatar, and one or two Latin American countries. The list of poor countries consists of all sub-Saharan countries, South and South East Asian countries and most of the Latin American countries. In between the rich and poor, there are some middle-income countries such as Russia, Brazil, and Mexico.

The World Bank also provides estimates of productivity and cost of living index to rank the countries. Norway tops this list.

She has large oil reserves and a strong industrial sector. All industrialised countries show high productivity levels whereas productivity in the agrarian economies is low. The cost of living index shows rich countries with higher wages and higher input costs and poor countries with low input costs.

Legatum Institute, a think tank, has started to publish a list of global prosperity ranking which compares countries on how they perform in areas such as economic, health, education and freedom. Norway, once again, is named as the most prosperous country in the world for the last six years. European countries dominate the top 30 places. The USA is 21st in rank which is lower than Uruguay and Costa Rica. Switzerland is 2nd and New Zealand 3rd on the list. Pakistan takes a 127th position which is 16 places up from the bottom. The ten bottom countries are all sub-Saharan countries except for Afghanistan, which is placed six up from the bottom. India ranks at 102 and Bangladesh at 104.

The traditional and modern ranking methods provide fairly similar results. The majority of the world population lives in poverty, but a sizeable number live in relative comfort. The rich countries differ from poor countries not just in per capita income but many other respects. For example, the rich countries have industrialised economies, democracy as a political system, fairly honest leadership, well defined and protected human rights, gender equality, better health and education levels, tolerance of religion, stable prices, slow population growth and lesser inequality. The relationship between economic prosperity and the factors mentioned above is a complex one. But none of these factors have a clear causal relationship with the economic development. Indeed, it may be possible to argue that it is the prosperity that has caused most of these characteristics. I explore this relationship in a later chapter in detail.

National Product and Productive Capability

The productive capabilities mirrors technological, industrial, and social conditions in each country and are reflected in the physical capital (i.e. machines, factories, houses and physical infrastructure), human capital (i.e. education, health, economic and social organisations, institutions, and social and political opportunities) and the technology embedded in the machines. These capabilities, in turn, determine the level of a national income and wealth.

Every generation inherits a stock of physical and human capital from earlier generations and increases it by its efforts and requirements. Any addition to a national productive capability depends on the ability of each generation to invest in the physical and human capital using full territorial natural resources and military strength. Human capital lays the foundation of great nations and can be improved. Basic education can create simple labour skills required in all industrial activities such as conducting and promoting low-technology, small-scale industrial activities and social duties. Higher technical-managerial education and vocational training are important for technically complex industrial processes. Advanced specialised training in science and technology enable nations to invent new technology and extend knowledge. The importance of advance knowledge grows in significance as industries reach frontiers of existing technology. Both quality and quantity of education must combine to play an effective role in the industrialisation and economic development. Physical capital with embedded technology ensures greater productivity in the production process. The accumulation process ensures that the depletion of capital stock is replenished and remains intact over time.

All three productive capabilities are strongly interlinked, and it is difficult to separate their individual contribution empirically or otherwise. A balanced improvement in all three is essential to avoid detrimental consequences. For instance, the physical investment without managerial or technical skills would result in production inefficiencies, high unit costs, and low labour productivity. The development of managerial and technical skills without the technological base and entrepreneurship would encourage skill people to migrate to other countries and would have a negative effect on research, inventions and innovations. The countries may be able to import technology, but it would be expensive and constricting.

Each nation-state has a unique set of productive capabilities, which determines its wealth and annual output level. Increases in productive capabilities (i.e. an improvement in physical or human capital or technology) open up new production opportunities to increase income and wealth of a nation-state. The wealth level is a stock which is like a fruit- bearing tree. It is the tree which is far more important than the fruit it produces at any one time. A nation without 'productive capabilities' can easily lose its freedom, wealth, and civilisation to more powerful nations. Most poor countries (i.e. ex-colonies) are agrarian with a lower level of annual output and wealth. These countries lack productive capabilities. Their poverty is such that individuals have no saving, knowledge or ability to invest in physical facilities or their education. The majority lack means to support investment in education, and those who have the means under-invest due to inadequate foresight, externalities or to avoid risk. The market system fails to provide universal education, higher education or technical training in poor countries. The poor lack physical capital, human skills and technology base which require time and resource consuming to develop.

The technological capabilities result from investment in machines and research facilities to encourage inventions and innovations. An invention creates new technology whereas innovation is an application of new methods and organisation in a production process. The first depends on the research and development resources and the creative genius of a country human capital and the second depends on the spirit of entrepreneurship of the individuals. The new technology can be imported to improve production and support indigenous technological efforts such as a variety of technical engineering, production processes and design and experimental work. Formal R & D is important for industrial efficiency and growth at higher levels of industrialisation and that is true even for those countries which rely on imports for basic inventions and innovations. All countries import technology from others, but the pattern of import differs from country to country. The technology import will depend on the technology strategy that defines the relative roles of foreign and local enterprise in building indigenous capabilities. The wholesale import of technology could result in creating foreign dependency as imported machines do not bring innovating processes with them and discourage local investment in technology development which can impact long-term deepening of technological capabilities in the importing country. For these reasons, it might be preferable for the industrialising countries to restrict foreign direct investment and import technology in 'unpackaged' forms. However, the mode of 'technology import' is not neutral. Some import modes are more beneficial than others for certain strategies and certain stages of development. For a country that wishes to develop and deepen its technological base, a restrictive foreign direct investment policy will be more beneficial.

The changing economic structure requires different institutions such as markets, property rights, Laws to regulate business and labour behaviour, financial institutions, public revenue, and internal and external security forces. Over time each economy goes through a set of structural changes and end up with different norms and institutions. The term institution in its broad sense refers to the political system, civil administration, judiciary, internal law and order, external defence, business organisation, banks, markets, property rights, and the accountability framework. But the term in the narrow sense refers to the body of rules to remedy the market failures in the development of industrial capabilities. The balanced development of 'productive capabilities' is essential to avoid imbalances and to transform an agrarian economy into an industrialised one. This will also transform a society's social structure from feudal to a capitalist system.

Commercial Policy and Productive Capabilities

The world is divided into nation-states and their interests are not always harmonious. Each state acts to further its interests. A policy measure that is beneficial to a rich state may not be beneficial for a poor. The foreign trade policy carries major consequences. The industrial capabilities can only be developed under protection and the effective demand can impact domestic goods. The free international trade mostly benefits technologically advanced nations. The extension of markets to foster development argument only comes into play, once a country has established a reasonable industrial base.

A sensible and proven course of action for poor countries is to develop their 'productive capabilities' to achieve structural change and economic growth. The industrialisation can only succeed if industries are protected from foreign competition in early stages of development. The protection of agriculture sector is of limited benefits, and the free trade in food and raw materials can be in the interests of a poor country. However, the situation changes when rich countries subsidise their agriculture sector than the poor would need to protect the interests of their agricultural labour force.

The protected industrialisation could be costly, but it can more than offset this heavy cost with larger output and lower price in future. The productive capability gains under protection can secure the nation an infinitely greater amount of material goods, industrial independence and national security against external aggression in future. Surely defence of State is of much more importance than opulence in the short run.

At the end of WWII, the super powers set up two world financial institutions, (i.e. the World Bank and the IMF), to create a new world order. The IMF was to facilitate international trade by providing financial help to avoid deflationary policies and deal with the balance of payment difficulties. The World Bank aimed to help the reconstruction and development of war devastated countries of Europe and ex-colonial poor nations of Asia and Africa, by financing infrastructure projects. The fall of Berlin wall and the debt crisis in poor countries in the eighties changed these two institutions dramatically. They started to dictate and took control of economic policies of debt receiving countries under the guise of the structural adjustment or poverty alleviation programmes. Their enforced policies provided them control over annual budgets, industrial regulations, agriculture and energy pricing, foreign trade, financial markets, capital movement, labour market regulation, and privatisation of national assets. During the 90's the international lending agencies expanded their areas of interests to include political systems, corporate governance, decentralisation of decision-making, and the central banks. Their policies did not change the economic structure but have positively harmed the development of 'productive capabilities' in poor countries. Meanwhile, the World Bank on the quite has started to finance NGO's operating in the poor countries to dictate distribution policies and to polarise societies. In one sense, these two international agencies (which are controlled and managed by the rich countries) have taken away the freedom of policy formulation from the poor nations.

Growth Models

In the aftermath of WWII, there was a visible change in economic thinking; the markets had failed to deal with stagnation or externalities and to provide external security or public goods. Russia had become a socialist state, and its industrial development was progressing with rapid speed. New independent countries which had come out of colonial chains were poor, and their citizens were living on a subsistence level. Russian development and social structure model presented a great deal of attraction for the ex-colonial people. The American financial aid under Marshall Plan was proving successful in industrialising the war-shattered economies of Europe. The cold war between socialism and capitalism provided an impetus to Western nations to concentrate on the economic poverty of nations. Some economists branched out from the mainstream to concentrate on poverty problems. A new branch of economics called 'economics development got established. The neoclassical discarded concept of ' Capital Formation' was to return once again to drive economic development. The teams of Western economists with their theoretical economic development models invaded poor countries in the second part of the 20th century to resolve their poverty problem. They employed mainstream economics to develop growth models for different countries to reduce their poverty. The following growth models are representative of the post-WWII period.

Two British academic economists (i.e. Harrods-Domar) of repute developed two long-run economic growth models in the 50's with embedded short-run fluctuations. They addressed two main questions: What are the requirements to maintain a study growth of full employment income without inflation or deflation? And will income grow at such a rate so as to prevent secular stagnation or inflation? They noted that investment has a dual character. It increases income directly but also increases productive capability which in turn increases output and employment. The business cycles (i.e. fluctuation in the economy) represent a deviation from the path of steady growth. The full employment output put a ceiling on upward swings and autonomous investment and consumption put a floor on downward swings. The full capacity growth is insufficient to absorb the growing labour supply into the production process resulting in unemployment. Consequently, a lower rate of population growth is helpful in maintaining full employment in the economy. These models employed unrealistic assumptions such as constant propensity to save, fixed factors input production function and fixed capital output ratio. They tried to explain the problems of unemployment and inflation in advanced countries in the context of general equilibrium. There was no empirical testing involved. The price changes were not allowed to change to consider their impact on steady growth. In the absence of price changes or factors substitution, the predictions drawn were of limited value.

Arthur Lewis model had emulated a poor economy with formal and informal sectors. The businesses had an unlimited pool of workers available at subsistence wage level. The formal sector consisted of capitalist institutions, industries with advanced technology, urban society, markets and wage labour with positive productivity and offered vast opportunities for investment in manufacturing and technological development. The informal or subsistence sector contained agricultural activities, inefficient technology and rural society based on personal ties. There was unemployment and disguised employment in the economy and public institutions and individuals' rights including property rights were ineffective. The enforcement authorities were corrupting and dysfunctional. The surplus labour could be transferred from informal to the formal sector without any adverse impact on output or wage level in the economy, which meant that marginal productivity of labour in the informal sector was equal to zero, which was an obvious fact.

Lewis wished to find out how an economy which was currently saving and investing 4 or 5 % of its national income would convert itself into an economy where voluntary saving and investment becomes 12 - 15 % of national income? At what point, the capital formation became self-sustaining in the economic development process? Lewis observed that increased investment in the formal sector with an unlimited supply of labour would raise productivity and profits without any increase in wage levels in the economy (another obvious fact). The generated higher profits were available for reinvestment to generate higher output levels in the economy. Lewis model was similar to the Soviet planning model which had relied on the supplies of factors of production to generate economic growth. The increased investment led to an increase in productivity and profits in the formal sector without increasing wage rate in the economy which implied that the aggregate demand would remain unaffected and have no impact on output level. The poverty problem, therefore, could be solved by simply transferring human and capital resources from the rural sector to the industrial and urban sector of the economy.

Lewis model is an interesting example where mathematics obfuscates the point of the analysis. The transfer of surplus labour to a deficit labour sector increases marginal productivity which gets confused in the mathematical exposition. Could it be that this perspective intentionally misses the entire logic of how the dual economy works and how it came into existence? Could it be that this duality had been intentionally created by the elites of the poor nations to produce a reservoir of cheap labour for their businesses and to keep wages at Ricardo's subsistence level? In one sense Lewis model, along with Walt Rostow (126) and Simon Kuznets (74) contains theories of the 'stages' of economic development based on their extensive knowledge of the history of industrialisation in developed countries.

Solow-Swam Models of Economic Growth

Solow and Swan, two of leading American economists, published their development models in 1956. Both are fairly similar in approach and use the national output as an indicator of economic growth. The Gross National Product (GNP) is a function of input (i.e. labour and capital). The addition to factors of production results in the higher output. The addition to the capital with fixed amount of labour leads to higher output because of increased labour productivity. But this increase in labour productivity will not be forever as the addition of more and more machines with fixed labour input will eventually bring about the diminishing returns to scale and declining labour productivity. The technological progress can delay setting of diminishing returns in the production process. The combining of labour with a steady stream of cutting-edge technologies can raise both the level and growth rate of output. Solow claims that the introduction of new improved technology in the production process increases total factor productivity which is the most important source of economic growth. Solow (147) improved his model by introducing technology as a separate input which enabled him to deal with the issue of diminishing returns and declining labour productivity. He suggested that better and improved technology will be an effective way to prolong the addition of capital with labour input to increase the level of output. Solow estimates his growth model using US data shows *that the technological input is the major contributor to the economic development. The labour and capital combined together explain only about 12.5 % of the variation in the level of output.* This finding was backed by Denison (24) in 1962 and 1974, and Easterly and Levine (27) in 2001. In some studies, the variation in output resulting from changes in labour or capital was equal to the respective shares of labour and capital in overall output. This insight allowed economists to estimate the impact of a percentage change in labour that will have one percent change in the level of output. Such quantitative causal relationships were often used to formulate economic policies in different countries. Mathews at al (86)conducted a supplementary study to the Slow-Swan models. They wished to explain the trickle down effect of international trade on the laggard countries and if it was helpful in the convergence of living standards between rich and poor. They used cross- countries data for different groups to estimate the relationship between labour productivity and trade. Their results were mixed in the sense that some supported the positive relationship between trade and labour productivity, but others found no such relationship or catching up. Baumol (9) undertook a similar study in 1986 with revised and different countries data. His results show that the rich countries were getting richer and poor were becoming poorer as a result of free trade and globalisation policies. This study has its limitations, but the results are very important. A large number of western economists have worked in this field, and Warsh (160) has presented a good summary of their work.

Kemal et al (60) and Khan (63) used similar time series data to estimate Solow's growth accounting models for Pakistan. They assumed GDP is determined by labour and capital input. The estimated coefficients determined input factors contribution to GDP. Total factor productivity got measured as a residual, which was assumed to capture components of GDP growth that were left unexplained by capital and labour growth. The 'residual' in both cases explained about 33% of the GDP growth, 47% from the capital and 21% from Labour. Each study gave a slightly different interpretation of the TFP. For instance, Khan states that TFP captures technical progress, political stability, economic policies, and institutional changes, but he has no way to attribute any numerical value to these variables. Both studies found that growth rates were much higher during army regimes compared with the civilian democratic rule. Some investigators have split up residual term into different factors such as education, research & development, and technological changes but have provided no empirical estimation. ES Reinert (120) has provided a different interpretation of 'residual estimates' across countries. He looks at the nature of growth activities and bases his explanation to accommodate qualitative differences in his explanation. He states that 'residual' in economic growth is activity-specific; the large 'residual' as in the USA (85%) results from diversified increasing returns activities and small residuals in poor countries reflect on agrarian economies with diminishing returns activities with very little innovation or technical change.

The Swan-Solow type growth models are part of the neoclassical equilibrium paradigm which has already been critically reviewed in an earlier chapter. But there are numerous problems particular to the production function studies. These relate to underlying assumptions, estimation techniques and the theoretical methodology. These models assume that the rate of economic development depends on the degree of utilisation and rate of increase of various explanatory variables such as capital, labour, and technology. But a Cobb-Douglas production function with constant returns is not capable of capturing many significant characteristics of these explanatory variables. The explanatory variables are not independent. These are interrelated and subject to changes resulting from social, political and economic forces of an economic system. Thus, the independent factors do not fall in any neat hierarchy of cause and effect. These models assume that technical change is exogenously determined by changes in climate, geographical location and institutions. This is contestable proposition as there is no empirical finding to back it. Furthermore, the models make a certain assumption regarding the nature of other complex forces such as human capital, trade, and investment policies which affect economic development. The generality of these growth models depends in part on the validity of assumptions, and if assumed relations vary over time and space. This makes these models space and time dependent. Can a government policy impact the rate of technological change? The answer is maybe. How come the pace of inventions and innovation differ from period to period or over societies? Can the technology be an endogenous variable? Romer (128, 129) points out that technological progress is unlikely to take place in most advanced countries unless sufficient incentives are created in the shape of imperfect competition for large benefits to be captured. Here he is defending the importance of an effective system of intellectual property rights that confers monopoly status on innovations for some period to come. More recently, Romer suggests that the State can stimulate investment and can bring about economic growth in the long-run. He states that the technological progress is an endogenous factor which means that it is determined by forces within the economic system itself rather than being exogenous to the system and being determined by such factors as climate. If one assumes technical progress as an endogenous variable then Solow's and others conclusions will not hold. In his later work, Romer states that technological advances are often a by-product of an economic activity itself and a product of deliberate investment of time and money by individuals, firms and states seeking to improve on what already exists and ultimately to use it commercially. The investment in knowledge discovery is extremely uncertain and provides one reason why statistical analysis mostly fails in capturing it.

I believe that the regression analysis is not a particularly good way of doing empirical work in social sciences including economics. Causal inference from observational data presents many difficulties. The underlying assumptions of these models often turn out to be unsupported by the data. If so, the rigour of these models is a matter of appearance rather than substance. The assumptions about expected value of error term being zero are hard to swallow. The relationship established on historical data may not hold in future. To hope, that a satisfactory relation based on past observations can hold for the future, is nothing but hope. Easterly in his 2001 study has expressed similar fears about the reliability of the estimation by saying that no standard variable, even investment in equipment, is consistently and reliably linked to economic growth. I conclude my dissatisfaction with quantitative models by quoting JM Keynes, '**The atomic hypothesis which has worked so splendidly in Physics breaks down in Psychics'**. *M Abramovitz (1,2) of USA had labelled the estimated error term as 'a measurement of our level of ignorance'*

Input-Output Growth Models

Leontief (79), a Russian-born American economist, developed Input–output flows of goods and services for an economy and in doing so, he quantified Walras general equilibrium theory. In 1941, he calculated an input-output table for the USA economy which reflected on its structure. He was awarded a Nobel Prize for his efforts in 1973. The input-output analysis shows an extensive structure by which inputs in one industry produces outputs for intermediate or for final use. The matrix of inputs is used to show the effect of a change in production of a final good on the demand for inputs. His basic planning model takes the following form:

X = (1-A) Y

Where X is output vector, (1-A) is an inverse matrix of intermediate goods and services and Y is a vector of final demand goods. The model can be used to trace the impact of economic policies on output, employment, and income. The multipliers are from closed economy transactions only. The production function is fixed proportion functions which do not allow any substitutions.

Institutions and Economic Growth

North (101,102,103) along with others has turned away from the modelling approach to explaining the process of economic development. They use the prevailing institutions (norms of life, culture, traditions, work ethic and law and order) of the countries to explain their poverty or riches. Richard Ely and his disciple John Commons pioneered institutional school in the USA by explaining that a large number of institutions support the harmonious existence of each society. They claimed that political institutions establish political order, property rights, and public management framework and others support markets, trade, and finance. Each society had constructed institutions to meet the emerging needs of changing conditions. The development history of Institutions clearly indicates that institutions were not a prerequisite but supplementary to the economic development process. Some of the so-called good institutions, however, may not be all that beneficial in the development process. Indeed, some may be positively harmful to the poor countries such as the stringent intellectual property rights, and antitrust policies. The patent laws simply force poor to pay royalties for longer periods and the anti –trust policies simply deny them monopoly surpluses as a source of new investment. Similarly, democracy is imposed on poor countries based on the belief that democracy and economic development reinforce each other. Some claim that democracy promotes free markets, which in turn promote economic development, which then promotes democracy. But there is no evidence that markets and democracy have any causal relation or play any role in the development process.

To conclude, the neoclassical growth models have been found wanting and unsatisfactory in explaining economic growth. Other economists have adopted a much broader approach to economic development process and concept. Some have developed theories of cultural change to explain economic development. But culture is difficult to define and can be changed over time. Max Weber (167,168) stresses the role of the Calvinist ethic in the development of the profit motive in western capitalism. Sombart (146) has emphasised the spirit of capitalism as the creative force in the evolution of capitalism. Pareto (107) developed a general cyclical theory of social change. Veblen (160,161) and Ayers (7) look at the cultural change. The relationship between social structure and economic development has remained a debating issue. Some saw it as the cause of poverty and others only a two-way correlation. Some approved a strong role for the state to achieve prosperity and equality and others have seen it as a source of coercion and inefficiency. Marx had proposed collective welfare as the basic motivation of human beings and his proposed a new framework for resource allocation and economic development others opposed it with individualism and self-interest as a human motive in the allocation process. Veblen societies bonded with admiration and envy of predatory class and in their modern version financiers who create boom and bust in the economy to make their money. Schumpeter had believed it is 'entrepreneur,' who creates a 'productive destruction' process with rapid use of invention and innovations, which increases 'productivity' in the production process to drive economic growth.

Gross National Product and Economic Welfare

Can one measure individual well-being or welfare of a nation? Can economic welfare encompass social welfare? In order to answer these interesting questions, the natural scientists define 'welfare' objectively by measuring daily intake of calories, integration of the personality in term of longevity. But in economic welfare is a subjective concept. In early days, it was defined in term of human happiness or utility. But over time, many rival theories (126) have evolved to compete against the utility theory. The mainstream economics makes a distinction between general 'welfare' and 'economic welfare'. A person's general 'welfare' depended on a large number of economic and none economic variables. The none-economic variables were assumed exogenous, independent and constant over time. Thus, 'welfare' was defined as a function of economic variables only. An individual welfare was represented by 'utility' as happiness. A nation's welfare was the sum of individuals' welfare. The problem of distributional inequality of welfare and utilities among different people were ignored. The happiness of one person could not be compared with the happiness of another. To avoid interpersonal comparison the utility was redefined as 'state of mind, which could objectively link to an individual's welfare choice.' If a person welfare map was identical to his preference map, he could show his preference among different situations, provided he had an opportunity of a choice. Thus, a nation's welfare would be higher in state A than in state B whenever state A was chosen. Majority decision rule could be helpful, but the total 'welfare' of the nation remained unmeasured and the problem of an aggregate utility function has not gone away.

The subjective 'welfare' analysis developed by J Bentham and Hume used utility as a measure of pleasure or happiness' which has got redefined over time. Edgeworth formulated a society's welfare as a collection of individual's welfare function. He ignored the interpersonal comparison problem, defined output narrowly as GDP which counted traded goods and services with attached prices plus public goods. Bentham had included goods and services as well as non-traded activities such as household activities, human health, and selected non-profits activities in the calculation of human happiness. Edgeworth welfare function, therefore, did not capture total human welfare. Two American economists namely W Nordhaus and J Tobin (98) realised this weakness and proposed an alternative set of accounts that included a *various form of nontraded activities in arriving at what they called 'Measured Economic Development.'* But their modification was only a simplification which did not help much in overcoming the difficulty of interpersonal comparison. Sometimes economists have tried to overcome interpersonal comparison problem by assuming that individuals face the same demand and utility functions and face the same common preferences and choice behaviour. Can such presumption allow the interpretation of the utility as a numerical representation of preference? The answer is no because the choice behaviour is not unique and a wide set of possible utility functions can represent it. Thus, all efforts to aggregate happiness have remained less than satisfactory.

The classical and neoclassical economics claim that an efficient allocation regime can directly impact human happiness or utility. However, in the real world, all allocation schemes can be equally good or bad. Hence, the selection of one or the other is based on the decision maker beliefs and nothing else.

Pareto used consumer choice to formulate a national 'welfare' function. His idea was a simple one. **If some people in a nation are made better off, and none worse off, a nation welfare rises, if some were made worse off, and none better off, a nation's welfare would decline. But if some were made better off and some worse off one just did not know what would happen to the welfare of a nation.** The optimal welfare criterion was summed up as such: **'It must not be possible to make anyone better off without making one other worse off.'** Such a *Pareto outcome depends on the efficient allocation of resources which in turn depends on an optimal initial distribution.* Since 1970, The market fundamentalists have employed Pareto optimality which assumes that the people who gain higher incomes can always compensate the losers. Thus they have supported free markets, free trade, free capital movement and deregulation unequal gains which can be used to compensate the losers. But the gainers do not compensate losers in the real world.

The utilitarian approach has merits as well as some demerits. The failures are fairly obvious that it fails to take account of distribution inequalities of welfare, difficulties faced in interpersonal comparisons because of human diversity and multiple human objectives or motives. The diversity of individuals (i.e. sick and healthy) will have quite divergent opportunities even when they have the same bundle of goods and services. Some believe that spiritual well-being is far more important compared with the material well-being and an increasing prosperity does not always lead to greater happiness. The economists have assumed this possibility away by making spiritual happiness as an exogenous variable. The huge flex of people wishing to move from poor to rich countries can indicate a human preference for more over less. But such an assertion becomes less convincing when a society has gained a high level of material well-being.

Two 20th century philosophers namely J Rawls (118) and R Nozick (104) have applied their minds to the development of a welfare function. Both are directly concerned with the distribution of income and wealth in a nation-state. *Nozick* published his book entitled '*Anarchy, State and Utopia*' in 1974, which states that it is illegitimate to use the coercive power of the state to make someone better off at the expense of others; his concept of justice requires the protection of property rights legitimately acquired or transferred illegally. He clearly supports Pareto's welfare theorem 'each *and every competitive equilibrium*' is an efficient one. *Rawls* book also came out in 1974. He uses a 'maximin principle' to justify substantial redistribution of income and wealth and makes a distinction between Pareto efficient outcomes. Nozick ignored the initial distribution question and suggested that given freedom of choice, the perfect markets will allocate resources using the marginal principle to maximise output and distribution. Rawls has questioned the initial distribution of resources and provides a framework for redistribution and suggest that given that initial distribution is optimal, the freedom of choice in the perfect markets will result in a maximum output and human well-being. It is worth noting that Mill had rejected the market-based distribution and had stated that the society could use any rule to distribute national output.

I conclude this section by paraphrasing Arthur Okun (106) on the subject. He says it is not possible to believe that GNP could be converted into a meaning-full indicator of total social welfare. Some things can make a nation better off without an increase in the real income. These include peace, equality of opportunity, the elimination of injustice and violence, better understanding among various section of a society and so on. Thus, it is not possible to put a price tag on all the social factors from one year to another. Thus the relationship between output and welfare is only tentative one.

Concluding Remarks

In the distant past European countries and in recent past, the East Asian countries have created 'productive capabilities' by protecting industries and investing public money in physical and human capital. They used different strategies to achieve high, sustained growth through their manufacturing. These countries now compete in the world markets in a broad range of industrial products. The State-directed industrialisation transformed economic structures, increased productivity and made these countries rich which has posed a serious problem for the neoliberal economics of individualism, impersonal perfect markets, and full employment equilibrium. It seems that the automatic adjustment process, which did not work in Keynes time, does not work anytime to ensure economic growth or full employment.

The State directed industrialised countries adopted different strategies reflecting on size, resource endowment or location of their economies. Small and large countries selected different technological options and different industries to pursue. The pace and extent of industrial deepening were a strategic choice which required matching of human resource development and incentives for infrastructure development. There can be many grounds for concerns about the efficiency of actual interventions, but the rejection of the State role is simply absurd. The efficiency concern may call for improving information and administrative capabilities and for instituting safeguards against excessive intervention, but not a total rejection of intervention.

The Western economists have tried to manipulate the East Asian industrialisation story by rejecting any relationship between economic growth and protectionist policies. That may be the case, but these two variables show a strong correlation which indicates that both exist together. The neoliberals also favour export-led growth strategy to explain the East Asian growth story. They claim that export- oriented strategies are more conducive for rapid, efficient and sustained industrial development. These industries are 'outward-oriented' and neutral of state interventions. They claim that the State incentives were cancelled with measures to make export attractive. Therefore, lower protection and export incentives generated benefits (scale economies and efficient allocation) and dynamic benefits of faster technical progress, greater receptivity to changes in technology and markets. The market prices provided correct signals for economic activities and ability to respond quickly ensured efficiency of allocation. Hence, the State intervention on supply side had become redundant, and successful industrialisation in Asian countries was the result of neutral regimes and efficient factor markets. Such an explanation offers a clever way to refute reality. The efficiency of perfect markets is miss-conceived and unrealistic and the nature of 'implied industrial efficiency' simply miss-interpret the experience of the East Asian countries. The devaluation cannot produce the 'supply-side' incentive factors needed for industrialisation.

6

ECONOMY TRANSFORMATION: STAGES OF DEVELOPMENT

Economic development is a grand theme of economic history, and its understanding involves an understanding of the economic transformation of economies. Is economic transformation an automatic process that results from free interactions of consumers and producers in the marketplace? There is no evidence available to verify this claim. The growth models discussed in the last chapter, have described the increase in GDP as a function of capital, labour and technology within the framework of markets equilibrium paradigm. The classical and neoclassical consider economic growth as an automatic process. Whereas, Frederich List and his follower s differ from the classical view and believe that a state must direct development process. So, who is right and who is kidding us. Both parties, however, agree that It is an increase in productivity which produces economic growth in an economy. Their differences rest with the role of markets and the state in raising the productivity.

The production activities, in different countries, use a different combination of factors of production to produce goods and services. Economic structures of rich and poor economies differ greatly. The essential problem relates to the transformation of an economy to achieve economic growth. Can a hypothesis be formulated on the economic transformation and growth that cannot be refuted? If so, then the inferences can be drawn for the growth strategies and policies.

European economies Transformation

How did Europe, which had been a backwater continent in early history, not only caught up with previous great civilisation but surpassed them? One may speculate that it was climate, energy sources (i.e. coal and wood), religious zeal, organisational abilities, intellectual curiosity, and institutional creativity or any number of other factors that combined to create conditions for an industrial revolution to take place. All we know is that the industrial revolution happened in Britain and not anywhere else. But once this event had taken place, the other European countries emulated it. One single policy that has contributed most to the prosperity and strength of Europe is the policy of emulation which relates to the present day, ideas of catching up and forging ahead. The policy had many dimensions such as protection of infant industries, the creation of monopolies for targeted manufacturing activities within selected areas, transfer of resources from agriculture to the industrial sector, provisions of cheap credit, tax breaks and export subsidies for targeted activities. The policy measures such as taxing raw materials export, protecting patent rights for valuable knowledge, and promoting technology provided strong support for agriculture and industrial development. In addition, the European colonialism virtually divided the world into their protected markets for cheap raw materials and closed markets for manufactured goods. According to Marx, colonialism provided a way for the capitalist system to avoid class struggle in the Western industrialised societies by exporting surplus capital and labour to the colonies.

Stages of Economic Transformation

A country passes through different stages (i.e. physical and human capital accumulation) in the course of economic transformation. A new 'stage' represents new condition competing with old conditions. Adam Smith described these stages in term of a sequence of hunting, pastoral, agricultural, commercial, and manufacturing. Marx described them as feudalism, capitalism, and socialism. List stated that each nation passes through five phases of economic growth: savagery; pastoral life; agriculture; agriculture-manufactures; agriculture-manufacturing-trade. Heilbroner (53) described growth stages with a concentration on a particular sequence of exchange relations: barter, a money economy, and credit economy. Gras (43) defined them using the range of markets: village, town, nation, and the world. Others have classified countries by the extent of their industrialisation or by the relative significance of capital goods. Hoffmann (55) measures the growth of industrialisation by the ratio between the net value of the output of consumer goods and that of capital goods. To him, the money value of consumer goods is usually 4 to 5 times the money value of capital goods at an early stage of industrialisation. During industrialisation, the output of capital goods rises much faster than that of consumer goods. In highly developed countries, the two types of goods are approximately equal and in some cases, the output of capital goods may even exceed that of consumer goods. The proportion of its working population engaged in primary production (agriculture, forestry, and fishing) declines and the proportion in secondary (manufacturing, mining, and building) and tertiary production rises to a maximum. All these classifications indicate the transformation that rich economies have gone through over time to become rich.

The above-mentioned classifications are vulnerable, as no single sequence fits the history of all countries and are not mutually exclusive, as each stage has hangovers from earlier periods. Thus, the stages are essentially composite and liner in conception with obvious limitations. A better way is probably to distinguish economies through characteristics of domestic economic structure and the extent of external relations in the context of world markets. The domestic structure can describe the composition of productive activities as subsistence or industrial. A subsistence economy is characterised with a very little division of labour, narrow markets, low capital formation, and dominant agriculture sector. Most poor countries fall into this category. The industrial economy is one in which specialised economic units perform different functions, a division of labour is extensive, markets are large, capital formation is large, and predominant form of economic activity is industrial combined with minor agriculture production. Markets and money relations dominate the production. Most rich countries are industrial economies. A country can be at the centre of the world economy or on the periphery. All industrial market countries are dominant players in the world trade and source of capital. All subsistence economies are on the periphery and mostly large importer of manufactured goods, exporter of raw materials or agriculture goods and a net importer of capital.

The automatic markets equilibrium process does not function in poor countries which lack knowledge, capital, technology and even markets. Keynes had pointed out this problem in explaining equilibrium with large unemployed resources. A poor country can remain poor for centuries and its economy may not go through any transformation process. In such economies, an effective state can play a dominant role in bridging growth stages by raising the rate of growth above the population growth rate. Britain achieved growth with the industrial revolution. Its investment in new technologies generated a high rate of economic development that was higher than population growth rate and real per capita income was able to grow over time. The horrors of Malthus predictions went into the dustbin of history. Industrialisation created economies of scale and increasing returns activities. The diminishing returns activities turned unimportant, and the Malthusian prediction became redundant. Steel provided metal for machines and coal provided energy to shape steel into machines. The innovating entrepreneurs provided extra help to establish industrial revolution which made Britain a dominant world economy. British economic transformation can be summarised as:

1. The industrial sector grew rapidly but individual industries grew at different rates to change their relative importance in the economy.

2. The rapid industrial growth helped in agriculture sector growth by increasing cultivated area and larger output.

3. The capital accumulation level and its rate grew rapidly benefitting from the technological progress.

4. The work organisation improved Significantly with the rise of the factory system, integration of market structure, and expansion of the banking system.

5. The transforming economy led to the establishment of Capitalism. Incentives, law and order, property rights got established and promoted by the State.

6. The markets for the industrial goods expanded through international free trade and protected colonial markets. Colonies provided cheap raw materials, cheap labour, attractive capital investment opportunities as well as empty spaces for the surplus labour forces to settle.

7. The real per capita income increased with an increase in productivity and check on population expansion.

A poor country called Britain was transformed through her industrial revolution. This increased productivity slowed down the population growth rate and turned her into one of the strongest countries in the world. Britain, under Tudor rule, had adopted protectionism as a policy to impose a total ban on imports (or imposed levied high tariffs), provided subsidies for manufactured exports, imported skilled manpower, and allowed monopolies rights to develop woollen manufacturing to transform the economy from a raw material producer into an exporter of manufacturing. Prime Minister Walpole in 1721 imposed high tariffs on imports and significant subsidies on exports of manufactured goods. He also reduced import duties on raw materials, established quality control standards for manufacturing to establish English brand, and banned any industrialisation in the colonies. He declared *'that nothing so much contributes to public well-being as the exportation of manufactured goods and importation of foreign raw materials.'* This policy remained intact in Britain for the next century. No one paid any attention to the classical free trade theory of comparative advantage. Once Britain had established supremacy in industrial power, she promoted free trade to destroy infant industries in other countries and used both military might and market forces to destroy others industrial base. The present-day imperialist, like Nail Ferguson (31), a historian, justifies British policy of the time by claiming that it was the cheapest way to guarantee free trade that benefited everyone. **But it did not benefit everyone**.

All European countries emulated Britain to industrialise their economies. Germany, France, Holland, Belgium developed industries under protection and human capital in the public sector. United States under the financial leadership of Alexander Hamilton (46) in 1789 proclaimed that the US must protect its 'infant industries' from foreign competition and applied protection measures such as import bans, high tariffs, subsidies, and a ban on raw materials export, tariff rebates on machines imports, patents rights and product standards to develop its finance and transport infrastructures. Hamilton policy remained in practice in some form or other until the end of WWII. By then the USA had gained industrial supremacy and started to liberalise its foreign trade policy to benefit from the free trade.

All European nations took a long time to transform their economies from an agrarian to an industrial base. In more recent times, some Asian countries have passed through the transformation stages in a relatively short period by adopting appropriate public policies. South Korea adopted a comprehensive industrialisation strategy to develop productive capabilities such as industrialisation, human capital development including institutions and technological capabilities and has created the most advanced and competitive productive base in the developing world. She imported foreign technology only in non-equity form and developed her industries under licensing and minority foreign ventures. She provided protection, tax concessions, cheap credit and foreign exchange, subsidies industries, invested in manpower and R & D, sponsored giant conglomerate to internalise economies of scale and to overcome various market failures. The strategy was successful in minimising investment risk in the development of advanced technology. Other East Asian countries (i.e. Singapore, Taiwan, and China) have used similar growth strategies to develop their productive capabilities to transform their economies. The available evidence suggests that the East Asian countries were the most assiduous and systematic in protecting their industries and building institutions to support industrial development. They set high standards for quality assurance, manpower training, information collection, technology diffusion, and support research institutions. Each of these nations was involved in promoting private industry participation in many public institutions, in particular, those groomed to enter foreign markets or technological developments.

To sum up, an irrefutable hypothesis can be formulated that prosperity without industrial transformation of the economy cannot be attained. Thus, if a poor country wishes to become rich it must transform its economy.

The next chapter provides some details of the different countries historical policies which led to their economic transformation. Was there an automatic process at work in Europe? Or did the state policies design it? The economic history of rich nations can provide answers to these two questions. But a brief answer to these questions is that each state established industries under protection to achieve economic transformation.

7

HOW POOR BECAME RICH?

Pre-industrial Europe

The Economic growth represents an increase in the gross national product (GNP). The development of productive capabilities transforms the economic structure to increase productivity and annual flow of the gross national product (GNP). The changes in economic structure turn poor countries into rich. All European nations learned this secret by observing the transformation of England as outlined in the last chapter. Let us look at a brief history of these nations.

Among the European countries, Italy had all the elements conducive to economic growth. She had fertile soil, a genial climate, prosperous coastal fisheries, roads and canal infrastructure, basic industries and trading connections with Greece, Asia Minor, and Egypt. The trade route to Asia most used at the time was over the northern seas. Italy at the time was not a united country and her cities or republics went through internal conflicts and self-inflicted destruction. The discovery of the new commercial route to India and beyond turned Lisbon in Portugal into a new hub of international trade.

Around 1241, Hamburg and Lubeck formed a league (which later on, incorporated all the cities of any importance on the coast of the Baltic and North Seas). It adopted the name of **Hansa and** went on to establish a powerful navy, monopoly fishing rights over vast sea areas and adopted a protective commercial policy by enacting a law that only domestic vessels could carry Hanseatic goods. Other nations, later on, emulated this policy. In time the Hanseatic got excluded from foreign countries. They had no home industry or agriculture and could not defend themselves against other strong nations.

In the meantime, The Dutch had limited natural resources which forced them to overcome the inroads of the sea. This generated a spirit of enterprise in them and they perused navigation, produced salt herring, meat, dairy products and exported manufactured goods to import grain, timber, fuel, and clothing. The art of *'salting herring'* established a *'monopoly of skill'* and provided large markets and higher prices. Charles V refused to give up the crown of Spain to gain Kingship of Germany, in consequence, province of Holland broke away to form a kingdom. Amsterdam became the centre of the world's commerce and attracted skilled migrants from all over Europe. It benefited from trade with Spain and forced Portuguese out of Indo-China. Up to the first half of 17th century, Holland surpassed the rest of the world in navigation, naval power, manufacturing, trade and colonial possessions. However, she was a small country and in the face of strong nations eventually faded away.

In pre-industrial Europe, the wealth was found in places which were not endowed with a great deal of natural wealth. The rich areas like Venice and Amsterdam had hardly any arable land but became rich. One may speculate that it was this lack of natural wealth that forced the citizen of Venice and Amsterdam to specialise in manufacturing and trade. Both cities possessed three unique features i.e. diverse basic manufacturing, controlled or monopoly markets for raw material and profitable overseas trade. These factors had created productive capabilities to achieve lower unit costs through increasing returns activities and created two important institutions; patent law and tariff, which were geared to protect knowledge, domestic manufacturing and technology and to stop its transfer to other countries. This protection policy played an effective role in promoting prosperity. Florence, another Italian Republic had learned quite early a basic wealth creation mechanism; minimum political and rent collecting powers for landed class, entrust state authority to none-feudal classes to create wealth through manufacturing, and ban the export of food and agriculture goods from the city.

Richard II of England emulated Hanseatic shipping protection policy and imposed navigation laws to encourage English shipping industries in 1381. But the policy failed because England shipping industry was not strong enough and England, at the time, was not powerful enough to enforce it by force. Henry VI and James I both tried to enforce shipping monopoly around 1461, but without any success. The English trade was in the hand of foreigners and was completely monopolised by the Hansards under the title of 'Merchants of the Steelyard' in London. The British goods were being carried exclusively in their ships. England, a poor country, exported raw materials and imported manufactured goods from other European nations at the time.

A century has passed, and Edward III (1327-1377) had realised that the export of raw wool was not in the best interests of the country. According to Davis (22), He took various policy measures such as the banning of wool export, incentives for Flemish weavers to migrate and produce cloth in England, and total ban on wearing of any articles made of foreign cloth. As a result, the woollen industry grew rapidly. This success brought some new restrictions on the trade of foreign merchants such as money earned from imports in England had to be spent in England. Edward IV adopted a harsher protective trade policy and banned the import of all foreign clothing. These restrictions got withdrawn for a short time but later on were re-enacted by Henry VII (1485-1509) who had learnt in his childhood that Burgundy prosperity had depended on woollen textile consisting of wool cleaning, and manufacturing activities both wool and cleaning material imported from England. On becoming King, Henry decided to make England a woollen textile producing nation. He introduced economic policy measures such as heavy export duties on wool, subsidies and monopoly to produce textiles in selected areas, tax exemptions for a given period, and incentives to craft men and entrepreneurs to relocate to England. The policy succeeded in establishing woollen textiles and sheep farming industries in England. Elizabeth I (1558-1603) imposed an embargo on all raw wool exports from England and banned all imports of metal, leather goods, and many other articles. She encouraged the duty-free import of timber to support domestic shipping industry. England acquired the knowledge and skills of 'salt herring' and 'whale fishing' from Holland and the Bay of Biscay. Elizabeth I also dispatched trade delegations to Italy, Russia, Persia, and India. The trading relations helped in establishing the Indian Empire for England. James I encouraged shipbuilding and fisheries using bounties. All types of industries were planted in England and groomed by care and protection for centuries. Each branch of industry provided stimulus for other related industries. Ramsay (114) has provided details of various acts (i.e. 1849, 1512, 1513 and 1536) which were enacted to ban exports of raw materials and imports of manufacturing in the country

The Tudors and their successors adopted a policy of industrial protection and navigation acts which laid down the foundations for the industrial revolution. Walpole's Act of 1721 proved to be a milestone in formulating a formal industrial and trade policy for Britain. It promoted manufacturing export, raw material imports and established quality control to create brand loyalty. For several hundred years British trade policy was based on one simple rule: import of raw materials and export of industrial production.

Post-Industrial Revolution Europe

Britain

Britain, in the second half of eighteen centuries, went through an industrial revolution which combined with colonialism and protective foreign trade policy provided her with a sustained economic growth. The technological inventions such as spinning jenny, steam engine, power looms, Cotton Gin, and the sewing machine changed transformed woollen and cotton textile industries. The new production techniques and organisation of work led to increased productivity and lower unit cost of production. The steam engine reduced transport cost with a reduction in travel distance and bulk consignment. The combustion engine helped in a number of industrial processes. The telephone and telegraph made information quick. The rapid development of woollen textile and its export had boosted coal mining, encouraged extensive coastal trade, fishing industries, and the naval power. The English navigation laws wrestled the control of fisheries and coasting trade from the Dutch. England captured 1600 Dutch vessels which made her a super naval power and gave her control over trade with Spain and Portugal. Her maritime supremacy established control over all sea routes. Jamaica was captured in 1655 to establish control over sugar trade. The Methuen treaty made Portugal a dependency of England and lay down the foundation of her Indian Empire. The Gunpowder invention made her militarily strong and combined with her naval power made her super power to control large areas of the world. The invention of printing press spread knowledge and skills throughout the country to increase productive capabilities of people. These developments ensured three rent seeking capabilities i.e. protected markets to provide cheap raw materials and customers for manufactured goods, monopoly over wool and ability to charge high prices and extensive overseas trade to benefit from specialisation and economies of scale. The industrial protection remained in place till she had established an industrial supremacy. With industrial supremacy established, Britain made some attempts to relax commercial policy to benefit from extended foreign markets and to halt industrialisation of European countries. The controls over banking and insurance, skilled emigration were withdrawn in the 1820's. The Corn Laws were repealed in 1864 and the Navigation Laws in 1853. There was a relatively free trade period from 1860 to 1880, but soon after 1880, under constant demand to impose tariffs, Britain re- introduce protection measures in 1914 which turned highly protective in 1932 and in 1939. The English history provides us with an irrefutable proof that the political policies and the national economy are an integral part of each other. The colonies were not allowed to industrialise during the British rule.

The State protected and guided the private sector to invest in the industrial sector and in public utilities such as telecommunication, railroads, canals, and waterworks. However, the State did not invest directly in the industrial development during the 19th century. But in interwar years and in the post-WWII period, the British State became more active in the resource allocation. The public utilities (i.e., gas, electricity, coal, and water) were nationalised; broadcasting; civil aviation; telecommunication and iron and steel. However, the iron and steel and road haulage industries were denationalised in later years. During the 1960's there was a lot of talks about centralised planning, but most of the planning apparatus got dismantled during late 1970' and early 1980's. The protection policies adopted during the 20th century provided protection to industries and generated large revenue which helped in the financing of National health and unemployment scheme. Both National Unemployment Insurance Act and the National Health Service Act had been approved in 1911 and 1946 respectively. The State used both fiscal and monetary policies to promote economic development and full employment.

Britain had a unique geographical location, and its productive capabilities stimulated ideas, arts, culture, political institutions and citizen rights of property and security of life. Her culture and political institutions helped in shaping political leaders, civil servants and judiciary to rule for the welfare of the people. Even in the present-day time, Britain is a mixed economy, a welfare state, which uses protection measures such as trade duties, patent and property rights to promote her economic interests.

France

In the middle ages, French economy was mostly agrarian. Francis I who succeed to the crown in 1515 was fond of good things in life, favoured silk garments and encouraged silk manufacturing in the country. He provided various money incentives to the artisans to promote arts and silk production. Henry IV (1589-1610) initiated the manufacturing of glass, linen, and woollen textiles. Richelieu (1585-1642) and Mazarin (1602-1661) were both cardinal and minister of the State. They worked hard to make France a superpower in Europe. Mazarin played a dominant role in achieving peace of Westphalia treaty in 1648 which aimed to achieve economic recovery of warring countries through public investment and protection of trade and industries such as silk, velvet, woollen, fishing and navigation. France transport infrastructure consisting of land bridge corridors and canals got established developed and was made operational. France promoted trade with Spain and exported corn, wine, salt, silk, velvets and other luxury articles in exchange for gold. A large number of French workers relocated to work in Spain. Mazarin protégé Colbert (1619-83) followed in his footsteps and refined emulation policy. He introduced protective measures to transform the economy around 1650. One such protective measure was '*The advantage of the other' meaning emulation of those policies and actions of your competitors where they had an advantage over you.* He established an efficient transport infrastructure of roads and canals, set up industrial espionage and encouraged relocation of skilled people and advanced machinery in France from other European countries. The industrial policies also helped agriculture to grow, but further measures were also taken to support agriculture by reducing levies on land, reducing interest rates and equalising the incidence of taxation. At the time of Colbert death, France had already established flourishing industries, fisheries, extensive mercantile marine and a powerful navy.

According to Milward and Saul (90), France adopted a policy of laissez-faire after Colbert death. The French industry and technology were promoted through industrial exhibitions, prizes for inventions, and business organisations, but these did not do much good. English flooded French markets with their high quality, low price products, and the French had nothing much to export except a bit of wine and few luxury articles to England in return. The free trade experiment ended in a disaster and resulted in ruining the French industrial base for a whole generation.

The Revolution and Napoleon's wars rescued French industries. Napoleon is on record to state 'that under the existing circumstances of the world any state which adopted the principle of free trade must come to the ground.' He had recognised the power of productive industrial capabilities in the prosperity of a nation and encouraged inventions and innovation and improved internal communications systems.

After the fall of Napoleon, the laissez-faire policy was re-enacted. France ancient dynasty rescinded under the influence of English power and gold, but free trade again brought havoc to the French manufacturing industries and forced France to adopt a highly protective trade regime. The new policy enabled France to double its productive capabilities during the period 1815 to 1827 and remained in operation till 1848. France used commercial treaties and domestic subsidies after 1850 to introduce limited free trade but it was reversed under the Tariff Act of 1892. Soon after that, the trade terms were relaxed once again and remained in practice until WWII. According to Nye (103), Britain was more protective compared with France during this period. In consequence, French industries suffered, and the authorities realised the folly of the free trade policy.

During the interwar period, France nationalised railroad and part of armament and aircraft industries; took a majority shareholding in numerous industries, established complete control over the central bank, high tariff, and extensive quota system during the 1920's. After WWI, France adopted national central planning for resource allocation. she adopted a broad agriculture support programme (i.e. high tariffs, grants, direct price fixing, and agricultural education) nationalised commercial banks, insurance companies, motor industry, steam shipping and airlines. The Monnet Plan selected six basic industries consisting of coal, electricity, rail transport, iron& steel, cement and agriculture machinery, for public investment. Two methods were used to implement the plan. It employed controls over credit, raw materials, and imports to direct investment into the desired industries and the State directly financed a large portion of the needed investment to re-established France as a major industrial power. Secondly, in 1948, all state funds were merged to establish a modernization investment fund to provide capital for modern equipment in both public and private sectors.

A study by R Juhasz in 1915 (57) has used a naval data-set from the Napoleonic blockade against English trade to analyse the effect of temporary trade protection on the cotton spinning industry with varying trade protection for different regions of France. It concludes that the better-protected regions increased their production capacity in the infant industry and other regions with lower protection benefited but their production capacity increased with relatively lower rates.

The economic history of France provides a clear evidence how the State policies transformed the French economy from an agrarian to an industrial base. The State direct public investment, protective trade policy, colonial markets and emulation of technology played a major role in the economic transformation process. Her experience with free trade failed time and again.

Germany

Up to the middle ages, German lived a life of warfare. Serfs and women performed agricultural activities. Later on, German settlements started on the Baltic, Alps valleys, Rhine, Elbe, and the Danube. These settlements flourished with fisheries, wine, navigation and sea and land trade under various influences. Still sometimes later, these settlements turned into cities, which formed various leagues to become sizable territorial entities, but there was no vision of nationhood.

The Hanseatic League established factories all over Europe to take advantage of cheap raw materials and shipped goods all over the place. They made money by *buying cheap and selling dear*. The monopoly over sea trade through vessels ownership enabled them to develop agriculture in Poland, sheep farming in England, iron industry in Sweden, and manufacturing in Belgium. They benefited greatly from their investment in industries, agriculture and free foreign trade. But when faced strong nation-states the Hanseatic League of private businesses folded. After the Hanseatic decline, Germany got involved in a thirty-year war with France and Ottoman Empire (1618-1648) that wiped out 70% of her civilian population in some parts of the country. The peace of Westphalia in 1648 left Germany in almost 300 small states. Mazarin, first minister of France, who had played a dominant role, in achieving this treaty made sure that France interests took priority, but he had made peace based on the economic recovery of all nations involved.

From this disintegration and devastation, the foundations for the revival of German nationality emerged. The house of

Hapsburg founded a hereditary monarchy on the South-East and the Margraves of Brandenburg established another kingdom in the North- East. While in the two western corners, two other republics were formed. The revocation of the Edict of Nantes played a crucial role in bringing back skilled Germans home as a part of the nation-building efforts. Austria and Prussia started industrialisation process and introduced trade and industrial protection policy in 1834. The tariff duties imposed proved insufficient to protect infant industries. In Austria, Charles VI (1685-1740), Maria Theresa (1741-1780) and her son Joseph II (1741-1790), introduced high tariff rates to protect and encourage industrial and agricultural developments. In Prussia, Frederick II (1712-1786) won the 7-year war and became known as Frederick the Great. He introduced reforms to modernise civil service and appointed noblemen to the judiciary to improve standards. He also took measures to support industries and agriculture.

The industries such as textile, weapons, metals, silk, sugar and others were protected from foreign competition and given monopoly rights, subsidies, and direct public finance to establish and grow. The development of transport and communication supported industrial and agriculture development. The high tariff duties were imposed to generate revenues and to ensure protection for the infant industries. Some technology factories were built as demonstration models and technical experts were appointed to guide industrial development. The banking sector was developed to facilitate financing in the economy. Prussia and Austria both banned raw materials export in order to increase supplies for the domestic industries.

Fredrick II was aware that military power and strong nations always dominate economic resources, so he started to develop iron and steel industry which was to help in the production of machines for all other industries. Trebilcock (153) states that certain other measures such as monopoly grants, cheap supplies of raw materials and direct public investment were used to achieve strong industrial base and economic development. *'The advantage of others'* policy guided the development process.

The French Revolution and The Napoleon's continental blockade were indirectly helpful to the German cause. German manufacturing started to improve and grow. With the peace, came the dumping of English manufacturing and the German reacted to introduce a new system of the customs tariff in 1818, which was based on the weight and not the value of the goods. This policy encouraged the import of refined goods only. Later on, a league was formed to encourage internal trade among German states by standardising custom duties. The extended markets helped division of labour, specialisation and economies of scale in production. An Institute of Trades was established in 1821 which subsidised experiments, trained individuals in the use of new industrial methods, and spread knowledge of new techniques. Germany also encouraged cartel movement, by making the cartel agreements legal and enforceable. The State provided financial support for the entrepreneurs to visit other countries and learn their technology. During this time, special help was given to steam engines and locomotive development. Along with public initiatives, private sector started to make a sizable contribution to the industrial development. After 1840, the State practised a more guiding role and got more involved in supporting innovation, organisation, exhibitions and development of cutting edge technology. During 1870 to 1910, the private sector became more active and grew and in consequence, the State limited its role to policy making.

Von Seckendorff, the founder of German economics, published *'Der* **Deutsche Furstenstaat** *'*(The German Principality) in 1656. Which examines the importance of industries, cities, navigation, and free movement of people and removal of duties on internal trade in achieving prosperity. According to him, *the success of a ruler* *was to be judged by the prosperity of his people.* Maybe this idea led to the creation of 'welfare state' in Europe. Another German economist of the time PW Von Hornick (1638-1712), published **'Economic Principles'** which suggested that the German states must emulate the economic structures of the rich European countries and make the best use of land to achieve the largest output of food and raw materials. He added that the use of all raw materials should be restricted to domestic use in the manufacturing process. The knowledge and skills of the population should be enhanced to suit both manufacturing and agricultural industries to avoid any wastage. Gold and silver of the country should remain within the country. The imports of essential goods either be exchanged for domestic goods or imported in raw material form and used in the manufactured at home. All efforts should be made to export country's surplus output, and finally, no import of foreign goods be allowed that are available at home.

During the 19th century, Germany undertook direct investment to accelerate industrial growth. By 1912, all railroads were state owned. German flirted with the free trade policy with the creation of the Zollverein in 1834. This allowed free movement of goods in a confederation of autonomous states. The external duties on manufactures were maintained and raw materials were either admitted free or subjected to very low duties. During 1834-48 periods, the duties on manufactured imports were increased. Later on, some duties were relaxed. Again, this relaxation trend was stopped in 1879 and complete protection for manufacturing was imposed. After 1890, there was a slight tariff reduction but not that much. During the 20th century, German continued with import tariffs to protect industries, and an extremely elaborate system of control over foreign trade was developed. In 1930's, the control over every foreign transaction was approved, and it remained intact until the end of Marshall Plan.

Germany passed national health insurance and old age pension laws before WWI and fixed minimum wage rates in agriculture and organised market associations to control prices. In 1930's, she imposed further tariff protection, granted subsidies for certain commodities, and undertook drainage projects to achieve agriculture self-sufficiency. Most of the manufacturing, transport, and utilities came under public ownership. The Nazi Germany controlled all aspect of production both in public and private sectors.

After WWII, the Marshall Plan ensured German industrialisation under protection with financial support. German invented a new policy known as co-determination after the WWII, which allows labour participation in the management of all industrial enterprises.

Russia

Russia, under Peter the Great (1672-1725), formed a national political unity and made great strides in developing civilisation, industry and national prosperity. The State directly developed transport infrastructure of roads and canals which encouraged large foreign trade and helped in agricultural and manufacturing development. Catherine II (1729-1796) provided incentives to foreign manufacturers and artisans to relocate in Russia and develop manufacturing industries such as iron, glass, and linen. At about this time, wars, continental blockade, and commercial regulations of other European nations forced Russia to use her raw materials domestically. With peace, the trade relationship with Europe resumed but greatly damaged the protected domestic manufacturing. The export of raw materials, however, increased and allowed Russia to pay for the manufactured imports. Later on, the European banned the import of Russian raw materials which eroded Russian agriculture and mining directly and industrial base indirectly. Russia reacted and developed an independent system of trade and industrial development with China, Persia, and other neighbouring Asian countries. The crisis proved a blessing for the Russian economy. The woollen industry, infrastructure, and international trade flourished. In the period between the abolition of serfdom in 1861 and the beginning of WWI, Russia protected her industrial sector and encouraged the inflow of foreign capital and skilled manpower which stimulated the growth of transport infrastructure and capital goods.

The Russian revolution completely changed the political and economic structure and provided new impetus to industrialisation. All economic activities and assets came under state ownership. The WW I and II had greatly devastated the country but after WW II, industrial development took off. The Central Planning Authority launched rapid industrialisation programme by diverting huge resources. Almost 25% of GDP was invested in heavy industry to create the base for industrialisation. The period between 1928 and 1960 saw the most rapid economic growth in the Russian history. The national income grew at 6% percent a year and in 1956 Nikita Khrushchev famously boosted *We shall bury you* and he was talking about the demise of the West and its capitalist system. One area of technology that Russian excelled was military and aerospace where they achieved superiority over by reaching the moon before anyone else.

The problems of coordination's and incentives became major hurdles in the smooth running of a planned economy. The West got Russia involved in a futile war in Afghanistan that sucked the blood out of Russian body and her socialist experiment collapsed and with it the hope of millions of a better life.

It is interesting to note that after the collapse of Berlin Wall, the Russian economy implemented the neoliberal policies which almost destroyed her economy. Her industrial base crumbled and folded up in the face of foreign competition. The free movement of capital created speculative boom and bust in the stock market, and her currency became a playing tool for foreign speculators. The capital flew out of the country. In consequence, Russia became an exporter of Gas and Oil which has sustained the economy. The country elected a new nationalist leader who reversed policies to stabilise the country. At present, the energy market has been flooded with excessive supplies from the Middle East. The Russian economy has taken a nose down but has survived. Given these realities, Russia has recently adopted the Asian model of industrial protection, control of foreign capital and support of raw materials and energy resources to gear her economy to the growth path.

Spain & Portugal

In the 10th century, under Islamic rule, the vast plains around Valencia were being cultivated to grow cotton, sugar, rice and silk. Cordova, Seville, and Granada were manufacturing centre for cotton and silk. Seville was a major centre of cotton textile containing about 16000 looms, and woollen manufacturing. It had about 13000 operatives in Segovia. Other branches of industry such as paper and arms manufacturing were well established. The Islamic state was defeated, and the darkness engulfed Spain. The Jews and the Moors were either butchered or expelled. The country lost the people with skills and capital.

Spain was the largest producer of wool around 1172, which it exported to Italy for its woollen manufacturing. In Philip II (1527-1598) time, Spanish Navy was one of the most powerful forces. Her coastal towns were centres of trade and fishing. The discovery of America and the trade route around the Cape enriched Spain and Portugal for a short time and turned them into trading nations. They bought goods from others sold these in their colonies for Gold and Silver and then exchanged this gold for the manufactured goods. They did not develop any domestic industrial base and in result became slave dealers. Elizabeth I who had become Queen of England in 1585 and her sea dogs, started to harass Spain sea trade and provided material help to Holland to separate from Spanish kingdom. Phillip II invaded England with his Armada, got defeated and lost most of the sea trade to England. This defeat helped English and Dutch to develop their naval power and productive capabilities. Later on, some Spain tried to reverse this destruction by imposing restrictions on manufactured imports. But the strong nations easily avoided these restrictions under different guises. Spain had failed to establish a strong industrial base to compete against English and Dutch, and the Methuen treaty between England and Portugal ended up making Portugal a dependency of England. The unwise national policies of Spain and Portugal led to their decline and relative poverty. The acquisition of gold and silver from their American colonies had destroyed their incentives to develop an industrial base leaving agriculture as the main source of national output. After joining the EU both countries have developed minor industrial bases but their relative prosperity has come from property investment by European national to enjoy the fine weather of these countries.

Sweden, Finland & Norway

Sweden recent pretensions that it has developed through free trade and market systems do not stand the test of scrutiny. In 1816, Sweden had adopted a protectionist policy of high tariffs and total banning of imports. The manufactured cotton goods import was banned and import duty on raw cotton was kept low to develop the cotton industry. During 1830-80 protective trade policy was relaxed to allow import of cutting edge machines, raw materials and food supplies but the protection for agriculture sector was back in 1880. In 1892, industry and engineering came under strict trade controls, and domestic industries were given financial subsidies and R&D support to implement cutting edge technologies. The trade control measures along with public-private partnership resulted in a rapid rate of industrial growth between

1892 and 1913. The public-private partnership was also used to develop communication and transport infrastructure, agriculture irrigation and drainage systems. The country established an Iron office to provide subsidies to steel and iron industry, geological knowledge and impose price and technology controls. In 1932, an 'employers versus employees' agreement was agreed with conditions that employers would invest heavily in welfare services and employees would agree to moderate wage claims. After WWII, the state played a dominant role in financing and upgrading the industrial base of the country.

Finland had adopted an import substitution policy in1850 which lasted many decades. Norway became an independent country in 1814. Her economy at the time was mainly based on agriculture and fishing, but she had ambitions to develop an industrial base to achieve prosperity for her citizen. Norway adopted a protective trade policy by imposing high import duties on Swedish good in 1847. This started development of industries which lasted many decades and led to a sound industrial base and rapid economic development. This industrial base has combined with the discovery of large oil and gas reserves and has turned the country into one of the richest in the world.

Netherlands, Belgium, and Switzerland

Holland became an independent country when it split from Spain. During the 17th century, she adopted the mercantilist policies, built a strongest naval force, occupied rich colonies in Indo-China, developed extensive trading capabilities to become powerful and prosper nation. The Dutch East India Company had exceeded all rivals and had become the most successful trading company of the time. William I (1815-1840) took several measures to establish an industrial base. An industrial fund was established in 1820, and a trading company in 1830. The fund financed and improved industrial capabilities by investing in cotton textile capabilities and the trading company procured monopoly profits from trade with Java and re-invested in other industrial development. From 1840 to the end of WWII, Holland relaxed her protective trade policy which proved harmful to industrialisation. The economy turned stagnant and many countries overtook her in term of per capita income. In the post-WWII period, Holland reverted to protectionist policies such as the public development of infrastructure, technical education, and financial subsidies for the regions and gas price support for the aluminium industry.

The current-day Belgium had become rich by developing woollen textile industry under protection in the 15th century. She expanded her industrial base after the industrial revolution and has maintained the strong industrial base since then. During the 19th century, she had become a leader in selected industries such as chemicals, metals, steel, and textile. She followed England to adopt a free trade policy during the latter part of 19th century. By then she had established a strong industrial base which allowed her to expand her manufactured goods export and to benefit from the cheap raw materials.

Switzerland followed England in industrialisation and by 1850; she had become one of the most industrialised countries in the world. She had attained *world leadership in textile by 1835*. The Napoleon blockade of trade had provided protection to her industries. Switzerland did not use strict protectionist policy because of her size and her rejection of other countries monopoly on patent rights which allowed her to copy other countries technology and in time refined it to higher technological levels.

More Recent European History

The European early economic history, from the end of the 15th century until the Second World War, explains how each country copied 'Advantage of the other' and established manufacturing capabilities under protection. Each country planted industries as one plants foreign plant species by providing a supportive environment. European nations had firmly believed that export of manufactured goods and import of raw materials enriches a country whereas import of manufactured goods and exports of raw materials makes her poor. Nations trading in manufactured goods enrich both parties whereas raw material exporters remain poor. Each nation learned through experience that industrial development needs protection in early stages of development.

The 18th and 19th centuries witnessed the Europe race to colonise the rest of the world, which culminated in the Berlin conference of 1884. Africa was carved up among the European states. Most of the Asian countries were already colonies. The USA by now had been an independent country for about 70 odd years, and she had started to expand, invaded Mexico from 1845 to 1848 and conquered vast areas i.e. Texas, California, Arizona, New Mexico and Colorado. The colonies expanded markets for manufactured goods and provided cheap raw materials for large-scale industrial processing.

In early 20th century, European nations went to war with each for economic gains and supremacy. WWI ended in the vast destruction of major economies. After the First World War, the victors wanted revenge. France wanted to destroy Germany's industrial base and her ability to conduct another war and insisted that the allies should force Germany to accept conditions which would lead to her total deindustrialization. Germany had to accept but soon realised the harsh reality of these conditions and the political climate that developed in its aftermath brought Hitler to power and led to the World War II. At the end of Second World War, once again, Henry Morgenthau Jr, US secretary of the treasury from 1934 to 1945, formulated a plan to keep Germany de-industrialised. Germany, he argued, had to be entirely de-industrialized and turned into an agricultural nation to avoid any future war. All industrial equipment was to be removed or destroyed; the mines were to become non-operational and flooded with water or concrete. His plan was approved in 1943 and implemented with German defeat in 1945. During 1946 and 1947, it was realised that the Morgenthau plan was seriously harming life in Germany, which is what British Economist Keynes had told them when the terms of surrender were being discussed but no one had paid any attention to him. De-industrialization had created huge unemployment, and agriculture productivity had fallen. The unemployed industrial labour moved to rural agriculture sector resulting in diminishing returns to scale. President Hoover was asked to investigate and report on the situation in Germany who concluded that if Germany was left as a pastoral state, it would lead to the extermination of the huge population unless 25 million people left Germany. The message was quite clear that an industrial state could feed and maintain a far larger population compared with an agrarian state, occupying the same territory. In other words, industry greatly increases the ability of the State to sustain a larger population. The labour specialisation in industrial processes increases productivity and output to support a larger population. Soon Morgenthau plan was quietly buried and the Marshall Plan was devised to achieve the reverse effect, namely to re-industrialize Europe and Japan under protection. In Germany, industrial base was to be returned to its 1936 level, which was considered the normal last year before the war. In addition to the reindustrialization, European farming was also protected. The industrial protection can achieve higher real wages whereas the protection of agriculture can protect farmers' income to fall far behind industrial wages. The protection logic for industry and agriculture differ from each other. The protection for agriculture protects employment and halt wages decline. It is clear that agriculture and manufacturing are two different types of activities.

Economic History of Non-European Rich Countries

USA

The USA economic history is interesting because periods of free trade and protection follow each other closely to create contrasting consequences. At the centre of this divergent experience is the clash of Alexander Hamilton and Thomas Jefferson. Hamilton supported protection and Jefferson free trade.

British did not allow industrialisation when the USA was her colony. Only basic manufacturing such as handicrafts was permitted. In 1750, manufacturing of hats in Massachusetts created uproar in the English Parliament and resulted in a total ban on manufacturing activities. Adam Smith *'Wealth of Nations'* had claimed that the USA would make a grave mistake if it attempted to develop manufacturing industries and in a different section had stated *'only nations that have a native manufacturing industry could win a war'. The two statements convey a completely different message.* The British banning of hats production had started a rebellion which eventually led to the independence in 1776. The manufacturing activities got underway under protection and provided support to the agricultural sector. The land prices and agriculture labour wages increased resulting in overall national prosperity. With the peace of Paris, the free trade was allowed and in consequence, the flood of English produce almost killed the US infant manufacturing. The prosperity vanished and a congressman stated, *'We did buy cheapest, and our markets were flooded with English goods which were cheaper in our seaports than in Liverpool or London. Our manufacturing was ruined, and even our importer became bankrupt, and land property became worthless.'* These conditions lasted until the formation of federal constitutions which authorised the Congress to form a unified protectionist commercial policy.

A protective trade policy was adopted in 1789, which proved beneficial. President Washington congratulated the nation in 1791 on the remarkable progress of industries, trade, and agriculture. The tariff duties in 1804 proved inadequate against English competition and the economy suffered. The declaration of war in 1812 provided protection to the domestic industries and huge stimulus to the domestic output which was sufficiently large to satisfy both domestic and export demand. The prices and wages increased rapidly and resulted in universal prosperity. After the peace of Ghent, the Congress doubled the previous duties in the first year to stimulate economic progress. In 1816, the trade policy was relaxed and import duties were reduced resulting in similar economic decline as was experienced in 1786 to 1789.

Hamilton, the first US secretary of the treasury had understood 'infant industry' argument and the dynamics of economic development. The American manufacturing was to be protected from the foreign competition to make his country strong and powerful. He had known that frequent financial crises were more common to the agriculture-based economies and importers of manufactured goods as import and export levels turn disproportion to each other in such economies. He went on to form a protectionist foreign trade policy

The tariff duties were increased in 1824 and 1828 respectively to safeguard the country's interests. The protected industries provided a ready customer for the agriculture goods. Monopoly was considered desirable to promote inventions and innovations. The banking was under central control between 1791 and 1836.The individual states were directly involved in developing productive capabilities and economic development during the nineteenth century. The U.S.A. has gone through periods of growth through Hamiltonian policies under Lincoln,

FDR, and Eisenhower and periods of drift and stagnation, led by followers of Jefferson such as Jackson, Bryan, Reagan and Bush. The story of growth is the story of strong, activist and effective government empowering the private sector through public investment.

DeWitt, a follower of Hamilton, became the mayor of New York City. He circumvented Jefferson by getting New York State to launch a massive bond issue to finance the building of Erie Canal, which linked Midwest with New York in 1825. A year after the completion of the project, the price of Midwestern grain at New York harbour fell by 90%. The New York boomed and the city became the financial and industrial centre. Jefferson had called the project *'a little short of madness'*. The Erie Canal proved the key to economic growth which turned the USA into a world economic power. The State took a risk which the private sector could not take.

In post-WWII, the growth in the U.S.A. was led by the high-tech innovations. Mazzucato in her recent book *'The Entrepreneurial State'* describes how all new technologies (i.e. LCD flat screens, multi-touch screens, lithium-ion batteries, GPS, communication satellites, the internet, cellular technology, SIRI voice recognition and more) which made the I Phone 'smart' were developed and sustained with massive government investments. The Apple was 'surfing' on a wave of state funded and state-led research and development. In the early years of the 21st century, USA is still carrying out a protective policy to safeguard her agriculture and industry from foreign competition. She protects industry under temporary protection measures, anti-dumping duties, and countervailing duties to offset the so-called foreign subsidies. Besides this, the US provides financial supports her failing industries. All this happens in spite of WTO agreements and when poor are being forced to adopt free trade policies of the Washington Consensus.

New Zealand

The British colonies with white settlers such as Canada, Australia, and New Zealand followed the example of the mother country and had embarked on programmes of industrialisation under protection to achieve their prosperity. The Asian and African colonies with no sizeable white settlers remained without their voice or freedom.

New Zealand was a low-cost agriculture producer but geographically a peripheral country. It has vast territory and very small population. Her natural resources were distributed to white settlers, on squatter's right bases. In her early history, she emulated industrial development policy of the European nations but failed because of huge transport cost and she did not have large markets to take advantage of economies of scale or specialisation.

Later on, she focused on agriculture as a preferred supplier of agriculture products, mechanised agriculture and used good quality input such as seeds and fertilisers to increase production for export. The expanding agriculture output allowed New Zealand to raise farming incomes, avoid adverse terms of trade, and maintain high living standards. The relationship with Britain became fractured when Britain joined the European market in the 1960s and raised import duties on agricultural goods to enforce EU common agriculture policy.

New Zealand started to face problems like other agrarian economies; her home markets were narrow, the competition for agriculture goods in the international markets was fierce. The terms of trade posed a serious problem. New Zealand had to find new markets for products in Asia and Australia, but prices for the agriculture goods were lower in these markets. New Zealand economic performance suffered, and population living standards started to decline. In consequence, New Zealand turned to industrialisation with very little protection. First, she built huge aluminium smelters and petrochemical plants in the 1970s, which could not compete against foreign competition and were written off as large losses. During the 1980s, she embarked on privatisation programme and cut-down annual expenditures by reducing social benefits which reduced effective demand and led to the even bigger economic decline. The country elected a new Labour government in 1999, which went on to scrap the free market paradigm and adopted protectionist industrial policies with considerable success. New Zealand provides a clear proof of the thesis that the industrial development needs protection in early stages, and a free trading agrarian economy would have a great deal of difficulty in raising or maintaining high living standards.

Japan

Japan had little contact with the outside world around 1639. Her political organisation was decentralised which had created pluralism. Markets were evolving with many advanced features of financial innovations. American came with gunboats in 1854, and turned Japan into a semi-colony and forced her to open markets with tariff rates below 5%. The flood of superior foreign goods killed her infant industrial base. The political subjugation undermined feudal political order. The Meiji restoration in 1868, restored Japan political independence but she was still bound by low import (i.e. 5%) duties treaties of 1858. Japan took on a more active role in the economic development process. The State established model factories for ship building, mining, textile and weapon manufacturing in the public sector. The rapid industrialisation restored some sort of confidence.

During the 1870s and 80's, Japan started to support privatised industries through large subsidies and directly financed and operated infrastructure projects, manufacturing, transport, telecommunication and other public utilities. The shipping industry grew with generous financial subsidised. The State invested in iron foundries, machine shops, silk and cotton spinning factories, cement, paper, glass factories and established Yawata Iron Works in 1896. After 1882, model factories were sold off to the private sector at a discount, but railroad, telecommunication, iron and steel, and public utilities remained under the State control. Japan made a significant investment in human capital at the same time when she was investing in physical capital. She trained managers, engineers, and labour force. The ministry of education was established in 1871 and the State encouraged the import of foreign technology, foreign experts, and foreign institutions such as criminal law based on the French model. Japan copied civil and commercial laws from Germany and banking from the USA and Belgium. She modelled her educational institutions on French, German and American schools and universities.

The West imposed tariff treaties ended in 1911 and Japan started to pursue interventionist and protectionist policies to foster industrial development on a massive scale. Some industries were given greater protection compared to others. From 1920 onward, Japan encouraged the formation of large cartels to avoid wasteful competition and to achieve economies of scale. The cartel policy encouraged concentration of economic power and monopoly practices which in turn allowed output and price decisions to create maximum surpluses for reinvestment in the industrial sector. The law restricted workers bargaining power in wage negotiations to keep national wages at a low level.

During 1930,s Japan invested heavily in both physical and human development and especially in heavy industries. This investment took a long time to show results. The bright young people were sent abroad to study foreign industrial techniques and given high positions on return. Japan also imported hundreds of foreign specialists to establish new industries. The State levied taxes on private banking, land and consumption goods to support education and industrial programmes.

During the Second World War, US conspired and brought Japan into the conflict and then destroyed her by dropping atom bombs on Hiroshima and Nagasaki. At the end of the war in 1945, General MacArthur introduced a Japanese plan to redevelop economy. The industrialisation under protection was encouraged and Japan embarked on a new industrial strategy for import substitution and high-quality consumer goods industries. *The concept of re-engineering was adopted to catch up and forge ahead.* A policy to subsidise targeted industries and large industrial groups was implemented to achieve increasing returns and high-value production. From 1950 to 1970, Japan experienced fast industrial growth and GDP growth rate of 8% per annum. Her industrial groups like Toyota, Sony, Honda and Panasonic became a household name throughout the world and Japan at one time became the second largest economy in the world.

Singapore, Taiwan, Hong Kong and other East Asian Countries

All East Asian countries had understood the importance of 'manufacturing multiplier' in generating national wealth. Their growth models contain free domestic markets, public investment in certain sectors and industries, investment in human capital and infrastructure and guided foreign investment. Each of these countries took the view that national welfare takes priority over individual's freedom at least in early years of development. They have achieved success by cultivating manufacturing under strict protection with high import duties, export subsidies, cheap credit and foreign exchange and central planning for resource allocation. The import of foreign technology was encouraged and subsidised and importers were allowed to operate under imperfect market conditions. Each state actively created environment and conditions to suit adopted strategy. However, their growth strategies differed from each other in the selection of target industries and enterprises, size and scope of technology development, types of industrial structures, and domestic or foreign ownership of industry.

Chang (17, 18) has narrated their success story in a convincing manner. They were successful in choosing correct industries and technologies. Each state promoted the formation of the large cartel by passing conducive regulation laws, investment and pricing policies, subsidised credit and foreign exchange to avoid wasteful internal competition and face up to the international competition. The monopoly surpluses were redirected into new industrial investment. Each state directly invested in human capital to meet industrial development manpower requirements. An effective manpower plan for each industry helped to smooth the linkage between human and physical capital formation. The financial institutions diverted domestic savings to the selected industries and firms which were favoured with tax breaks, exclusive licenses, government contracts, and protection from foreign competition. The foreign direct investment was controlled and encouraged to form partnerships with local companies. Only certain sectors could receive foreign investment and under certain conditions such as transfer of technology to local partners. Each state, directly and indirectly, supported the development of basic infrastructures such as roads, water, sanitation systems, education, law and order, finance and basic scientific research. The rest of the economy was allowed to operate under normal market conditions.

The Taiwan political leadership took the decision that the most effective way to promote prosperity would be to encourage the development of the export industries through cheap finance, tax incentives, and subsidised exchange rate. They kept local currency undervalued through a pool of US Dollars from export earnings. The foreign exchange was made available to the export industries at subsidised rates. The machine tools manufacturing industries received financial support and protection from foreign competition. The investment in human capital targeted selective skills and sent talented people abroad to study managerial and technical skills. They were encouraged to achieve excellence in scientific fields and learn leadership skills. On return they got responsibilities to head newly formed ventures. All these measures turned Taiwan into a vibrant hub of manufacturing and innovation. The country became a leader in design and production of new products. Another important feature of the Taiwan industrial strategy was to encourage foreign direct investment to build large production plants hiring a large number of locals, but one of the conditions for the foreign investor was to buy components and services from the local companies. The domestic component production helped in process innovations and encouraged local government bodies to encourage and support local entrepreneurs to initiate new ventures all over the country. Taiwan has developed mainly small and medium enterprises with institutional support for technology import and its and diffusion in the country.

Singapore strategy relied on foreign technology import, incentives for investors to relocate, bring cutting edge technology to the country. The state invested public money in human capital to meet the expanding physical capital formation and services sector.

Hong Kong strategy relied on the specialisation of light industry. She invested heavily in human capital to build skills base, entrepreneurship, trading know-how and infrastructure. She encouraged and supported selected export activities. such a strategy requires less state intervention compared with the 'comprehensive industrial' strategy of South Korea.

Concluding remarks

The prosperity and welfare of any nation at any time depends on accumulated human and physical capabilities. The intelligence, literacy, freedom, morality, health, and industry of people represent cumulative human capabilities. The stock of capital goods and embedded technology determines the physical capabilities. Each nation state provides suitable public institutions and security to encourage personal ambitions and social cohesion and her policies, directly and indirectly, help in creating the size and quality of 'productive capabilities'.

Every rich nation developed her 'productive capabilities' by transferring a larger share of GNP to savings and investment. This transformed economy from an agrarian to an industrial base. The industrial activities with increasing returns to scale increased productivity in production and led to higher level of output. The infant industries were protected with a restrictive commercial policy to avoid foreign competition. In summary, one may conclude that all rich countries had effective states with purposeful leadership and economic and political stability to implement national policies. Each state provided and supported investment in human and physical capabilities including research. Having established a sound industrial base, each state then encouraged international trade to benefit from international specialisation and wider markets. Britain industrial revolution, restrictive trade policy and colonialism made her rich and other European emulated her to achieve prosperity. The USA copied actions and deeds of Britain and not words. Japan and East Asian states used more refined policies compared with the early European to achieve prosperity. They used diverse industrial protection measures such as tariffs, subsidies, tariff rebates for exported goods, granting of monopoly rights and cartel formation, cheap credit and much more in early stages of industrial development, which supported agriculture sector and achieved balanced growth. The parallel development involved an interplay between increasing returns activities of the industries and the diminishing returns activities of the agriculture and created synergies among activities, entrepreneurship, knowledge, and leadership.

History teaches us that the restrictive trade policy is a natural result of the different national interests, and unless the whole world comes under one law these interests will remain. The dominant industrial powers always benefit more from free trade.

PART 3

NEOLIBERAL ECONOMICS: DOMINATION OF A NIGHTMARE.

With the fall of Berlin Wall and the collapse of socialism, the neoliberals have enforced their philosophy of individualism in the shape of neoclassical economics on the world with the claim that it presents default conditions for economic growth or poverty reduction. The West accepted paradigm as their victory and the poor were forced to accept it as 'structural reforms' or 'poverty reduction ' conditions for loans, which were needed to deal with a current account or balance of payment deficits. The ruling elites of poor collude with the lenders to lace their pockets without caring about the consequences for the country or poor. Thus, the *end of history* paradigm has turned into a nightmare for the poor of this world.

There are potentially three main regimes of resource allocation, individualist utilitarian, collectivist utilitarian and a combination of individualist and collectivist utilitarian. In reality, the pure individualist or collective utilitarian regimes exist only as a theoretical possibility.

The neoclassical equilibrium model is underpinned by individualist utilitarian resource allocation which represents only a theoretical possibility. The allocation of resources and distribution of output is done by the markets and rest on '*to each according to his ability and want*'. Under the utilitarian collectivist regime, the national resources are collectively owned and allocated by the directions of a central authority to ensure efficiency and maximum happiness of generations. This approach is based on *"from each according to his abilities, to each according to his needs"*.

Both allocations regimes have strengths and weaknesses. The market allocation can be rigged, fails to take a long-term view and cannot deal with externalities or public goods. The central planning can be corrupted to become a vehicle for special interests. Both systems aim to create societies where individuals will enjoy maximum freedom and happiness. But fail in their set ambitions. Both can achieve efficiency under strict assumptions but in reality, such an outcome is impossible.

All economies of the world are mixed economies of individualist and collectivist utilitarian and differ only in the size of the State budget. The national resources are allocated partly by individuals and partly by the State. In most countries, about 30 to 40 % of GDP is collected as taxes and duties and is spent on public goods and transfer payments. The markets and the State allocation operate side by side. The public allocation choices are made by the political representatives who can be inconsistent and corrupt. The election processes can be rigged, and the political parties can indulge in horse-trading. The preferences may not be formulated accurately of the public expressions. Amartya Sen in his recent work accepts a mixed economy framework where markets and state both play role in resource allocation. He describes development as a process of extending personal freedom and the State education and health (both semi-public goods) policies can promote it.

The next two chapters' details the failures of neoliberal economics.

8

NEOLIBERAL POLICIES:
A POVERTY TRAP

After WWII, The USA had become new super power and leader of the free world. The American universities turned into research centres of excellence and attraction for the world's brightest minds. A large number of East European scholars' escaping from the tyranny of Hitler, sought refuge in the USA. Some of them are famous economists such as Machlup, Mises, and Hayek. The others are Arendt, Berlin, Polanyi, Popper, and Talmon. They would in time generate new ideas and thoughts.

The 'individual versus social welfare' debate would become a central issue in economics. The Soviet socialism had started to become a model for the poor people and countries. The East European economists had seen and suffered from the violent state coercion and hopelessness of the individuals. The neoclassical economists like Hayek, Friedman, Solow, Arrow, Fisher, Lucas and others, started to refine and improve individualism as a mean to human prosperity. It is collective thinking of these individuals which has separated economics as a science of resource allocation from its roots of political economy. Keynesian ideas needed to be destroyed and Hayek and Friedman took the responsibility to do so. The State and its power got turned into an evil concept that must be curtailed and made harmless.

In order to make liberalism as a utopia, the neoclassical economists turned the classical system of economic freedom into a new mathematical model of *general equilibrium. Which gave economics* a status greater than any other human-related discipline. Walras had provided a mathematical demonstration of the 'invisible hand' by assuming humans as *Homo Economicus* who live under false and unrealistic conditions. So individuals maximising self-interest, self-organise into functioning economies. The free markets turned into self-regulating entities which reconcile supply and demand exactly ensuring optimal level of output for the given amount of resources. There was no need of top-down regulation by the State and it should stop meddling in economic management. The metaphors like 'invisible hand' were kept alive to make powerful claims of efficiency and optimality.

The neoliberals have combined the assumed efficiency of general equilibrium model and philosophy of individualism to formulate a policy menu that has become a dominating paradigm since the fall of Berlin wall in the second part of the 20th century. The poor stagnating economies and free- falling transition economies of Eastern Europe were turned into laboratories and their citizen into lab rats to observe the consequences of the neoliberals' policies in practice. The corrupt leadership in poor countries accepted their policies in exchange for loans and aid to enrich them in the name of economic stability whereas the newly liberated transitions countries accepted them to get rich quick but soon learned that blind acceptance always brings about nasty consequences.

The Washington Consensus Policies

The term Washington Consensus describes neoliberal policy measures formulated by John Williamson of the USA. These are accepted and agreed by most free-market economists of the western world. The IMF, the World Bank, and the US Treasury use these measures as a default policy for the poor to get rich. A summary of these measures is given below.

1. **Freedom of Individual Choice**: Individuals' act in self-interest. Markets should operate freely, and no attempt should be made to regulate them by social or political actions. Any intervention in individual choice or markets operations distorts resource allocation.

2. **Open Markets**: Markets should be deregulated to encourage startups and measures should be taken to remove all restriction on internal and external competition. The neutral and perfectly competitive markets achieve allocation efficiency.

3. **Financial liberalisation**: Transition to market–determined interest rates and the opening of financial markets to foreign participation will bring new investment in the economy to generate greater productivity and output.

4. **Foreign Exchange rates**: The competition in foreign exchange will determine equilibrium level of the foreign exchange rate which would encourage rapid growth in non-traditional exports.

5. **Foreign Trade**: Free movement of goods and services across borders. All quantitative and qualitative restrictions to be abolished, tariffs to be reduced to a minimum or abolished completely. The free trade extends markets to achieve universal resources allocation efficiency.

6. **Freedom of Capital Movements**: Abolish all barriers impeding the entry of foreign direct investment. Allow capital to move in and out of the country for greater productivity.

7. **Privatisation**: The government should not provide goods and services or own productive assets. The existing state-owned assets should be sold off. The economic role of the state should not extend beyond the enforcement of contracts and protection of private property rights.

8. **Fiscal Discipline**: Budget deficits should not exceed a noninflationary level. Marginal tax rates should remain at a minimum level with an enlarged tax base. Taxation should not be used to redistribute income and wealth.

9. Better Protection for property rights, especially in the informal sector.

10. New spending priorities should favour human and physical infrastructure, etc.

11. Some neoliberals consider that anti-monopoly policy is needed to preserve the competitive markets but others reject it.

12. The independence of the central bank and the financial institutions is desirable and the monetary policy must be preferred to the fiscal measures. This ensures a minimum role for the State in economic management.

The above-given policies are based on the neoclassical general equilibrium model and this paradigm has been supported by academic institutions, media houses, and think-tanks in the rich countries. However, their support is ideology based and the market fundamentalism of Hayekian type lies at the root of proposed policies. Fischer (32), an American Economist, have supported these policies in his study of 2003. John Williamson the father of the Washington consensus, however, admitted in 2004, that after fifteen years of experimentation he now favours a larger State role in the management of the economy. He claims that he had intended his policy measures to act only as flexible guidelines but others had turned them into a rigid model for all developing countries irrespective of their economic conditions or stage of development. He accepts that his policies have failed to deliver economic growth in Latin American and transition economies. Rodrik (125) has argued that the neoliberal paradigm has failed to deliver the predicted results in the countries which had been forced to adopt it. One cannot find a single country where neoliberal policies have resulted in economic stability or prosperity. This failure has become known, and yet these policies remain intact, favoured and foisted on highly indebted poor countries like Pakistan. It does not matter if the borrowing country is facing high unemployment, falling exchange reserves because of adverse terms of trade, declining national and international demand and capital shortages because monopoly profits are being taken out of the country by the looters. All poor countries are the same and one pill will cure all problems but the pill does not cure, it increases the illness.

The rich countries including the USA have used their aid budgets and promises of access to their domestic markets as an incentive for the poor to accept these policies. The WTO has played a major role by forcing trading rules that favour free trade of goods, free capital movements and direct foreign capital investment. The hidden agenda (not so hidden anymore) of these so-called structural reforms programme, was to engineer a far more market radical practice in poor countries for legal exploitation.

Failures of Neoliberal Paradigm

Neoclassical General Equilibrium Model and Markets Failures

As a deductive argument, the freedom of choice and free market framework can deliver efficiency of allocation, but it is only a theoretical possibility. The Dynamic Stochastic General Equilibrium macro model based on micro foundations is equally unrealistic and has no empirical backing. A central planning agency (with different unrealistic assumption) can do the same. If both systems can achieve the same logical end, there is no ground why one should take any preference over the other. Besides, there is not a single country in the world which can claim to represent the neoclassical free market economy. It is difficult to accept that a theoretical possibility without any empirical evidence can represent a real-world economy.

The textbook failures of the market framework rest with unrealistic assumptions of human motivation, instantaneous reactions, perfect information, certainty, none provision of public goods and externalities. These are well documented. The failure of demand and supply functions to capture production theory and qualitative differences in labour poses a further serious problem. The quality difference in productive activities (output) can lead to material differences in income. The implied equality of human capabilities, perfect information, and economic activities across nations is not possible or empirically proven. The assumed rational selfishness of *Homo economicus* preference negates human nature and the myth of self-regulating markets has collapsed in the aftermath of the financial universe meltdown in 2007. The supply and demand do not resolve anything and everything as we were told by the Chicago Boys. Privatise everything including State-owned enterprises, pension, curtail unemployment benefits, open borders and so forth. They had thrown away the Keynesian insight regarding unemployment, the ineffectiveness of monetary measures in determining the level of unemployment and output and uncertain future. In short, the myth of the prosperity-generating markets has been dispelled.

The greed and selfishness of individuals are not always good as it can destroy individuals and cost nations their freedom. The certainty of future outcomes is simply not valid in a changing world. The financial crisis of 2007 and inequality within nations and across nations has provided a clear proof of markets failures. The model based on individuals' greed, as a motive, is no longer accepted or acceptable. Human nature is such that a person will do everything to survive but beyond this the concern for others also becomes important. If we are devoid of these concerns, who are we? Hayek had accepted that individual may not be the best judge of his interests, as he takes decisions with partial or incorrect information, therefore, his decisions cannot lead to an optimal output. It may be that superstructure of human values does not accept pure greed as the basis of human civilisation. Human motivation is complex and multifaceted and even inconsistent over time and space. Hayek knew that information will always be incomplete and imperfect, and markets can only vaguely indicate the directions of individuals' wishes and fail to take account of risk. The assumption of numerous sellers in the market is another myth refuted by the existence of large multinationals that control the supplies and the markets for various goods.

The neoclassical trade cycle model (DSGE) treat variables as if these are drawn from a 'data-generating process' that unfolds over time and this data-generating process is known. Such an assumption is simply ridiculous as no one can access to the mythical Holy Grail of the 'data-generating process. The efficient markets did not anticipate the enormity of the problems of unregulated financial markets. There is no reason to believe that the variables come from the stochastic probability functions with known means and variance. Keynes had already pointed this fact in his work on probability by stating *that people behaviour facing uncertainty cannot be predicted.* The markets have no in-built automatic mechanism and the monetary policy of zero interest and lower taxes cannot deal with stagnation or secular stagnation of present day.

The markets are corruptible like any other man-made system and privatisation of state assets and deregulation of markets does not result in greater economic efficiency or elimination of corruption. The perceived economic efficiency comes from the conversion of the public into private decisions. The corruption disappears because politicians and civil servants lose authority over resource allocation to extract bribes. But private short-term decisions could be in conflict with national interests and corruption is ripe even in rich countries. Moreover, the neoliberals' market role comes in the shape of private contractors and more frequent contracts; which will simply increase bribe taking opportunities and waste of national resources. The false accounting, insider trading, and tax cheating are a sort of corruption and are endemic and quite common in the rich countries.

The markets efficiency leads to democracy which in turn leads to economic growth. It is claimed that in democratic systems fear of re-election becomes a check on the bad behaviour of the politicians and market-based allocation ensures economic efficiency and development. But democracy and economic growth have no causal relation and the principles underlying democracy and market are different. In a democracy, it is one man one vote, whereas it is one $ one vote in the market. The wealth carries a greater weight in the marketplace and could subvert democratic decisions. In reality, the rich can buy politicians to subvert the interests of a layman. The democracy and markets can both be manipulated with consequences for the allocation efficiency. The classical economists had not favoured democracy because they feared that poor majority would adopt policies against the rich minority interests to kill incentives.

The neoliberals accept that income and wealth distributed by the markets represent differences in the productivity based on differences in effort, talent, and skill. This implies that 1% of the world population that controls 99% of the world assets have such skills or talent not found in the 99% of the world population. The argument that state intervention in the distribution represents coercion is rather a bogus one. A fair distribution leads to an equal and fairer society which promotes economic development. All rich countries redistribute income and wealth to promote fairer societies. Rawl has shown that economic efficiency can remain intact with a new income and wealth distribution.

The conflict of interests between generations on the one hand and the State and individuals on the other has implications for the allocation process. For a state, development of 'productive capabilities', take priorities over individuals' consumption level because this ensures higher output for the future. The current sacrifice is more than compensated by the larger output in future. To accept self- interest as a motive for individuals' choice and discounting future streams of benefits in investing decision implies a preference of present over future and buy the cheapest as a choice criterion.

The national interests of different nations are not always in harmony. Each nation uses various degrees of direct participation in the initiation, direction, and protection of her economic interests. The countries such as Japan, USA, Germany, Britain, USSR, China, and East Asian are examples of state-sponsored development. The poor countries lack human and physical capabilities and have stagnant economies. There is no automatic adjustment mechanism to correct stagnation. The poor suffer from low saving and investment levels and lack private sector to invest in high risk and public goods. The state participation becomes a must under these conditions.

To conclude, the human motivation cannot be summed up by self-interest, markets are neither neutral nor perfect, future is uncertain and efficiency of general equilibrium model is make-believe efficiency of false assumptions and claim of maximum welfare is deceitful.

Property Rights

The property rights are an essential feature of the neoliberals paradigm. Individuals are the best judge of their interests, and unless there is protection for the rewards of their efforts, they will not perform to the best of their abilities. Thus 'property rights' must be accepted and protected in the free markets economies. The legitimacy of property rights turns controversial if the property has been acquired by force or cheating. There is 'crime behind every fortune' can be observed in every society. Mill and Veblen both had high- lighted this fact in their work. *Let them steal and they will steal.* Russia went through this looting in the post-1989 period. Her economy had collapsed as a result of the long war in Afghanistan, and she had accepted and implemented the Washington Consensus policies to generate economic growth. The free movement of capital enabled corrupt politicians, officials and businessmen to steal and take their loot to the foreign safe heavens. Pakistan is going through this stealing and looting at present as there is no one there to make ruling elites accountable for their corruption and looting.

More recently the debate on property rights has become a debate on intellectual property rights which have been enforced through WTO agreements. The property rights have evolved through changing economic conditions to facilitate transactions and therefore cannot be an independent causal factor in determining economic performance. In early years the individuals did not have property rights and it has not done any harm to the Chinese economy. The strict imposition of intellectual property rights creates monopolies and help rich at the expense of poor.

Free Foreign Trade

The globalisation was to bring blessing in its wake but its magic spell has gone. Ricardo's theory of comparative advantage provides the underpinning for the free foreign trade theory. It is claimed that extended markets allow greater specialisation, the efficiency of allocation and benefits for all trading partners. But it does not benefit all trading partners, only the industrialised economies.

Ricardo had claimed that free trade benefits all trading partners even when one country can produce everything more cheaply than others. The efficient country benefits by specialising in the production of goods with greatest cost advantage whereas the least efficient country gains by producing goods with least cost disadvantage. *With this theory, Ricardo condemned colonial countries to permanent poverty, by arguing that colonies would still benefit from trade if they were to produce raw materials where they had the least cost disadvantage.* The acceptance of this theory implies that existing technological base of each country is her permanent state, and her comparative advantage cannot change. A recent free trade theory by Heckscher-Ohlin-Samuelson reach the same sort of conclusion by stating that the different countries comparative advantage is based on the relative endowment of 'factors of production' and not on technology. Every country uses the same technology to produce; therefore, the country's comparative advantage is determined by how suitable is the technology used for each product and how intensively it uses its factor of production (i.e. labour or capital). Again, this theory is based on the unrealistic assumption that countries have the equal capabilities to use advanced technology. The fact is that poor countries lack this capability, and that is what makes them poor. The acquiring of new technology matched by human capital development changes 'productive capabilities' and comparative advantages to produce more complex and expensive goods with high value added to increase economic development.

A country's development process takes time and experience to develop technical and organisational skills, physical capabilities and ability to absorb new technologies. During this process, newly created capabilities need protection from international competition. The protection period usually has its cost, but the future gains compensate for it. The sacristy of cheaper and better-imported products in the present is compensated by the larger output generated by the new physical capabilities and help to break out of the vicious circle of poverty.

Now a day's rich countries claim that they became rich because of free trade policies. But history tells us a different story; every rich country became rich by applying protective policies such as high tariffs, subsidies for manufactured exports, restrictions on foreign investment and regulation of capital movement. Once their protected industries had matured, they embark upon an act of 'free trade imperialism' to halt industrialisation of others and to keep them as suppliers of raw material. Britain had adopted this policy of 'free trade imperialism' in the 18th century, and USA did the same after WWII. Indeed it can be argued that the American economy has been successful simply because it ignored free trade policy. American cities spend billions of public funds to establish incubators for high- tech industries and provide financial help to foreign companies to establish industrial plants. The financial incentives generate extra income from newly established plants which recover the costs of the subsidies. The USA Small Business units spend about $2 billion public money to support private American companies each year. It seems that the Washington Consensus policies are exported to poor countries but not applied at home.

The fact is that the free trade theory promotes short run efficiency over long run productive capability and economic growth and its acceptance by poor means that they are happy to remain poor forever. The neoliberals have forced liberalisation of free foreign trade since debt crisis of 1982. They were supported by WTO agreement in 1995 and in consequence, poor countries tariff revenues have shrunk, annual budgets deficits gone up, unemployment levels have increased, and infrastructure investment in education and health have reduced.

Infant Industry arguments

The free foreign trade keeps poor countries agrarian as any effort to industrialise is wiped out by the competing efficient foreign countries. An 'infant' industry like an infant, needs protection and help to grow up and be strong. Even as an infant it adds to productive capabilities and under imperfect markets, it generates a large surplus for re- investment. in time, the infant grows up, learn through experience to achieve declining unit costs to face up to the eventual foreign competition. The industrial activities are increasing returns activities which provide opportunities for division of labour, specialisation and expand production with declining unit costs and increasing profitability. The dynamic of industrial development with higher employment and higher wages supports higher demand and output in the agriculture sector. Industrialisation transforms economic structures and opens up possibilities of changing comparative advantages (which are mostly the result of past decisions).

The neoliberals reject protection and financial support argument on the ground that in most cases the 'infants' never grow up and impose a heavy cost on the society. They claim that if there was any chance for 'infant' industries to grow up to become internationally competitive, then the capital will be available from international markets for investment and there would be no need for the State financial support or protection. An extreme version of this claim sees no disadvantage for the poor countries in remaining agrarian economies. One can counter these objections by stating an obvious fact that creation of 'infants' is beneficial to a static economy because of increased 'productive capabilities' and learning possibilities even if 'infants' never grow up. The newly established industries will still produce and add to GDP by creating new employment for previously unemployed labour. The benefits from the higher rate of economic growth with fewer unemployed resources can more than compensate the static costs. Besides, foreign capital does not fly to small poor countries to develop their industrial base but to take advantage of cheap raw materials. The borrowing from international capital markets with imperfect or asymmetric information is impossible, and no correction of markets can rectify this situation as one correction will bring about numerous others. Frederick List had argued that if an economy lacks productive capabilities, a state can justifiably use scarce financial resources to develop these capabilities. For a state, all generations are equal, and it does not need to discount future to determine new industries feasibility. Indeed, this is what happened in East Asian countries to promote industrialisation. The claims of potential benefits of agrarian economic structure depend on the comparative cost advantage. But no consideration is given to the potential changes in the comparative advantages, gains from increasing returns activities, specialisation in imperfect markets, and declining terms of trade for the additional agriculture goods.

Like every policy measure, the protection policy has a trade- off between generations. Trying to create a viable domestic industrial capability against foreign competition imposes a cost, but it is more than compensated by the expanded 'productive capabilities', greater future output, higher employment and higher labour productivity and wages. The new capabilities create internal synergies and learning experiences leading to innovations, declining marginal costs and externalities. The industrial development always becomes the protector and supporter of the agriculture sector by increasing its productivity and wage rates. The higher productivity and wages increase effective aggregate demand for output and capital goods and accelerate economic development. Stiglitz and Greenwald (153) support the view that industrial development under protection can transform economies and change their comparative cost advantages. Aghion et al. (3), in their 2012 study concluded *that China in the presence of market failures protected her industries to achieve a remarkable rate of economic growth. It is, therefore, not unreasonable to support a broad protection policy to protect dynamic sectors of the economy. Which is innovation enhancing; skill-intensive and can help in the specialisation process to become drivers of economic growth.* Krueger and Tuncer (68) in 1982 show that the protected firms and industries, increased Turkish employment in the industrial sector and national GDP.

The arguments so far advanced relate to the protection of industries from the international free trade. It is important to draw a distinction between freedom of trade between nations and within a nation. The restrictions on the internal trade are not compatible with the liberty of individual citizens, but in the case of international trade provide the highest degree of individual liberty. Indeed, it is possible that the greatest freedom of international trade may result in national servitude.

Freedom of Capital Movement and Market Exchange Rates

It is a fact that the saving rates in most poor countries are low as most people live on a subsistence level and the corrupt and super rich launder their money to foreign bank accounts. The low levels of saving and investment result in low level of economic growth rate. The neoliberals argue that countries with surplus capital should be able to invest in capital poor countries to supplement local capital formation and economic growth. The capital inflow will increase economic efficiency by investing in productive projects and improving organisational capabilities with best practice policies. The poor must open their financial markets and remove all restrictions on exchange rates and flows of capital to benefit from free capital movements.

The foreign capital movement takes many forms, such as grants, debt, investment, and foreign direct investment. The Grants are money given with conditions. The debt consists of bank loans, government and corporate bonds. Investment is equity investment and consists of direct physical investment or purchase of equity with management control. The neoliberals dislike grants on the ground that these create dependency and corruption, but forget that grants are given to seek favourable treatment for rich countries businesses or to finance NGO's. The financing of NGO's creates a parallel government structure in poor countries by polarising and destabilising society. The NGO's mostly act as pressure groups to advance the interests of the aid donors and can be used as spying cells.

The bank loans and bonds and equity without management controls are extremely volatile and always harmful to the poor, as money comes in and goes out at the wrong time. The capital flows in to buy equities at low prices which are sold off at higher prices rise for the capital to fly out of the poor countries. The assets bubble becomes a common occurrence and stock markets in poor countries become playing fields for the foreign fund managers. The opening of financial markets brings regular and endemic financial crisis, and the net result is always the net outflow of capital from the poor countries and the control of financial markets simply passes on to the rich country's financiers. The market-determined foreign exchange rates play a very useful part in this exploitation process. The market exchange rates are limited value to the poor countries as their export base is narrow and exports are mostly raw materials. The devaluation in such cases would not do any good as there is nothing much to export and the imports of capital goods become so much costlier, which makes development process sluggish and in some cases come to a halt.

The foreign direct investment is slightly different in character. It can bring new productive capabilities, new technology, higher employment, managerial know- how, as well as increased productivity to increase national output. In the past, foreign direct investment used to be stable and long-term in character and benefited the recipient countries, but more recently, FDI has been made more liquid with the opening of capital markets and market exchange rates. The fixed assets can now be disposed of quickly, and capital flies out of the country with great speed. Another difficulty faced with DFI is that it can create the opportunities for 'transfer prices' by international companies with operation in numerous countries, which allows them to avoid taxation in the poor countries. The technology which comes with FDI in poor countries is not cutting edge, and yet most of the domestic producers are wiped out through increased competition. The exploitive power of FDI is well known for a long time, and that is why rich did not open their financial markets to outside competition or allowed foreign direct investment. Finland only relaxed its control over financial markets and foreign capital movements in 1987. US Banker's magazine in 1884 expressed the view that it will be a happy day, when not a single US equity, is owned by foreigners. Some powerful poor countries such as India have imposed and kept controls over foreign exchange rates and movement of capital across borders to avoid the outflow of capital.

Fiscal Discipline or Loss of Economic Sovereignty

Each country manages its economy through monetary and fiscal measures, and neoliberals following Friedman prefer monetary policy over fiscal. They believe price stability takes priority over unemployment, and monetary policy is a better instrument to manage it. Keynes had argued that state behaviour should be opposite to the individuals' rational behaviour in dealing with inflation and unemployment. A rational individual behaviour in a downturn is to save (cut spending) for difficult times, but this behaviour is likely to reduce effective demand making unemployment problem worse. The State, therefore, must increase spending to increase effective demand and reverse unemployment trends. He had rejected the effectiveness of monetary measures in dealing with unemployment. In an inflationary situation, the State must cut spending (individuals increase spending) to reduce effective demand to reverse inflationary trends.

The monetarists, like Friedman, had argued that price stability is the foundation of economic prosperity, therefore, an independent central bank should control the money supply to ensure price stability but the money supply is endogenous and not exogenous to the system and it is not effective in dealing with unemployment.

The State spending crowd out private spending and reduction simply crowd in private spending to make fiscal measures ineffective. The fact is that reduction in interest rates or cheap money does not increase demand for funds if there are no profitable opportunities and high interests do not deter demand for funds if there are profitable opportunities with higher rates of returns. The financial crisis of 2007, however, has exposed false premises of monetarist thinking, and their orthodoxy is now dead and buried. But the poor are still being subjected to their condemned thinking; monetary discipline is being imposed on them as they do not have the self-discipline reflected in twin deficits to keep money supply under control or maintain price stability. The international lenders of the last resort have become the enforcer of this discipline. The borrowing by the poor is approved if they agree to accept structural reforms (monetary policies) programmes and thus relinquish their economic and political freedom. A restrictive monetary policy cuts down investment, reduces effective demand, increases unemployment and reduces output. The reverse of what a poor country needs facing twin deficits. The tyranny of financial power has no limit. Keynes fiscal policy has been discarded because it was assumed to encourage stealth taxes, distributes income, and hurts fixed income groups.

Fisher, a neocon's American economist, insists that inflation rate of between 1 and 3% per annum is an ideal. Inflation usually accompanies economic growth. South Korea had an inflation rate of about 18 when it was growing by 7% per annum in the 60's%. Brazil per capita income grew at the rate of 4.5% from 1960-80 when its inflation rate was almost 42% per annum. Bruno and Easterly (12) have shown that if the inflation rate is below 40%, there is no systematic correlation between inflation and growth rates. Robert Barro (8) a neoliberal economist, accepts that less than 10 % inflation rate has no impact on economic growth. No one can argue that hyperinflation is good for economic growth; it is not, as it creates uncertainty which is not conducive to investment or long-term planning. But moderate inflation has been helpful in growing economies as it increases effective demand, employment and protects current and future incomes. The control of inflation with high-interest rates reduces effective demand, increases unemployment and dampens down productive activities. The financial meltdown of 2007 exposed the hypocrisy of neoliberal economists when they were clamouring for zero or negative rates to generate higher investment spending which proved ineffective and exposed 'make-believe' nature of monetary policy in dealing with the stagnant economy.

The desire for an independent central bank is a desire to minimise the role of the State in economic management. The central bank cannot be detached from the State as it is to serve the national interests. The commercial banks and the financial sector serve the interests of financiers at the cost of manufacturers and general public, and there is strong need for the regulation of these institutions

Anti-Monopoly Policies

The logical deduction of general equilibrium model depends on the assumption that no single producer has the power to manipulate the market or charge a price above the marginal cost. The neoliberals never get tired of boosting the superiority of their model and telling poor countries to remove all anti-competitive practices to achieve allocation efficiency. However, all rich countries live with imperfect markets. Their international companies virtually operate as monopolies or as cartels and reap monopoly profits to maintain monopoly power in the world. A group of radical libertarians oppose even anti-monopoly laws to cut down the State power. They claim that only coercive State can create monopolies. Individuals do not have coercive power, so there would be no monopoly in the marketplace. Armentano (5) has provided a good summary of these views.

Concluding Remarks

The Washington consensus policies favour capitalist system because of its values such as individual freedom of choice, neutral markets, and efficiency of competition. The dark side of the capitalist system is forgotten or brushed away. The market system logic is a human construct and has no empirical backing. The individuals' decisions are not always based on self-interests and the markets are neither perfect nor neutral. The system creates inequality among individual's and nations. Alternative voices claim that fixing a false objective and then constructing a framework to achieve it, does not turn such a model into a natural or superior. Marx and Veblen had exposed the fundamental features and underlying interests of a capitalist class and how it subjugates the rest of the society. The increasing inequality in rich countries has remained hidden behind the magic word of competition.

Economic development involves profound structural changes in the economy and society. These changes work through the use of knowledge and technology in the industrialisation process and form new institutions, life capabilities, opportunities, moral values and political regimes. The State plays a dominant role in these changes. Who is to enforce legal rights of individuals or harmonious operations of markets if not a state? Who is to regulate large international corporations? Who bears the risk of the business failures? What would have happened if the USA and European had not bailed out their financial institutions in 2007? Marx's and Schumpeter's had exposed capitalism consequences of inequality and how it contains seeds of its destruction. The question of unfair distribution has not gone away it has become more urgent reflected in the misery of billions of the poor people.

In 1953, Kuznets (73) had brushed away the issue of inequality in his paper entitled '*Economic Growth and Income Inequality*' by claiming that internal logic of economic development would remove inequality in due course of time. His conclusion gave rise to the theory of 'Kuznets curve', which explains that inequality usually follows a 'bell curve.' It increases with industrialisation as only a small section of society benefits and then as the economy reaches maturity it decreases because all section of society shares the riches. Kuznets had based his observations on faulty USA data which included periods of shock. He also allowed himself to become an agent of political forces, which wanted to keep poor countries under their control. Over time, his theory has been blown away. There has been no automatic mechanism within the development process to reduce unemployment or poverty or to create wealth. A French economist, Piketty (110)has demolished Kuznets theory in his recent work. He has extended Mark's analysis of income distribution by looking at the personal distribution of income and wealth in France, UK, and the USA, for the last three centuries. He concludes that whenever the rate of return (g) exceeds the rate of interest(r), it usually leads to extreme capital concentration and inequality of income and wealth in societies. The inequality comes from greater rewards going to the capital compared with the labour. Such inequality and concentration of power in a very small section of society are socially as well economically harmful for social structure. Thus, the State must find a way to reduce inequality as the market system and various taxation regimes have failed to do so. This work has blown away all pretensions of the free marketers that mixed economies can promote greater equality of income and wealth by increasing wage rates or taxation policy.

The persistent promotion and enforcement of privatisation, the opening of financial and goods markets, free capital movements combined with the restrictive monetary policy have created economic disasters for the loan and aid-receiving countries, who have dubbed these policies as a new imperialism.

9

NEOLIBERALS NEW THEORIES OF POVERTY

Get the 'price right', open up your markets to foreign competition and invest in sectors of the economy where you have a comparative advantage, and you will get rich. The neoliberals forced this prescription for curing poverty when poor took the medicine, it did not make them rich but poorer. Their 'infant industries' got destroyed and the neoliberals' policies imprisoned them in permanent poverty. The free movement of capital did not bring about the equalisation of wages or more investment but robbed them of their capital as it flew out to be deposited in the foreign banks. Any expansion in their agriculture sector ended up in lower prices in the international markets. The so-called structural reforms of the international lending agencies enslaved them in new chains. The ideology of free market system is a human construct and has a dark side. It creates inequality among segments of communities within a country and across borders. The poor countries remain excluded from the proclaimed benefits of the market system. The poverty cries out for social justice, and yet a Japanese –American academic (34) had already accepted the superiority of the capitalism and declared *End of History* in 1989.

The neoliberals deny the exploitative nature of colonialism by saying it did a lot of good and implied that inferior races were taught new knowledge, the art of management and economic development. The colonialism covers almost four centuries of European aggression, brutality and exploitation. The colonies were kept as closed markets and denied any industrial development. European countries got industrialised by protecting industries from each other, exported manufactured goods and obtained raw materials cheaply from colonies, provided job to their unemployed as soldiers and civil masters in foreign lands, and invested surplus capital to facilitating trade. They extracted maximum wealth, destroyed economic and political structures, and established institutions to protect their interests beyond their colonial rule. It would be difficult for anyone to disagree about repression, plunder and mass slaughter of subjugated and yet it is done by the neocon's historian of the present day and especially Ferguson. They invent new history to serve their interests. The story of South Africa is slightly different compared with other colonies. Here the climate suited European and they established their settlements and developed an Apartheid state. The blacks had no rights and provided cheap labour for agriculture and mining sectors. The white rulers imposed a different set of frameworks on developing industry, commerce, agriculture, and education facilities. *The dual economy of South Africa provides a perfect historical proof; how industrialisation and restrictive trade could lead to prosperity and how the lack of it results in squalor and poverty. The colonial legacy is difficult to eradicate.*

A comparison between the end results of impersonal forces of free markets and colonialism shows that both end up creating poverty. The globalisation is a very similar process as colonialism; both discourage industrialisation, encourage raw materials and infrastructure development, and free movement of capital in poor countries. The neoliberals are the new imperialist of today and they are helped by the emergence of the multinational corporations as the principal agencies of investment across the world. The multinational giants such as Coca-cola, Shell, Microsoft, Amazon, and Nestle locate their manufacturing or processing operations in many countries which change the flow of capital in two ways. The capital is invested in basic technologies in poor countries and it combines with cheap unskilled labour force without allowing labour wages to rise. This scheme of things allows big businesses to capture new markets and import cheap goods back into developed countries to keep labour wages under constant pressure.

The neoliberals' policies have failed to reduce poverty but they refuse to accept this failure or change or modify their free market-free trade paradigm. They have started to claim that there are other factors that need correction for the paradigm to succeed. Each time they add a new factor to the mantra of 'right price' to end poverty, each time prosperity eludes the poor. Easterly (28) cries out about the tyranny of experts and waste of $2.3 trillion as aid but no one wants to hear. The market equilibrium model is too sacred a cow to be slaughtered. The symptoms of poverty or the factors which evolved because of the industrialisation are presented as the cause of poverty. They should know that dependent variables cannot be considered as independent. Is this an intentional diversion? R Wade (163) has called these efforts as 'the art of paradigm maintenance'; where new features are added without changing model to protect the core of the theory or paradigm. The allure of keeping mathematical model comparable to physics achieves a status far greater than any other human-related discipline. It does not matter if the model is detached from the real world or cannot be improved by incremental changes.

The core of poverty problem (i.e. the activity based nature of economic development) is still being denied. The success of Marshall Plan that had established a link between wealth, civilisation, and urban activities had no meaning and no lessons for the neoclassical economics which claims all economic activities are the same and the State intervention in the markets distorts allocation. Full employment (not unemployment) is a default condition of all economies and specialisation is strictly based on current comparative advantages. The neoliberals' paradigm has ruled supreme since the fall of Berlin wall and there is no escape for the poor.

New Theories of Poverty

The neoliberal paradigm is unrealistic and has no empirical backing and yet its edifice remains standing in one spot adding to its height and spewing out toxic policies. Should it not be discarded or modified? The answer has to be yes but few dare to say it aloud. Here are their proposed new theories of poverty which do not explain but highlights symptom or consequences.

Geography, Climate, and Diseases

In the colonial time, it was claimed that poverty is caused by race and geographical location of people. French had proclaimed without any evidence that *'if the history of the world were to repeat itself without any changes on the surface of the earth, it would end up being the same'*, in other words, material conditions of life and social activity would not change in different parts of the world. This idea established a link between geography and human development and it was accepted by the subjugators. Huntington (57) of Yale University claimed that geography could explain the physical and cultural development of different countries and regions. Some say Huntington was simply linking environment with temperament, merit, and wisdom but others believed it provided a link that geography had made 'Blacks' happy and lazy compared with 'Whites' and explained the poverty of non-white races and countries. Such explanations were an echo of the racial period when intellect and performance got explained by race. The poverty of subjugated races was obvious but can it be claimed that race and geography were independent factors which caused poverty? The racists of the time and of the present time were and are happy to hold these views.

The race, geography, climate, and diseases are back in writing on poverty problem. Lendes (78) *observes that most poor countries are located in the tropical and semi-tropical zones. Nature is unfair, so the poverty is the result of unfair geography.* He supports his argument by stating that in tropical zones living standards are low and human life is short. Geography in the form of climate has a direct effect on human body. But then it is claimed that hot climate effect is much greater than cold climate, and it makes people lazy and idle causing poverty. This myth of laziness can disappear if one refers to Adam Smith, who states '*In all European colonies the culture of the sugar-cane is carried on by Negro slaves. The constitution of those who have been born in the temperate climate of Europe could not, it is supposed, support the labour of digging the ground under the burning sun...*' so we know who is lazy and idle and who is hard working and capable of doing hard work in the most hostile environment. It does not require much imagination to state that climate conditions can change as in the south of United States. The cities like Atlanta, Houston, New Orleans and many others are prime examples, how industrialisation can overcome hostile climate to achieve prosperity. Two East Asian countries of Singapore and Malaysia, are just one degree above the Equator. These countries are not poor and have achieved prosperity through successful national industrial policies to overcome disadvantages of geography and climate. The most common and biggest killer in hot climates is Malaria which was endemic in Europe for hundreds of years and was eradicated by draining the swamps. A similar exercise was carried out by the French in Algeria around 1840 and deaths from malaria declined by 61% over a ten-year period. So 'draining the swamps' get rid of stagnant water and can eradicate Malaria worldwide. *The climate-related diseases are a symptom rather than a cause of poverty.* By stressing Geography, Climate and Diseases as causes of poverty, a focus is being moved away from the paradigm failure

It is unbelievable that in the first quarter of a 21st century, partial observation can be tolerated and used in explaining poverty. The existence of poverty in hot climates is a direct result of colonialism and might show correlation but to turn geography as a cause of poverty without any proof beggars' belief. If climatic conditions can be changed and overcome through industrialisation then it is not an independent causal factor.

Culture and Religion

The neoliberals have argued that some cultures and religions produce societies where values and behaviours discourage material prosperity and therefore cause poverty. The differences in societies are reflected in attitudes to work, saving rates, education, cooperation, trust, authority and numerous other aspects which directly affect economic activities and national prosperity or poverty. Huntington and Lendes (78) had supported this argument by claiming that cultures create a difference in the economic development of nations. Fukuyama (36) supports cultural hypothesis by arguing that some culture lack trust beyond family members thus limiting the size of business organisations and economic development. The argument assumes an unchanging behaviour determined by culture, religion or 'habit of national heritage'. The argument was discarded in the early part of the 20th century but has been revived more recently.

The culture and religion generated behaviour is flexible over time and space. Marx had noted that transformation of productive system changes superstructural of human values (i.e. culture, religion, and behaviour) which in turn can change the productive system. History has witnessed that many countries have gone through social, political and religious changes through industrial transformation but the resulting superstructure of values have failed to change the productive system. Public policies can change human behaviour and a number of societies have successfully done so. The neoliberals' argument has confused correlation with causation and a changeable variable such as culture cannot act as an independent causal factor.

Culture has numerous aspects and it is difficult to establish a distinction between a good and a bad culture as every culture has good and bad elements. A century ago, Sidney Gulick (44), called Japanese lazy and utterly indifferent to the passage of time. Webb (165) declared 'Japanese have no desire to think.' British considered German to be untrustworthy in the 19th century. Mary Shelley (140) found Germans lazy. So, a century ago, Japanese and Germans were lazy and dishonest. How come these two nations have changed their culture and behaviour so completely? Could the economic transformation of these countries explain this change? Similarly, East Asian Confucianism a religion practised in China and East Asian countries, was blamed for rigid social hierarchy, and biased against professions and law. But more recently it is claimed that it promotes hard work, education, frugality, cooperation, obedience to authority and economic development. Could this new appreciation of Confucianism be a direct result of the economic transformation of that region? Islamic culture and religion are being blamed for all sorts of things including causing economic poverty in present time. Some say it opposes diversity, entrepreneurship, wealth accumulation, female education and participation, investment in human capital, economic development, and glorifies holy war and the afterlife. But Islam does not contain any social hierarchy like Hinduism or British class system and promotes knowledge, industry, commerce, enterprise, encourages geographical and social mobility. It promotes rational thinking, teaches tolerance and provides a contractual framework for human and property rights. These are two different pictures of the same culture and religion. Islam can and have produced markedly different behaviour pattern over its history. Spain and India both had their glorious periods of prosperity and harmony under Islamic rules.

In poor countries, where people rely on nature and agriculture to live, busy times are season related, and no one needs to keep to time as in automated factories or societies. People work long hours and yet it looks as they do nothing and are lazy. The West interprets different work pattern as laziness and fails to understand that poor countries suffer from mass unemployment and if there is no work, how do you keep busy? It is interesting to look at the unemployed in the West and how they spend their time in pubs or watching endless TV programmes. Would they call them lazy? There is evidence available if one looks at the migrants in industrialised countries. Are these people lazy or more hard working compared to the locals? Thus, many of the cultural aspects assumed anti-development are the product of agrarian economies which disappear with the industrialisation.

Population

Once classical economists had considered population as a major factor affecting economic growth, but with the industrial revolution and better family planning, population lost its importance in the development debate. The neoliberals have reverted to the population as a problem. The poor are put in 'no win' situation in the debate. They can not argue against 'too many/few' reality and any dissenting voice gets brushed off in the uproar of white noise. Malthus work has been revived and articulated. Population growth outstrips economic growth; hence, poor are forever condemned to a losing struggle between multiplying mouths and the insufficient stock of food and other provisions. The gap between population and the food supplies growth rates has to be bridged, and nature achieves this balance through infanticide, war, famine, and diseases. The neoliberals bring religion into play by stating that some religions do not support birth control measures which result in unchecked population growth. The population growth rate exceeds capital accumulation rate to keep 'vicious circle of poverty' intact.

The history is ignored in this blame game. The industrial transformation of the European economies delinked population and economic development. With economic prosperity, family planning overcame the natural desire to reproduce. The industrialisation lowered unit cost, increased output, raised employment and wage levels which increased effective demand and speeded up economic development. The higher economic growth generated a higher rate of capital accumulation embedded with cutting edge technology, which in turn leads to more industrialisation, more employment, higher wages and higher incomes. *There is increasing evidence that industrialisation and increasing per capita income has a direct negative impact on the population growth.* The social structure of the society changes with a change in economic structure; people start to plan their families just like in the rich countries. Birth controls, declining fertility rates, change in the custom of marriage age, and large-scale migration to increasing returns countries can help in overcoming perceived overpopulation. Malthus theory was forgotten like a bad dream. *But neoliberals do not accept that such a situation can last long and assume population growth rate is an exogenous variable* which it is not. It is generally accepted that there exist two-way causal relationships between population growth and per capita income. A moderate increase in population is essential for economic growth and an increasing per capita income can lead to a reduction in the population growth rate. Industrialisation is an obvious answer to the population problem but it is conveniently ignored.

Entrepreneurship, Invention, and innovations

Schumpeter 'entrepreneurs' took the risk to introduce invention and innovations to lower unit cost of existing products or to produces new products. The re-organisation of production or new inventions generated growth in the economy. This process of 'creative destruction' turned into a driver of economic growth. The neoliberals have adopted Schumpeterian idea to claim that lack of entrepreneurship in poor countries is the main cause of their poverty. **Yet Schumpeter analysis is not a part of neoclassical general equilibrium model and they oppose any state funding for research and higher education in poor countries.**

The spirit of 'entrepreneurship' is reflected in all sorts of activities for survival in poor countries. An Individual deprived of a job and other means employs wit and entrepreneurship on a daily basis to survive. So, it is not 'Entrepreneurship' per say that is lacking in poor countries. In advanced industrialised economies, people have unlimited opportunities in jobs, businesses or training to think about improvements or new ways of doing things. Industries are clustered and located in specific locations with Klondike effect. Research activities take place in both private and public sectors. The synergies among activities create invention and innovation possibilities. In comparison, the agrarian or subsistence economies do not have much scope for inventions or innovations. Here greatest enterprise is to remain alive.

The industrialisation opened up opportunities for inventions and innovation in all industrialised countries over time. The USA had gone through a steady technological change during the 20th century and the introduction of new 'information and communication' technology led to 'destructive creation' in all sorts of ways and without any significant inflationary pressures. New Entrepreneurs emerged to take advantage of new technological possibilities to lower unit cost of existing and new products to make wealth beyond imagination. Greenspan, the chairperson of Federal Reserve Bank, *observed at the time that American economy was behaving by the Schumpeterian theory.* The States in all advanced countries create conditions and incentives which promote innovations and inventions. The incentives and investment in public knowledge lead to new innovation and inventions that result in cheaper or new improved product with higher price, profit and wages. The competitiveness of the rich countries based on product invention leads to higher real wages and incomes. The poor countries have no incentive, lack advance knowledge or industrialisation to encourage innovation or inventions. The process innovation enforced in poor countries results in lower unit cost, lower unit price and competitive edge in raw materials activities. The adverse terms of trade add to their misery and poor have to run faster and faster to stand still. Thus, the poor are being forced to specialise in the art of how to remain poor. Their competitiveness based on process innovation leads to lower real prices in the international markets, lower wages and lower income. So, the 'competitiveness' is a pill that makes rich people richer and poor people poorer.

Be competitive mantra is a doggy one. At the single firm level, the term is easy to define. It describes the ability of a firm to compete and grow profitably in the marketplace. On a national level, however, it poses a problem. Porter (111) defines it as national productivity'. But it fails to capture the nature of the productive activity that a nation chooses to be productive. The consequences are different If a nation chooses to be competitive in the increasing returns (i.e. high value added) activities compared with the diminishing returns activities. Scott (137) define 'competitiveness' by stating 'Competitiveness reflects on the ability of a company, operating under open market conditions, to produce goods and services that meet the test of foreign competition while simultaneously maintaining and expanding domestic real income'. Here it is worth noting that the company is operating under open market conditions not under perfect competition. Indeed, it may be operating under imperfect competition to reap economies of scale, increasing real wages and national income. The businesses operating under open market conditions compete in international markets to make money and add to the prosperity of the nation. The rich countries have open markets but the poor are forced into perfect markets. In the post-Berlin Wall era, the term 'competitive' has turned into a universal mantra without really meaning much. Reich and Krugman, two eminent American economists, both have expressed their dislike of the term, although they are on opposite side of the industrial and trade policies. In concluding it is obvious to me that lack of entrepreneurship and lack of invention and innovation capabilities are a symptom of poverty and not its cause.

Corruption

Corruption is endemic in most poor countries and some time has resulted in a change of political regimes in countries such as Pakistan. Thus, the extent of corruption has a direct bearing on the political and economic stability of the country but can it be a causal factor? Corruption violates people trust in authority, destroys the sense of loyalty to organised society, harm institutions and incentives, and can damage national interests. But can one jump to establish a causal relationship between corruption and poverty? The answer is not clear cut. Corruption is widespread in public administration such as public works, purchasing agencies, licensing authorities, custom and tax collection authorities, national railways, utilities, universities, policing, judiciary, and other national organisations. The abuse of discretionary powers can provide favours in return for cash payments. The officials share bribes with politicians with authority to influence careers. The political class abuses vested trust in numerous ways such as misuse of development funds, cheap credit, monopoly licenses, discriminatory prices, misuse of the customs system, and tax privileges. They can also bestow favours on foreign businesses, cronyism and nepotism, and in the sale of the public organisation at knock-down prices. The reforms schemes to control corruption never get implemented.

Corruption is morally and legally objectionable as it transfers resources from productive individuals to mostly parasites in societies. Does this transfer lead to economic inefficiency? The answer is that it does not have an unambiguous negative economic consequence. The negative effect depends on how the transferred money is used. If it gets invested in an equally productive project, there would be no negative consequence but If it is wasted in conspicuous consumption, it would result in negative economic consequence leading to higher unit costs, higher prices and lower output. There is, however, a third possibility, where bribe money gets invested in a more productive project which can result in greater economic efficiency and growth.

If bribe money flows out of the country, the country suffers from the lower capital investment, lower additional employment and output. In most poor countries including Pakistan wider loyalty to country is missing and corrupt take money out of the country and the country suffers from low investment and devalued the currency. The corruption poses an acute problem in Pakistan as society is based on family and tribe loyalty rather than national loyalty and individuals' interests take priority over national interests. The law and order have become subservient to the wishes of the ruling elites. The Corruption, however, can lead to different consequences in different countries. Some corrupt countries like Zaire and Pakistan end up with ruined economies; others have not suffered too badly such as Indonesia. Whereas some countries like South Korea, China, Italy, Japan and Taiwan have done very well in spite of their rampant corruption. According to Nield (98), most rich countries had achieved their industrialisation and prosperity despite the fact that these societies were spectacularly corrupt at the time. Britain, Holland and Scandinavian countries were all rife with corruption when they were going through their development process. The economic transformation of these economies, however, led to changes in socio- political structures and created middle classes with strong moral values. The ruling classes established high standards of public service.

The wages and salaries were increased to discourage corruption. The transformation of the productive structure, establishment of high moral values and accountability framework all contributed in reducing the impact and level of corruption in rich countries.

It is obvious that the corruption is a symptom of poverty and not its cause. Its scale presents a problem, but a manageable one.

Public Sector Governance

Hayek, in his book *'Road to Serfdom'*, has detailed the tyranny of the state by stating how the lack of information, coordination, and intervention in the marketplace creates inefficiencies. The politicians, civil servants, and other state functionaries are mostly corrupt and use institutional resources for personal gains. The corruption, taxation and excessive interventions in the markets distort allocation efficiency. The liberalisation, privatisation, and minimum state policies are based on the political ideology of liberalism.

The public sector *'governance'* is defined as the exercise of political authority and use of institutional resources to manage society's problems and affairs. The hidden agenda is to cut down the current account and balance of payment deficits by cutting the size and role of the state. The measures to reduced state role are clouded in the coded language of 'good governance'. The International Lending Agencies enforce their structural reforms policies on poor to promote free trade, cut down public spending, sell off public assets, and change political systems. The liberalisation, privatisation and minimum state policies result in higher twin deficits, reduced productive capabilities, unemployment, lower output, lower per capita income and increased poverty in agrarian economies. The frequent private contracts for public works increase corruption. The political participation polarises poor societies. The 'poor states' are mostly agrarian with little specialisation, unskilled labour, and competitive in the export of raw materials. The social structure is pre-capitalist feudalism. There are no middle classes in the country and the society lacks cohesion. A suitable structural reform for such states is foreign trade protection, control over capital movements and industrialisation. But the structural reforms of lending agencies make them competitive in the production of raw materials with diminishing returns, low productivity, lower wages, lower prices, lower effective demand and living standards. So *'good governance'* ends up making poor even poorer.

Education and Health

The investment in education and health amounts to an investment in people, which increases productive capabilities of a country. Healthy mind and bodies are essential for human wit and will, as knowledge becomes the main driver of productivity. The poverty is a major reason for illiteracy and ill health and investment in education and health can improve both literacy and health levels. This two-way relationship indicates a correlation between two sets of variables but the linkage is not tight from a policy point of view. Yet, human capital development remains important because it improves the quality of human life, an ultimate objective of all development efforts.

The neoliberals policies make human capital development a contentious issue. They promote free market mechanism as a solution to illiteracy and poor health. They argue that the private sector can supply education and health at the right price, cut down current account deficit, minimise state role, and improve allocation efficiency. These arguments can be countered. First, the history of rich countries tells us that in each country, the state played a major role in providing health and education provisions. The public funding of these provisions is cost-effective and can achieve universal basic education and health in a very short period. Second, both services are consumed collectively by the society, a characteristic of a public good where market failure is well established. Environment preservation, Epidemiology, and public health care are pure public goods. A malaria free environment can benefit all without any exclusion. Education, however, is a mixed case; the basic education provides shared benefits which can transcend the gains from the person to the society, which in turn can lead to social change by lowering fertility and increasing labour force mortality and productivity. The market mechanism cannot capture collective benefits and therefore is less than effective in providing an optimal output for these services. Given these advantages, it is rather remarkable and deceitful that neoliberals force free market solution for public goods in poor countries.

Property Rights

I have already discussed these rights briefly in the last chapter where a question was raised about the legality of the ownership. The main argument for the enforcement of the property rights rests on human incentives. It is claimed that poor countries are pre-capitalist economies which fail to protect property rights and investment incentives. The individuals turn work shy, uncertainty ceases long term investment and development efforts stop. The well-established and well-protected rights, therefore, provide strong incentives for the individuals to work hard resulting in prosperous societies. This argument turns GDP as dependent and 'property rights' as an independent causal variable. But the history tells that *property rights* evolved from changing the economic structure and cannot be assumed as an independent. China presents a prime example. Besides the 'property rights' have many elements which cannot be measured in any satisfactory way and no one has empirically tested the hypothesis that output is a function of property rights.

The security of 'property rights' cannot be justified if the property has not been acquired by hard work or by legal means.

Mill, Marx and Veblen had considered property ownership a sort of theft. In most poor countries, the property and wealth have been accumulated through political corruption, deceit, fraud and coercion. The cheater and looters have designed and manipulated institutions for personal gains and to prolong their power. Similarly, 'property rights' enforced in the colonial times enhanced, protected and safeguarded the mother country interests and these rights have remained intact after independence. In the presence of such unfair distribution of income and wealth, the violation of property rights and the creation of new rights could prove more beneficial for economic development. History tells us that once old property rights gave way to the new rights, economic development gets a boost. The countries such as Britain, Japan, South Korea, China and many others have shared this experience. So, what matters for economic development is not the protection of existing but just rights and moral values which would provide correct investment incentive for economic development.

There are varying views on the intrinsic merits and demerits of private property. Some take property rights as a constitutive feature of human development and argue that all restrictions should be lifted on ownership, inheritance, and use of the property. The property income should be free from all taxation. Others have been repelled by the inequalities of ownership and have gone to demand the abolition of private property to avoid inequality. Nozick libertarian theory has given preference to extensive classes of rights including property rights over the pursuit of social goals such as removal of deprivation, destitution, equity or well-being. He places an absolute priority on 'property rights'. Others disagree with this 'absolute priority' because intense economic needs related to life and death matters and cannot be of lower order compared to personal liberty or property rights. Rawls in his book '*Political Freedom*' seem to have accepted the weight of economic need argument and have tried to accommodate it within the structure of his theory of justice. Should one accept that all property distributions are valid, and need protection? Should property obtained through corruption, fraud, and other illegitimate means be protected? Williamson now recommends redistribution of income in poor countries. The protection of property rights usually requires effective state but the neoliberals' minimum state reduces the State effectiveness

On the back of 'Property Rights,' the West has pushed hard for the protection of patent rights in the world. They have argued that the protection of patent rights is essential to ensure investment in new ideas, inventions, and innovation to generate higher productivity and new products. The protection of 'patent rights' however create monopolies which distort allocation efficiency. History tells us that scientific curiosity and desire to benefit humanity have played a much bigger role in promoting new ideas, inventions, and innovations compared with material incentives. The granting of these rights imposes a cost on society, distorts income distribution, generate a social loss and distort resource allocation. The productivity gains do not offset the losses from misallocation. The most sinister impact of the patent rights, however, rests in its ability to block knowledge flowing to poor countries that need new ideas and technologies for structural changes. The ideas and new technology have always flown from one country to another to help in the development process. Most European countries had copied each other ideas and machines to advance their technologies. In more recent times, Japan and other East Asian countries have copied European technologies to develop their economies. There was no legal protection for intellectual property up to second half of the 20th century. Borrowing ideas were encouraged, and extensive counterfeiting was a common practice in Europe. The enforcement of these rights have extended period of monopoly rents for the international corporations and rich countries and has made 'reverse engineering' impossible.

In conclusion, one may say that enforcement and extension of 'patent rights' have provided the rich nations legal means to keep poor countries poor?

Institutions

Every discussion on the poverty of nations somehow ends up with a talk on institutions. The neoliberals state that dysfunctional or extractive institutions create disincentives and serve elite classes interest at the expense of poor which encourages inequality and poverty. The new requirement for poverty eradication is to get the institution rights, which covers all aspects of human life. These include the judiciary, civil administration, armed services, political system, markets and financial institutions. Some economists also include public finance and social welfare administration in the good institution's list. Many countries are offered as an example where extractive institution and poverty co-exist to support their argument. However, correlation does not mean causation as institutions evolved to support changing the economic structure and not the other way around. The changing eco-political structures needed markets, exchange contracts, property rights, insurance, limited liability, financial markets, regulation, employment and safety laws, and political participation. The division of labour led to exchange and markets. The long-distance trade required some sort of insurance. The exchange needed proof of ownership, which in turn needed a central codification and enforcement authority. The changing power of classes within the society required political representation of different economic interests. The need for these institutions arose from the structural changes in the productive system and different nations constructed different institutions to support changing conditions. The development results from new knowledge and new technologies.

D Acemoglu and JA Robinson (4) have argued that extractive institutions cause poverty in some African, Asian and South

American countries. North Korea poverty is offered as a proof of non-existent human and property rights under the communist regime. It is claimed lack of individuals rights have taken away all incentives to achieve prosperity and economic well-beings. Uzbekistan poverty results from one family political rule which has used national resources for personal interests. They imply most African and South American countries have similar institutions, which enable ruling classes to extract huge economic benefits at the expense of the vast majority of people. One may, however, wish to highlight that the political systems are the result of prevailing poverty. It is absurd to turn correlation into a causal relation. The extractive institutions are the symptom of poverty but not its cause. Veblen had explained how productive system shapes social, political and cultural institutions. Mark's had said the same thing that it is a productive economic system which changes the social and political system of society. How can 'institutions' be the independent variable, if these change with the change in the productive system?

It is questionable if the lending agencies have any right to intrude in the internal governance of poor under the cloak of structural reforms. Do they have any legal right to do so? The answer is no. Besides, the West's institutions may not suit the social norms, religion, and cultural values of poor countries. But merely increase their public spending and current account deficit.

Ha-Joon Chang (18) has provided an excellent historical perspective of western institutions and economic development. His main thesis is that the Western institutions were developed to meet the growing needs of the economy and therefore cannot be a cause of poverty. He argues that evolving human societies required institutions for the smooth functioning of economies and political authority and therefore cannot an independent causal factor in economic growth.

Political Participation

The neoliberals' claim that democracy or mass political participation is a must in order to promote economic prosperity. **Most poor countries have no mass political participation and in consequence, these countries remain poor.** Acemoglu and Robinson's book promote this idea. But the history of nations provides sufficient evidence to support the fact that democracy is an outcome of an industrial system and not its cause. It is claimed that there is a relationship between democracy and the market system. Democracy promotes free markets and checks the extractive behaviour of ruling elites. Free markets flourish and provide incentives to invest and generate wealthy people who can counter the power of ruling elites and seek more participation in the decisions making that affect their lives. *The argument seems to ignore the fact that markets and democracy are not natural partners because markets bestow power on wealthy and democracy on individuals.* One person, one vote had haunted the classical economists who thought it would enable poor to impose policies that could work against the interests of the rich minority. In recent time, this fear has come true in British EU referendum of 2016 when the poor majority voted to leave EU against the wishes and interests of the rich minority. Such fears had restricted voting rights in the past when only people with economic power had the voting rights. If one cannot allow the poor majority to exploit rich minority, then one cannot allow a rich minority to exploit poor majority either. But this is what privatisation and budget cutting policies achieve.

History tells us that rich countries, when they were getting rich, did not have universal democratic systems. The voting rights were restricted to a small minority of property owners and male educated classes. The universal suffrage came quite late, in some cases later than some poor countries. For instance, the UK, the mother of democracy, introduced its male suffrage in 1918 and universal suffrage in 1928. Canada introduced male suffrage in 1920 and universal suffrage in 1970. France introduced male suffrage in 1848 and universal suffrage in 1946. The USA introduced its universal suffrage in 1965. As against this, some of the poor countries like Pakistan introduced universal suffrage in 1947, South Korea in 1946 and Indonesia in 1947. The second largest economy in the world, China, still has not introduced universal suffrage.

Given these contradictions, it is difficult to accept that democracy can be a default condition for economic development. Every political system gets abused including democracy and in poor countries where the productive system is still feudal, and the majority of the population live on a subsistence level, democracy has been high-jacked by powerful groups who can buy votes and manipulate elections. The elections get rigged, and the elected members use their membership periods to enrich themselves in collaboration with the civil servants and other state functionaries. Most of the national decisions end up as short-term, and the long-term interests of the nation get ignored. Democracy becomes a mean of corruption and economic instability and polarises society. When sham democracies are overthrown, political and economic stability returns and public mostly welcome such a change. *There is enough evidence now available to state that democracy in poor countries creates political and economic instability, destroys incentives through endemic corruption and discourages economic growth.*

Civil Administration and Judiciary

Everyone agrees that honest and effective civil service and impartial judiciary is essential for an effective state, efficient public funds allocation, investment incentives and a fairer society. It is also a fact that in most poor countries, both civil and judiciary services are corrupting and inefficient. The civil service abuses its discretionary powers and Judiciary prolong cases and dishes out biassed judgements to lace their pockets. These abuses happen as there is no transparency or accountability. The political representatives themselves are corrupt. Unfortunately, these institutions in ex- colonial countries were established by the foreign rulers to preserve and prolong their rule, these have remained intact after independence and have turned extractive to serve the interests of new indigenous corrupt political regimes.

There is a clear need to reform and improve these services, but *'new public management'* enforced by the neoliberals (outsourcing and more frequent contracts) do not provide any respite to the poor countries. Indeed, the suggested cure aggravates the conditions by putting an extra burden on public revenues. Weber's has stated that the measures such as merit-based selection, long term career path, and rule-bound management can help in developing honest and efficient civil servants. But these measures are already part of poor countries civil service selection procedures and have failed to remove corruption or inefficiencies. It seems more likely that ineffectiveness of states, prevailing poverty and neglect of human capital development may have strengthened the corrupt ex-colonial institutions. What is needed is the transformation of the economy to change the socio-political structure, reconstruction of state institutions and development of moral values.

Corporate Governance: Financial Institutions and Markets, Public Finance, Welfare Policies and Institutions

The neoliberals claim that poverty is the result of poor corporate governance, and unless poor adopt the Western laws and practices they will remain poor. The corporate governance concept covers bankruptcy law, limited liability, financial reporting and audit. Limited liability evolved to socialise risk and raise investment in changing economic structures and increasing foreign trade.

The failure of businesses either because of dishonesty or otherwise led to the enactment of bankruptcy laws. It is important to have an effective mechanism to deal with dishonesty and fraud and the competing claims against the failed businesses. The businesses fail regularly in a capitalist system and create difficult situations which require the transfer of resources to deal with employees demand quickly and fairly. It is extremely difficult to have an objective criterion to do justice to different categories of claims. UK law favours creditors; USA law favours debtors, and French law is employee friendly. Each country has gone through a process of perfecting bankruptcy laws with a desire to punish dishonesty and to create a balance between the competing interests. There is no agreement how to deal with conflicting interests but everyone agrees on the desirability of bankruptcy law.

The correct information is needed by the financial institutions and shareholders to base their lending and investing decisions. In rich countries, accounting and auditing organisations have been given the responsibility to provide accurate business information but do not always act with honesty. The self-interest involved in winning contracts to provide information can encourage the provision of misleading information. Given the poor quality of auditing and greed of auditing companies in rich countries, the enforcement of these practices on poor, without a clear cost benefits analysis, can increase their financial difficulties and in some cases, make them non-competitive in the marketplace.

The banking system evolved and became crucial to sustain and promote changing economic conditions in all rich countries. Its ability to create money can lead to huge financial crises. This requires tight regulatory mechanism. Some countries started regulation at an early stage whereas others left it quite late. The neoliberals opposed regulation on the ground that markets can avoid all crisis. The efficiency of markets and especially financial markets is based on an unrealistic assumption of rational expectations. The regular financial crises are proof of this fact.

The neoliberals also support the central bank independence, which has a monopoly on note issuing, money supply, and acts as lender of last resort. They claim that an independent central bank can use monetary policy more effectively. Should a central bank be free of political control? What is its role in managing unemployment and inflation? The answer to these questions depends on political beliefs rather than economic merits. The monetary policy has repeatedly failed to deal with stagnation.

With the failure of Soviet socialism, the stock markets promotion has become a mantra to press poor countries to establish and open their stock markets to foreign competition which would open up the possibility for foreign investors to bring money in the country. Germany and Japan have used a bank-led financial system for industrial development as against the Anglo-Saxon stock market led financial system. There are supporting arguments for both systems. History tells us, stock markets bubbles have led to extreme economic instability many times. Foreign investors have destroyed poor countries currencies through speculations and have facilitated the transfer of resources from poor to rich countries. Stock markets open up opportunities for fraud in securities transactions, insider information, and willful misrepresentation. The regulatory regimes are always a step behind frauds, and 'Ponzi, schemes always hurt small investors and poor countries.

It is argued that poor countries are not very good at managing their money, spend more than revenue collected and end up with chronic current account deficits. There may be an element of truth in this argument. The ruling regimes often lack political legitimacy, which is crucial in taxation acceptability by the paying public. If people believe that taxes are not fair or not used in public interests or pocketed by ruling elites, then they would use every possible mean to avoid payment. The corruption of tax collecting agencies adds to the loss of public trust in the fairness of the system. The neoliberals prefer indirect taxes, new administrative mechanism, and better collection methods. *However, indirect taxes are mostly levied on essential goods and services which put the main burden on the poor. Rich can use bribes, tax avoidance schemes and simply refuse to pay as they are ruling elite.* Thus, the public finance reforms simply create more poverty, greater corruption and higher financial burden of collection.

The rich countries developed taxation regimes to finance welfare spending as their economies grew. The industrialisation had created conditions and needs for the welfare laws and these were implemented in stages. First came public provisions of health and education, the factory laws, and finally unemployment benefits. These laws have proved helpful to stabilise societies and increase production efficiency. But these involve costs before any benefits which poor cannot afford. The neoliberals insist on a 'minimum safety net'. There is no mention of potential costs (such as coerciveness and legitimacy of taxes) only the potential benefits. There is no mention that the industrialised nations established these welfare institutions between the last quarter of 19th and the first quarter of 20th centuries. The enforced implementation of welfare laws in poor countries simply diverts their limited resources from industrial development to consumption expenditures. The poor are being pressed to pass governance laws before any economic structural changes or industrial development. The passing and implementation of these laws simply encourages dishonesty and socialising of risk hides a 'moral hazard' that can encourage excessive risk taking, shirking by managers and make business owner lax in monitoring hired managers.

Target Setting Policy

The Washington Consensus policies of free trade, small governments and free capital movement have failed to improve economic conditions in the loan receiving countries. Indeed, their poverty has increased as a direct result of enforced policies. Under attack, the neoliberals have started to promote a new 'scheme ' called 'target setting,' which divert resources to specific problems and specific sectors to alleviate poverty. But it does not do anything of the sort; instead, it diverts attention from economic transformation and imprisons future generations in the vicious circles of poverty.

The neoliberals target setting schemes aim to improve health, child mortality, literacy levels and the environment. On the surface, these goals deal directly with urgent social problems and look worthy of praise. However, there may be a hidden agenda which allows neoliberals to hijack control of economic distribution policies and allocation management. The structural reforms had given them control of economic management and 'target-setting' give them control over distribution policies in loan receiving poor countries. The poor are free, and yet they have no freedom to choose their economic policies. The hidden agenda shifts focus from industrialisation to symptoms of poverty. But poor know that suppressing symptoms does not cure the disease.

I am aware of one 'target-setting' NGO operations in Pakistan which have set poverty reduction targets (49). Some locals have been given jobs with large salaries to promote and publicise the scheme. A foreign economist directs it and knows real long-term objective. The World Bank provides finance and uses it as a policy instrument. The poor countries like Pakistan have no choice but to accept foreign financed 'target- getting' schemes. The money coming into the country is surely a good thing for some in the starving nations. It does not matter to the corrupt leadership if it takes away their control over the social and redistribution policies and increases national dependency on others. The desire for self-sufficiency and autonomy disappears and with it control and ability to form national economic and social policies. The massive transfers of aid funds channelled through NGO's create passivity and disincentives to work, provide food to eat but do not provide tools or skills to earn a living. There is an added problem that these transfer payments are easy to withdraw or cut down to show donors disapproval. The resulting loss of employment and income could create political unrest and provide a control mechanism. NGO's indirectly strengthen the indigenous political elites to hold on to power. The promotion and financing of NGO's enable donor countries to exert direct influence and control over poor countries. It is also known that NGO's act as intelligence network for the finance providers. Some rich countries consider these transfer payments as a price worth paying as it keeps poor countries as raw materials and semi-manufactured goods producers with diminishing or constant returns while they enjoy and maintain increasing returns industries and benefit from free foreign trade.

Concluding Remarks

The mainstream economics, devoid of qualitative aspects of production, ends up highlighting symptoms as the cause of poverty. Such a shift allows them to divert attention from the main causes of poverty and take control of economic policies of the loan receiving nations. The historical way to eradicate poverty is to transform economic structure through industrialisation. European nations had become matured industrial countries by 1910 and started to refine their institutions. Each country regularly borrowed ideas and copied laws and institutions from others.

The neoliberals, new poverty theories, blame poor for being born in geographical areas and culture that breed poverty. The poor are poorly educated, have poor health, bad people to rule, wrong types of institutions including shaky property rights and were unfortunate to be colonies at some times. Their markets are narrow and non- competitive, and they use protective trade policies, lack entrepreneurship, innovation, and inventions. Poor should develop agriculture and mining or dead-end industries to benefit from their comparative cost advantage and forget about industrialisation as their markets are narrow and lack trained or capable manpower to make a success of value added activities.

The symptoms of their poverty are causes of their poverty. There is no need to transform economies from agrarian to industrial base under protection. They should adopt democracy to polarise their societies and import costly goods and services and promote more corruption to end corruption. These new theories of poverty are based on deceit and are nothing but red herring.

PART 4

ECONOMIC DEVELOPMENT HISTORY OF FOUR ASIAN COUNTRIES: A COMPARISON

Part three has detailed the neoliberals' theories and policies of economic growth and their consequences for the poor loan receiving countries. Part four briefly details the economic development history of four Asian countries which became independent at a similar time and faced similar economic conditions of fractured economies and poverty.

The comparison of these economies shows huge differences. Some of them have been more successful at facilitating industrialisation and economic development than others. An investigating into the quality of leadership, effectiveness of States and their role in creating economic conditions and pattern of development can provide insight into differences in performance. Pakistan, South Korea, China, and India, are chosen for this comparative analysis.

The next four chapters provide their differing historical growth paths and contributing factors such as political systems, national objectives, growth strategies and quality and ambitions of leadership. The 5th chapter compares their performance and draws inferences for the different levels of achievement.

10

RUINED DREAMS: PAKISTAN

Introduction

The present day, Pakistan shared its history with Northern India from 1193 to 1770 under Islamic rule. Once the Mughals Empire went into decline, the present day, Pakistan came under the Sikh rule in 1770 which lasted up to 1849. The British captured Lahore in 1849 and by 1858; the rest of Pakistan came under direct British rule which ended in 1947. The British distributed land to create a loyal class to be responsible for supplying fighting men and collecting revenue introduced civil, armed and judiciary services and invested locally raised finance in irrigation schemes and infrastructure to boost agriculture production especially cotton. The economy at the time was agrarian and education and health facilities were non-existent.

The Indian nationalist movement had failed to become a mass political movement in present day Pakistan territory and the 'divide and rule' policy had manipulated religious differences to weaken or break up nationalist movement. Muslim movement for freedom opposed British and Indian Congress scheme to leave India in the hands of majority Hindu population. It was a short-term movement which played in the hands of British in providing them with the opportunity to create instability in the sub-continent. The Indian National Congress political stand on Federation helped British in their scheme of things. As WWII folded up, British came out Victor but economically weakened and under intense nationalist political pressure left India in 1947. The country was divided into two separate countries i.e. India and Pakistan. The British had used this 'divide and rule' in 1905 to divide Bengal into Hindu-West Bengal and Muslim-east Bengal. A similar policy was used in Ireland to divide it into two countries in late 1920's. Millions of people lost their lives through partition with lasting problems that have kept both countries at loggerhead ever since.

Pakistan had two wings separated by thousands of miles of Indian Territory, race, language, and culture. Two of its provinces i.e. Punjab and Bengal had no natural borders. The two wings had only one thing in common i.e. religion. Pakistan's socioeconomic conditions and its physical split, at the time, did not provide much confidence about the long-term survival of the country, and this is what Indian political leadership had expected. They had believed, faced with difficult economic problems and internal division, Pakistan would fold and be reunited with India. Pakistan did split into two countries i.e. Bangladesh and Pakistan, but she has not folded. The creation of Pakistan had not resulted from any growing national consciousness or sense of public purpose. It was not a product of a revolutionary ideology, and there was no clear understanding of the constructive role a state can play in the development of its people.

Pakistan in 1947 was still a colonial construct. She had inherited territorial lines, feudal ruling elite, colonial institutions of the judiciary, armed and civil services, an agrarian economy with low productivity, and illiterate population, multiple languages, migration problems, no industry, and a semi- functioning skeleton ex- colonial administration. Her share of Indian Army and civil service contained very few officers trained under British indoctrination of staying above politics. Misra (93) has claimed that some Muslim ICS had not passed the merit test but were recruited to keep communal balance. Besides, Indian civil servants were trained as a generalist and had no training in specialised tasks such as industrial or trade policies, building technical institutions, promoting scientific knowledge, or economic development planning, which a sovereign state would require. Pakistan as a state had hardly any capability to undertake basic political and social changes. She depended on existing economic, political, social and administrative frameworks. She had no manufacturing sector, small-scale mining, large, illiterate and divided population, no business traditions or business community, no shipping or transport, very little infrastructure, long borders and hostile neighbours.

Pakistan is a subtropical zone country, her land resources and man/land ratio is a reasonable size, but land fertility is low. She produced mainly cereals, cotton, tobacco and other minor raw materials and did not possess many known energy resources. Her mineral resources have remained unexplored due to the limited geological survey, and her water resources flow from Kashmir, which is unlawfully occupied by a hostile neighbour. Her main exports consisted of cereals and cotton. She had basic agriculture goods markets but no financial institutions in 1947. The income and wealth were unequally distributed, the result of land ownership concentration. Her feudal political leadership did not have nationalist aspirations and had no understanding of the State role in the development process. The socialism was an alien ideology and had no place in the land of the pure.

Pakistan's economy of 1947 was totally different compared with the rich countries' 'take-off' economic conditions of climate, small energetic population, pluralism, fertile land, powerful navies, reasonable levels of foreign trade, colonies, basic industrial structures, coal and iron reserves, and a strong sense of nationalism and nationalistic leadership. Pakistan's economy, however, was fairly similar to other Asian ex-colonial economies of the time. All were agrarian, with a large population, low education levels, minor industrial sectors, different political systems, and ideologies, varying quality of leadership and the State capabilities. The newly independent countries had one common factor in their favour compared with the European countries at their take-off stage, that they could start with a clean slate, promote the latest knowledge, establish most suitable institutions and buy advance technology to transform their economies in short time. Whereas European nations had to go through the process of industrial revolution, the evolution of knowledge, development of institutions and technology to transform their economies which took considerable time. Thus, the fate of ex-colonial countries rested with them. It would be the visions and capabilities of their leaders, political and administrative systems and their selection and adoption of economic policies, which would either improve or waste human and physical capabilities.

Pakistan has survived and made considerable progress in spite of adverse conditions. It is still a very poor country in 2016, but it is also a nuclear power. At her birth, her founding father had visualised her turning into a welfare state but with his untimely death, that vision got lost. Pakistan faced the daunting task of setting up a modern state. The USA became pattern saint of Pakistan, provided it with financial and defence support, encouraged army takeovers, granted generous aid and loans which created a dependency culture, supported agriculture development, free markets system and used her against Russian socialism. Pakistan dependency on foreign aid and loans has impacted economic and foreign policies and economic development path. She has failed to develop a strong industrial base or expands her tax and export bases to achieve self-sufficiency and in consequence, carries low esteem among the comity of nations.

A narrative of macro development indicators, such as per capita income growth rates and the structural changes in the economy are a common way to describe the historical progress of a country. A second narrative is of changing political regimes and their impact on capital accumulation and economic performance, which can provide an insight into the concrete political and economic factors that determine rates and pattern of capital accumulation, industrialisation, and economic growth. I have used both narratives to describe the historical progress of each country. In Pakistan, political versus Army rule provides an obvious way to make a distinction between regimes.

Micro Indicators of Economic Performance

Pakistan's development efforts have produced mixed results. Up to 1958, its economy grew at an average growth rate of 3.5%, but the real average growth rate was only 1.1 % per annum. The next decade saw economy growing at the rate of 6.7%, which then dropped to 4.6% for the next ten years. In the eighties' growth rate increased to 5.9%, but for the next decade, it dropped back to 4.3%. The economy grew at an average rate of 5.4 % for the first six years of this century but since then it has dropped back to 3.6%. The population has grown at the rate of about 3% since 1947, which means that real per capita income has increased at varying average growth rate of 1.1 to 3.6% over the same period.

Table 1 provides details of GNP, population, and per capita GNP growth rates in average percent per annum term. The pre-independence growth rates have been measured using numerous assumptions and are merely intelligent guesswork. The post-independence figures are no better than indications.

Table 1: Pakistan Annual Growth Rates of GNP, Population and Per Capita GNP (% per year)

Variable/ periods	1900/47	1947/60	1960/70	1970/80	1980/90	1990/2000	2000/06	2006/14
GNP	0.9	3.5	6.7	4.6	5.9	4.3	5.4	3.6
Population	0.8	2.4	2.9	3.0	3.01	3.02	3.01	2.5
GNP per capita	0.1	1.1	3.6	1.6	2.9	1.0	2.4	1.9

Source: for the colonial period. Sivasubramonian (141) for others: Government of Pakistan various surveys.

Table 2 below reflects on considerable structural changes since 1947. At the start, the agriculture provided almost 90% of the output, with virtually no industrial output. Over 70% of the labour force worked in agriculture, and agriculture goods export earned 90% of the foreign exchange. It makes it easy to speculate that the distribution of income was highly unequal because land ownership was concentrated.

Pakistan industrial development has remained limited since 1947. There was hardly any industrial growth till 1960, but the next decade saw the average growth rate of almost 11%, which fell back to 6.5% during 1970 to 1990. These figures are deceiving because starting from nothing makes limited development relatively large. Since 1990 it has been reduced to about 4.0% per annum. The manufacturing has fluctuated over the years from 10% to about 4% in recent times. By the end of last century, Industry and Manufacturing contributed about 21% of the national output, but agriculture still contributes nearly one quarter and services about 51% of the GDP. However, services growth is based on the expansion in defence, administration, and made up services to hide large or disguised unemployment in the country. The 60's was a period of highest industrial, manufacturing, and services growth.

Table 2: Sectors Growth Rates (%) of Pakistan economy 1956-2000.

Sectors\ Periods	1956/60	1961/70	1971/80	1981/90	1991/2000
GDP	3.5	7.2	4.7	6.3	4.0 (100)
Agriculture	2.2	5.1	2.4	4.8	4.4 (24.9)
Industry	--	10.8	6.1	6.8	4.3 (8.1)
Manufacturing	--	9.9	5.6	7.3	4.2 (15.7)
Services	--	6.8	6.0	6.7	4.4 (51.3)

Source: Pakistan Economic Surveys Various Issues. I do not consider these figures to be exact only tentative indicators. The figures in brackets are average total.

Besides sectors and overall growth indicators, there are other important economic indicators that are helpful in understanding the performance of an economy. These are shown in Table 3 below.

Table 3: Other Economic Indicators of Economic Performance since 1947.

Variables/ periods	1947/60	1960/70	1970/80	1980/90	1990/2000
Ratio to GDP (in %)					
Domestic saving	10	8	7	13	12
Domestic Investment	11	17	15	17	15
Private Investment	--	9	6	7	
Public Investment	--	8	11	9	6
Foreign Direct investment	--	--	0.1	0.4	1.1
Trade	10	24	30	33	39
Exports	4	9	11	12	16
Imports	6	15	19	22	22.01
Foreign aid	--	6.5	4.2	2.6	2.0
Foreign Debt	--	27.5	41.0	42.1	55.6

Source: Government of Pakistan Statistical tables.

Capital formation creates new productive capabilities which increase the rate of economic growth. Pakistan's poverty has kept domestic saving rate around 10% since 1947. The investment rate has exceeded saving by an average of 5.5%. This difference can be explained by the foreign financial assistance available in various years. Most of the public- sector investment has come from foreign financial assistance such as aid and loans. The foreign direct investment has remained insignificant and less than 1% of the GDP.

There are some changes in the composition and size of the foreign trade. In 1950, imports were 6%, and exports were 4% of GDP. By 2000, imports have gone up to 22% and exports have increased to 16% of GDP. The trade deficit has remained a problem since 1947. The composition of export has slightly changed but the base has remained very narrow. The share of raw materials and agricultural goods such as textile has remained the largest component of the export.

The availability of foreign aid and loans had been subject to foreign donors' whims and interests over the years. The foreign assistance was quite large during the 60s, 80's and the early years of the 21st century when US interest was directly involved in the region and declined as the West interests became less important. In the 60's, Pakistan received foreign aid amounting to 6.5% of GDP, but it had declined to 1.8% of GDP by the end of last century. The drop happened when Pakistan refused to obey and exploded Atom devices. The USA aid rose, once again, during early years of the 21st century when she attacked Afghanistan and Pakistan's help was needed.

Pakistan's foreign debt has risen steadily over time, and it stood at 55.6% of GDP during the 90's. The foreign debt in absolute term has risen from $3 billion in 1970 to $36 billion in the year 2000 and $70 billion in 2013. This has increased debt interest payments as well as payment of the principal. Pakistan's domestic debt burden stood at 28% of GDP during the 60's, rose to 41% of GDP during 70's and 80's and to 56% of GDP in the 90's. The debt service ratio in Pakistan has ranged between 21 and 31 percent.

Pakistan has mostly relied on foreign aid and borrowing to supplement low domestic saving and capital formation, and this dependency has allowed foreign powers to dictate her investment policy. The large foreign debt burden has increased debt servicing payments and has put an extra burden on the balance of payment, increasing her economic vulnerability. The budget deficit which used to be fairly small and manageable for the first 15 years have risen significantly ever since. Political ideology, corruption, mismanagement and expansionary policies, have been contributory factors.

US invasion of Afghanistan has directly caused internal strife and macro instability. The increase in food and energy prices have increased poverty. The capital has flown from the country, and the value of the currency has fallen by about 40% since 2007. In spite of huge foreign loans, the economy has failed to recover. However, remittances from overseas Pakistani have remained the only bright spot and saviour of Pakistan economy. The following table described Pakistan's economic reality in 2013.

Table 4: Estimated Pakistan economy's Indicators 2013(US$)

GDP (ppp)	54.1 billion
GDP (at official exchange rate)	236.5 billion
GDP per capita (Ppp)	3100 (Current US $)
GDP growth rate	3.6% per annum
Population below poverty line	22.3%
Budget estimate:	
Revenue:	29.71 billion
Expenditures:	47.97 billion
Budget deficit:	18.26 billion
Industrial growth rate (estimate):	3.5%
Balance of Payment Estimate:	
Exports (estimate):	25.05 billion
Imports (estimate):	39.27 billion
External debt (estimate):	65.5 billion
Foreign Exchange and Gold Reserves (estimate).	11.18 billion

Agriculture Products: cotton, wheat, rice, sugarcane, fruits, vegetables, milk, beef, mutton and eggs.

Industries: textiles and apparel, food processing, pharmaceuticals, construction materials, paper products, fertiliser, shrimp

Source: CIA World Factbook.

In summary, the path of long-term growth in Pakistan has remained a difficult one. In 2016, she is still a poor country, and politically and economically unstable. After 68 years of sovereign existence, there is nothing much to celebrate or be proud of. Decades of corrupt and incompetent leadership, political disputes, and visionless economic struggle have led to slow growth and underdevelopment. Agriculture has remained the largest provider of employment and contributes more than 25% of GDP. Pakistan's main exports have remained raw materials and basic textile with very little high-value-added contents. Her trade base is still narrow and is vulnerable to the adverse terms of trade. There is high unemployment and the official figures relating to an unemployment rate of 6.6% are highly massaged and misleading.

Given the above given performance, did the State help and guided the economic development process? To answer one needs to look at the Economic planning in Pakistan.

Economic planning in Pakistan

Economic planning in Pakistan has been nothing more than an exercise to follow the fashion of the time. Pakistan set up a planning commission in 1958. The country went through the notion of approving eight five years' plans covering 40 years of its life. None of these plans except for one was ever completed or followed in any serious manner. Sometimes when one regime implemented a plan, it was soon discarded by the incoming regime. During 1970's, when a socialist party came to power, it discarded the existing plan, favoured nationalisation and used annual budgets as a framework to run the economy.

One reason for such neglect could be that Pakistan simply did not buy socialist ideology or planned economy concept because of its people deep rooted religious beliefs or being USA client state. The socialist societies were Godless and Pakistan was a religious state. The second reason for the neglect points to the shortsightedness of the country's political and administrative leadership which was undisciplined, self-interested and mindless of long-term national interests. The uncertain availability of resources to finance planned projects might have contributed to this neglect as well, and finally, the USA influence positively discouraged planning through expert advice, aid policies, and promotion of free market system. National planning got turned into an exercise in futility. Here is a brief history of development plans.

The first development plan was approved in 1950 to guide investment in infrastructure and industrial development. It got abandon lacking human and financial resources. Again it was revived in 1955 with new priorities, targets, and assessment. Once again it got abandoned as no compromise could be reached on resources division between the two wings of the country.

The second five-year plan (1960-65) surpassed all its set targets. All sectors of the economy showed considerable growth during this period. The plan had encouraged private enterprise and development of import substitution industries under protection. USA aid and loans provided financial support for the plan. The war with India in 1965 diverted attention and resources to defence and planning and development went on the back burner. The third plan (1965-70) did not get enough resources and did not get implemented. The 4th Plan (1970-75) got abandoned as India defeated Pakistan to turn East Pakistan into a separate client country Bangladesh and the socialist leadership abandoned national planning. Zia regime re-introduced planning by draughting 5th five-year plan (1978-83), it was to stabilise the economy but once again it got abandoned due to lack of resources which got diverted to defence needs and to pay for the new rise in oil prices. Some industrial controls introduced by the socialist regime were relaxed during the plan period. The 6th plan (1983-88) shifted priority to the development of the private sector. The public-private cooperation led to significant improvement in the performance of the economy. However, the plan was less successful in raising agriculture sector productivity or to lower dependency on imported energy. The 7th five-year plan (1988-93) prioritised energy, transport and communication, physical infrastructure and housing, and human resources development.

The industrial sector was given low priority in allocation. The public-sector corporations were to become self-financing and private investment was to be encouraged to drive growth. The plan did not achieve any of its set targets. The 8th five-year plan (1993-98) sought cooperation from the private sector making them a partner in the planning process. The plan got discarded due to political instability. In brief, the national planning has been an abject failure in Pakistan.

Political Economy of Pakistan

Historical growth of macro indicators and economy's structural changes provide an overall view of changing conditions but what has caused these changes? I happen to agree with Schumpeter who believed that history is a story of the impact of leadership on the mass of society. It is the driving force of leadership that bring changes and development. only a nationalist leadership turn a state into an effective organ to transform poor economies rapidly. The real leadership rests with only a tiny minority.

There is no automatic process to put poor on a steady growth path. Political participation in poor countries promotes short term compromised decisions which may not serve the long-term interests. Pakistan has lived with 38 years of 'parliamentary form' of democracy and 30 years of Army rule. Political regimes created inequality, chaos, political infighting, corruption, low capital formation, mismanagements, macro instability, and a stagnant economy. Army regimes brought political and macro stability, high level of public and private investment in infrastructure, human and physical capital, effective management, relative honesty, and a higher rate of economic growth. Both civilian and army regimes failed in providing a nationalist leadership or long-run vision for the country. There are similarities between Pakistan and South Korea military takeover of the countries except that South Korean Army Leadership had a vision for their country, and they were ruthless to achieve it.

Parvez Hasan (48), an ex-employee of the World Bank, is very much aware of this disparity in economic growth rates under different regimes and yet claims that the rapid growth during the Army rule was the result of the USA financial support which increased inequality and loss of political rights and freedom. He does not provide any objective or normative indicator to back his accretion of increased inequality. It is true that the USA financial support was significantly greater during Army rule *(but aid did not stop during the civilian rule)*. But they were paying to compensate the increasing costs of Pakistan's involvement in the US international conflicts. Hassan's third claim of loss of political rights is laughable. Political participation without economic freedom becomes meaningless in poor countries. The civilian rule in Pakistan has repeatedly undermined and destroyed political rights through lawlessness and lack of accountability. The fact is that Army rule provided macro stability which encouraged both external financial assistance and domestic savings and investment resulting in faster growth rate. Having made these general observations, I turn to look at different periods of Pakistan political economy in chronological order.

Survival Amid Political Chaos (1947-60)

The founder of Pakistan, MA Jinnah, a political giant and man of vision, died in 1949, just a year or so after the creation of an independent country. With his death, Pakistan lost his vision and may be the purpose of her creation i.e. an Islamic welfare state.

Pakistan had inherited a parliamentary system of democracy but had no experience of conducting national elections. There was only one political party made up of landowning class with divergent interests and no mass membership. The country consisted of two wings, different languages, culture, and divided by 1000 miles of Indian Territory. Pakistan's first election brought landowning class to power as they were the only one to have money and influence over rural population to contest elections. The conflicting political ambitions, ethnic cleavages, regional economic disparity, corruption, and weak administration all played a role in the creation of political and economic instability. The daunting task of setting up a new state, millions of refugees settlement, floods, insecurity against external enemies and foreign intrigue also contributed to the chaotic conditions. India started a hostile currency war in 1949 because Pakistan had refused to devalue its currency. It is difficult to side with those who considered Pakistan's refusal to devalue its currency along with Indian devaluation in 1949. Pakistan had very little to sell in the foreign markets, foreign demand for its cotton and jute was fairly inelastic in the short run and she had imposed import restrictions to avoid possible adverse effects of its policy. This policy and high demand for agriculture products from Korea proved fruitful, and the country achieved its first trade surplus during 1950/53 period.

The first prime minister was killed in 1951. The next seven years from 1951 to 1958 witnessed 5 Prime Ministers and political bankruptcy of legislators, for whom holding on to power became an end itself. The centralised civil bureaucracy kept the fragile country intact but got politically involved in a power struggle among various factions of ruling elites. During this time, one civil servant acted as prime minister and the other as the Governor General of the country. The colonial subjugation and feudal society norms and power structure had turned population dependent and slavish in nature. An active armed conflict broke out in Kashmir, a disputed state between Pakistan and India.

The fear of socialism had drawn USA attention to Pakistan and under the guise of financial support and experts' help; it started to play a (destructive) role in the affairs of a new and not so sure or secure country. The foreign aid, loans, and weapons seduced Pakistan into submission and made it a begging country. Pakistan did not get enough time, which was needed, to transform itself from a colonial country to an independent sovereign state. The ruling elite tempered with appointments and promotions in the administration and judiciary services and made 'land distribution' policy ineffective. The professionalism of the bureaucracy and the independence of the legal systems got compromised. The internal promotions depended on connections and loyalty to politicians. The civil service kept technocrats at-length, adopted short-term objectives, to please their masters and enrich themselves at the cost of long-run national economic development and human welfare. Political elites put priority over law and order and the civil service was happy to maintain the traditional colonial status of master-servant relationship with Joe public which created a mismatch between development ambitions and state capabilities. This lack of capability became quite clear during the 70's. The socialist regime of the time made civil service responsible for economic management of nationalised industries, which failed miserably, and most of the industries under their management became economically bankrupt. The civil service, a generalist service, failed in providing an appropriate guide to private and public sectors investment or technical policy formulation or its implementation.

Pakistan established its central bank, two commercial banks and a planning commission in the 50's. The planning commission was to guide resource allocation. Pakistan got lucky as Korean War started in 1950, which created high demand for agriculture products and provided a stimulus for the economy. This export-led boom ended with the ending of Korean War. At the same time, Pakistan agriculture sector was devastated by heavy floods of 1951/52 and 1952/53.

Pakistan adopted a free market mixed economy system under the American supervision. The agriculture price controls and restrictive trade policies were adopted to extract surplus from agriculture to finance industrial development. The restrictive (i.e.

high tariff) foreign trade policy was to raise revenues and protect infant industries. Both cotton and jute industries grew rapidly. Pakistan used incentives such as tax breaks, low-interest rates, and high tariffs on imports and subsidised foreign exchange for machines imports to promote industrial development in the private sector. The strategy worked and industrial sector started to grow, but the private sector investment went mainly into cotton based industrial units or light industries. New industrialist took advantage of protected markets and monopoly position and turned into rent seekers. Tax authorities were too lax or incompetent to extract monopoly rents for a new capital formation which ended up as conspicuous consumption. The monopoly prices for industrial goods and internal agriculture price control discouraged efforts in the agriculture sector and created a spirit of hopelessness in the rural population. During this period Pakistan suffered from current account and balance of payment deficits which were dealt with USA financial help.

In mid-50's, Suhrawardy, a prime minister from East Pakistan, introduced a programme of collective farming which wasted a huge amount of money without any success. An effort was made to re-enact the first plan in 1955 with new priority to develop agriculture and reduce the imbalance between two wings (i.e. East and West Pakistan), but it got abandoned because no compromise could be reached between conflicting interests. The politicians from East Pakistan claimed that foreign exchange earning of jute export were being used to develop industries in West Pakistan. In fact, it was Karachi, the capital city at the time that had benefited most through centralization of power. The politicians formed a single unit of four provinces of the west wing to counter east wing population majority. This act simply increased inter-provincial bitterness and macro instability.

In the early years, the feudal had taken advantage to strengthen their economic and political hold by investing in industries under protection, created provincial economic disparities, filled public services with less intelligent incompetent personal and refused 'land distribution' policy. The expansionary fiscal and monetary policies fuelled inflation. The foreign aid and loans lace the ruling class bank accounts. The internal price controls stagnated agriculture. The fiscal and trade deficits widened, and unemployment got worse over time; food shortages became common day occurrence, and the inequality widened. Inter-provincial bitterness reached a new peak, natural disasters like floods destroyed agriculture, external aggression posed a serious threat and lack of financial and technical skills created inefficiency. The political instability became too acute, tensions between different tiers of government reached a breaking point, and the management of country almost collapsed.

Under these conditions, civil order started to dismantle. Political and economic uncertainty reached to such level that the country could not go on for very long. In consequence, the Army was called upon by the President, with the American blessing, to take control of the country around 1958. The parliament was dissolved, martial law imposed but the Army had no experience of running a country or economic vision to guide its economic policies; however, it had discipline, honesty, and integrity. The financial help and economists arrived from the USA to manage Pakistan economy.

Ayub Era (1960-70)

Gen Ayub ruled for the next ten years. The Army takes over created certainty, improved economic management, reduced corruption by sacking 400 corrupt civilian administrators and diverted a sizable spending to human development.

The Second Five Year Plan (1960-65) was a revised and improved version of the first plan. At that time USA policy was to support the industrialisation of poor countries to shield them from the socialist evils. The private sector was to play a central role in the development of the country with the active state support. Industrialisation, promotion of scientific knowledge, development of transportation and agriculture were declared priority sectors. The set target of 20% growth in GDP over five years was exceeded. The political certainty and macro stability encouraged private saving that increased from 8 to 10% of GDP. The domestic investment went up from 12 to 17% of GDP. The private and public investment established import substitution consumer goods industries and infrastructure. Most of the public investment went into the development of water resources, agriculture technology like tractors, new seeds, and fertilisers. The investment funds were provided by the international agencies, as long-term loans. The public investment funds came from foreign aid or loans. The USA financial support helped in building up armed services and bridging fiscal and trade deficits. The private sector was offered incentives to develop consumer goods industries and capital formation in the private sector increased by almost 13% per annum. The main driver of economic growth was a large public-sector investment. The industrial sector grew at the rate of 10.8% per annum and the agriculture growth rate increased to 5.1% per annum. The economy grew at the rate of 7% per annum. The high growth rate in agriculture sector led to rising income levels in rural areas, which stabilised rural population.

A conservative monetary policy and mildly expansionary fiscal policy were implemented to maintain price stability and to encourage trade, but the level of export remained low because of limited capacities of consumer goods industries. The country remained dependent on imports for most of the industrial goods which brought a progressive deterioration of the balance of payment deficit.

Some Pakistani Economists have claimed that the restrictive trade policy created industrial inefficiency which led to the deterioration of the balance of payment. Such an argument is just silly. Pakistan at the time had not created a solid industrial base to take advantage of the free trade opportunities. Her existing trade policy had created a balance of payment difficulties and had discouraged further industrialisation in the country. The trickle-down policy, a favourite of American economists, failed to increase wages or level of employment in the country. The investment in public goods (i.e. education and health) amounted to about 6% of the development expenditures. The USA financed the family planning programme, but it failed to control the population explosion.

The disparity in resource allocation and resulting unequal growth rates between East and West Pakistan increased regional bitterness. The creation of one unit in West Pakistan to counter larger population of East Pakistan and building of the new capital city, Islamabad, in West Pakistan further increased political tension. The relatively rapid industrialisation of West Pakistan provided further support to the argument that the central government was biassed. All these factors increased political division and inflamed unrest in the East wing. A war with India on Kashmir issue ended in a stalemate in 1965 but resulted in diverting resources from industrial development to the defence needs of the country. Pakistan got a new constitution in the 60's that discarded parliamentary form and adopted a Presidential form of political structure. An electoral college consisting of local representatives was to select the President. Ayub Khan was elected President with a rigged election that touched off civil disorder. His desire to legitimise Army rule created political and economic uncertainty in the country and he was forced to leave, handing power to another Army General in 1969-70. The period (1965-70) was marred with political unrest, external invasion, and economic uncertainty. The foreign aid declined as a result of conflict with India which reduced public investment. The fiscal deficit started to get larger, and the balance of payment difficulties became acute. Pakistan went to IMF three times during the 60's for financial help. All three loans were a short-term arrangement.

Pakistan industrial take-off suffered badly. It is unfortunate that at that time when the global economy had become open to manufactured goods from developing countries, Pakistan failed to take advantage of this situation whereas South Korea took full advantage of this opportunity and adopted export-oriented industrial growth and export promotion strategy under its Army dictator to transform its economy.

The rate of growth, over ten years of army rule, averaged around 6%. The population grew at the rate of about 3% over the same period. The first nine years of the Army rule provided political and economic stability. This increased foreign aid, public and private investment and country made a considerable economic progress that was quite unmatched in the developing countries at the time. The restrictive import policy promoted import substitution industries. But there was no grand vision of Pakistani leadership to make their country rich and strong. The investment in the human capital remained low, inequality of income and wealth increased, and no policy measures were taken to correct the imbalance between two wings of the country which led to the separation of two wings as two separate countries. The water treaty with India reached in the 60's has proven to be deficient in protecting the interests of Pakistan.

Socialist Chaos Years (1970-80)

This decade saw the return of parliamentary form of democracy, a new constitution, and a civilian socialist regime. A new election took place in 1969/70, where a political party from East Pakistan won a majority of seats in the national assembly but was not allowed to form a government. The political chaos spread, India took advantage of civil strife and invaded East Pakistan and got it separated as a client independent country call Bangladesh. The 4th five years plan (1970-75) got abandoned in the aftermath of an Indian victory in East Pakistan.

In the new country of Pakistan, power was transferred to the socialist party, which had won the majority of seats in the west wing. Z. A. Bhutto, a feudal in a socialist cloak, bypassed virtually every plan and conducted the country business on his whim and used annual budgets framework to manage the economy. He had sold a pipe dream of removal of poverty, land reforms, reduction of industrialists' power, and minimization of civil and military powers in his election speeches. These slogans turned out to be more symbolic rather than real commitment. Bhutto initiated a nationalisation programme to include banking, insurance, basic metals, iron and steel, heavy engineering, vehicle assembly, chemicals, petrochemicals, cement, public utilities, shipping, oil distribution, cooking oil, and education institutions. The export trade of cotton and rice also came under public control. The civil service took control of the nationalised industries, but it had no capability to manage business enterprises. The poor management and political chaos bankrupted most of the nationalised industries. The nationalisation of banks benefited numerous cronies and friends but failed to provide lending to the general public. The foreign financial assistance which had previously supported public investment dried up and the economy turned stagnant.

Bhutto initiated a 'poverty alleviation' scheme, but it had no substance. A land reform scheme got announced which could have helped in redistribution of wealth, but it did not redistribute any land. A security policy for the land tenants was promised but never implemented.

The country had been in a coma having lost half of its territory. Middle East conflict sent the crude oil price soaring that put a great financial burden on foreign reserves and created fiscal and balance of payment deficits. Nature also turned against the country; floods battered the agriculture sector and the economy stalled because of sluggish demand. The failure of management and militancy of the trade unions led to the destruction of limited industrial base created during the last decade. New civil service powers made them all powerful as no business activity could take place unless it had received the paper authorization. A lot of business people left the country to settle abroad and took their money with them. The nationalised industries and businesses went into decline mode, and the culture of entrepreneurship, risk-taking, and innovation simply folded up. The politicians and their cronies obtained large loans from the financial sectors for personal luxuries and either refused to pay back or got them written off. This open day robbery turned financial institutions mostly insolvent.

I am not sure if Bhutto had any ambitions for Pakistan and its people. Once he got power, most of his promises remained promises. His policies of nationalisation, encouragement of trade union militancy, and mismanagement of some large public projects (i.e. integrated iron and steel plant, Indus River West Bank highway and highway tunnel), created an uncertain environment, which saw a 50% drop in private investment and more than 50% drop in manufacturing. By 1978, Private investment had dropped to less than 30% of 1970 level. Private capital had fled the country or went into small scale manufacturing and real estate. The industrial output turned stagnant and brought a near collapse of the economy and slower growth rate of 4.6%. There was no significant reduction in the poverty and unemployment. The agriculture and industrial sectors turned stagnant over this decade, and unemployment increased significantly. The currency was devalued to increase export of agriculture goods but it made machines imports very expensive. The State bank increased interest rates to boost domestic savings but higher interest policy also discouraged domestic investment. The domestic private debt increased manifold and foreign aid got cut by foreign donors. The fiscal deficits went through the roof which was a direct result of oil price rise, expansion in the public sector and wage inflation. The macro economic instability increased and the expansionary fiscal and monetary policies resulted in a much bigger trade gap. In 1977, Pakistan once again had to beg IMF for a loan to safeguard the sinking economy. IMF agreed to bail out by approving a short-term loan of $1193 million.

With higher oil prices, Middle East countries embarked on numerous infrastructure projects that increased demand for labour from Pakistan. South Korea won those contracts to gain experience and made large sums of money. Pakistan exported his young and their foreign remittance considerably lightened her foreign loan repayment burden. The remittances increased from $136 million (17% of export earnings) in1972 to $1.2 billion (41% of export earnings) in 1978. Pakistan managed to export its youth to build other people countries and their foreign exchange earning did not find a home in investment opportunities in Pakistan but was taken out of the country and deposited in corrupt leadership foreign accounts.

The feudal turned socialist, Z.A Bhutto rigged elections to get re-elected for the second term in office, and the political chaos followed. He had under-estimated the USA hostility to socialism. The money had been flooding in religious parties' deposits to strengthen their organisation, which collectively rose up to challenge 'God-less' regime. Bhutto regime tried to control it by asking the military for help, but the situation had reached such a point that the Army takeover became inevitable and was welcomed by the masses. The Prime Minister was arrested in 1977 and hanged in 1978. The political and economic instability caused by autocratic rule ended up destroying the small industrial base, increasing civil service inefficiency and corruption, abandoning central planning, and reducing the overall rate of economic growth.

Bhutto's socialist revolution was a fraud against the people of Pakistan. However, if I am charitable, I might say that his intentions may have been good, but he underestimated the opposing forces. He took advantage of political instability and economic poverty of the time and sold the dream of bread, clothing, and shelter to millions of poor people of Pakistan. But he did not distribute land and underestimated the power and control of the feudal system. He did not dismantle ex-colonial institutions of parliamentary democracy, civil service, judiciary and armed services, which had been constructed to maintain status quo and could not be part of a revolution. His nationalisation programme and political neutrality did not find any sympathy in the USA and Pakistan was too important a country to be allowed to go in the socialist camp. Pakistan did not have enough trained managers and technical experts, who were committed socialist, to take control of nationalised industrial units to make it a success. Pakistan civil service did not have the capability to act as economic managers of nationalised units to run them on commercial footings. The output from nationalised units dropped considerably, and huge losses resulted in increasing budget deficits and slow economic growth. One notable achievement of ZA Bhutto was his initiation of a nuclear programme that would deter any enemy to invade Pakistan or endanger its existence in future. It was this programme which eventually resulted in the development of a nuclear bomb that was exploded in the 90's to make Pakistan a nuclear power. *Some economists have questioned the rationality of this project because of its large cost, but I am not one of them. The security of the state is a primary function which takes priority over all other functions.*

Zia rule and Russian invasion of Afghanistan (1980-90)

The USA conspired with the Army to over-through the socialist regime and Gen Zia took control of the country in the late seventies. The constitution and parliament got suspended. Zia was visionless but his rule restored some normality in the country.

The new President introduced 'Islamization' programme by establishing 'Zakat' and interest-free banking. Zakat is a tax to finance welfare activities, and Islam does not allow usury. Ushr Ordinance got promulgated in 1980; it is a tax levied on agriculture produce at a fixed rate of 5% of the value of the produced but just like every other time rich and powerful did not pay it. The religious elements, who had helped in creating political unrest had to be comforted. They were appeased by passing Islamic laws, declaring certain section of the population as non-Muslim and making Pakistan the Islamic Republic. This religious appeasing policy will cost Pakistan dearly in the future years.

The political and economic certainty returned. The currency was allowed to fluctuate in the market to encourage exports. Private investment was liberalised and encouraged. Large scale American financial support flooded in to support the fight against Russia in Afghanistan and overseas Pakistanis remitted large funds back home. The increased capital formation increased economic growth, and the economy grew at an annual rate of 7%, with 4% annual rate in agriculture and 9% annual growth rate in the industry. The large inflow of funds (loans and remittances) helped to deal with higher oil prices and encouraged private and public investment in industries such as fertiliser, cement, steel, and water resources. The rate of domestic savings remained at around 9% of GDP whereas the domestic investment rose to around 17% of GDP. The public investment in education and health increased which created a feel good factor.

The fiscal and balance of payment deficits were controlled and managed with foreign aid and loans. The USA aid was generous because of Pakistan's direct involvement in the fight against Russia. IMF and the World Bank, by now, had adopted more activists approach to dictate their terms as a part of loans provisions. The restrictions on the size and scope of public sector activities were a precursor to the Washington Consensus policies.

The boom ended sadly with the Russian defeat; the USA cut back its financial support and Pakistan ended up with 3 million Afghan refugees, which added extra pressure to her economic and security problems. The harsh weather conditions in 1986 and 1987 impacted agriculture output and its rate of growth declined to 2.2%. Some structural reform policies were implemented such as reduction in fiscal deficit, encouragement of private investment and public enterprises as self-financing entities. In August 1988, Gen. Zia was killed.

The rate of growth for the period 1878-88 had gone up to 7% per annum, but the last two years of the decade were low growth period and as a result, the growth rate fell back to 5.9%. Once again, the country was gripped by financial problems. The budget deficit rose to 8.5 % of GDP; inflation rate went up to 10%, and the current account deficit doubled from 2.1 to 4.3% of the GDP. The debt-service ratio increased to 28% of the export earnings, and the foreign exchange reserves fell to less than three weeks of imports.

Return of Political Chaos (1990-98)

Zia's engineered death provided opportunity and the USA brought back civilian rule in 1989-90. A new civilian government took office in 1990 but lasted less than three years. After that, an employee of the World Bank was imported as a Prime Minister of Pakistan. He brought policies of liberation, deregulation and privatisation with him. In 1994 a new government took power but continued with policies of structural reforms. The politicians brought old problems of mismanagement, corruption, and flight of capital with them. Denationalisation or privatisation policy topped political agenda, and it provided unimaginable opportunities for corruption and money making for the politicians and their partner in crimes. A large number of national assets were privatised at nominal prices. The miss-management of the economy resulted in huge increase in expenses and low revenues collection pushed up fiscal deficits to new heights. The relaxation of free trade bankrupted few remaining domestic industries and created a balance of payment problems. The foreign currency reserves fell to a record low, raising fears of loan default. The government went to the international lender of last resort. The loan was granted with conditions. Pakistan had to agree to fiscal discipline, opening up of the markets, competition, and free movement of capital, privatisation of the state enterprises and removal of all subsidies on electricity, gas, petroleum products, fertilisers, and interest rates.

The structural reforms policies cut down current account deficit in the short-run but led to higher prices, reduced effective demand and slowing down of the economy. The high-interest rates increased investment cost to discourage new investment, reduced industrial operations, and increased unemployment. The liberalisation of trade resulted in flooding domestic markets with imports, which put more pressure on the balance of payment and destroyed infant industrial sector. The freedom of capital movement encouraged capital flight out of the country. The reduction in new investment and existing industrial operations dampened down economic activities and economic growth. The deflationary policies of structural reforms were opposite of the expansionary measures that Pakistan needed at the time. The loss of effective demand adversely impacted agriculture sector and its growth rate fell to 4% per annum. The industrial and manufacturing sectors turned stagnant. The higher prices, unemployment, and political infighting led to political and economic unrest. The government folded once again, and opposition party formed a new government.

The country was drowning in economic chaos, and politicians were busy conducting the political musical chairs show. The incompetent and corrupt do not become competent and honest without any accountability or new skills. The twin problems of budget and balance of payment deficits resurfaced. The government froze foreign currency accounts to deal with the worsening currency reserves situation; this backfired, as foreign remittances fell significantly during this period. The Privatisation of public enterprises had opened up new ways of corruption. The profit making public enterprises were sold off at nominal prices to the politician's relatives or proxies. Some public enterprises were intentionally turned into loss-making so that these could be given away on nominal charges. Naqvi and Kemal (97) in their paper 'Privatisation, Efficiency, and Employment in Pakistan' have stated that Pakistan divested 86 manufacturing units, two commercial banks, one financial institution, 10% of the PIA and 12% of the telecommunication business in the first instalment of the privatisation programme. In the second instalment, the rest of the manufacturing units, all commercial banks except National Bank, remaining telecommunication business and 500 MW of thermal power got sold. They observe that the efficiency of the privatised units did not increase with privatisation. The private buyers reduced employment, increased prices and did not invest in improving efficiency or new capacity. The new owners became monopoly rent seekers. Some privatised industrial units folded up and their land holdings were sold off for real estate development. The privatisation programme helped the ruling elites to get rich, and the country lost productive capacity. The sale revenues simply disappeared in fiscal deficits or politicians overseas accounts.

The freedom of capital movement did not increase foreign direct investment, but it made it easier for the foreign currency to fly out of the country to the politician's bank deposits in the western countries. The freedom of capital movement also made the stock market as an instrument of foreign exploitation. The prime minister of the time was directly involved in the money laundering. Pakistan paid a heavy price for conditional international borrowing in the 90's. The structural reform policies killed a significant number of domestic productive capabilities, encouraged capital outflow, cut down import duties revenue without increasing export earnings.

Pakistan exploded atomic devices following India and the USA and allies imposed economic sanctions on Pakistan in 1998. Pakistan's currency lost value against all foreign currencies which made import of capital goods very expensive. Economic instability discouraged domestic savings and investment. Remittance fell to $984 million in 2000. Foreign exchange reserves came under pressure and fell to less than three months of imports. Foreign loans went up to $36 billion to become 58% of GDP.

The successive political governments (led by MNS and BNB) failed to understand the foreign loan conditions and did not apply correct economic policies to deal with serious and mounting economic problems facing the country. The rising unemployment, rising consumer prices, and open corruption stories had people up in arms and this shameful period of corruption and incompetence ended with the takeover of the country by the Army for the third time. Once again people celebrated the disposal of the corrupt ruling elite by distributing sweets in the streets.

Musharraf Rule and USA Invasion of Afghanistan (1998-2006)

The Army rule and political stability returned to Pakistan in 1998, and the rate of economic growth once again picked up. Unfortunately, Pakistan was dragged, once again, into an American war in Afghanistan, but it brought USA financial assistance with it.

The new administration, faced with huge problems, managed to deal with national debt by paying back international loans and cutting interest payments. The USA aid and loans helped in repayment of debt as well as helped with the balance of payment deficit. The expansionary fiscal measures reduced unemployment and export subsidies raised export earnings. The debt services charge declined with reduced debt level. The increased effective demand stimulated economic growth. The aggregate investment went up from 15.5% to 23% of GDP to accelerate economic activities. The improved revenue collection stabilised and cut down budget deficit which eventually declined to an acceptable level of 4% of GDP.

The political and economic stability resulted in higher and effective use of existing capacity and effective management of remaining public enterprises resulting in higher productivity and reduced financial support. The easing of economic sanctions proved helpful in increasing exports, and favourable weather helped agriculture output. The higher economic growth rate, larger exports and increased overseas remittances improved economic conditions in the country.

The Army chief, who had been acting as the President of the country, went into self-destruct mode under foreign pressure in 2006. He agreed with the USA to legitimise his rule to allow political parties to contest the election and the winning party would elect him as the President. The USA had already planned that PPP would form the next government in Pakistan. Once the election campaign started, the chairperson of a political party (PPP) was killed. In sympathy and with American help, her party won the rigged election, and once again the tales of corruption, incompetence, and patronage started. AAZ, the husband of murdered leader, became the new president of the country. The civilian government politicised and polarised all state institutions. The corrupt politician promoted bendable civil servants to obey their orders. The police became an instrument to protect and enhance the interests of the ruling elite. The president of the country became known as Mr 20%, as everyone had to pay him to conduct any business in Pakistan. He also facilitated the USA to capture Osama Bin Laden.

The endemic corruption became a norm, and the economy got derailed from its growth path. The USA imposed conditions on aid and the global financial crisis of 2007 made matters worse. Once again currency lost value against international currencies, and capital flew out of the country. The balance of payment got worse as the country's exports declined. The PPP government went to IMF for help. IMF agreed to 'bailout' and approved a 23 month, $7.6 billion loans to avert a current account deficit and a potential default on foreign loans. In 2013, a new government headed by NS took control of the country. The new finance minister has borrowed from the International agencies and raised money from the foreign markets. The foreign debt has risen to $80 billion. The foreign loans have severely impacted the country's economy and hurt ordinary people. The stories of corruption and failing industries, money laundering is rampant. The Prime Minister is prosecuted for money laundering and corruption. The terrorist activities are rampant and the civil-military relations are at the lowest ebb.

Summary

Since 1947, Pakistan has managed to survive but has turned into an ineffective state without any long- term vision. She has failed to attain national respect or prosperity. Her political and economic instability has kept domestic saving and investment at a low level which has made her dependent on foreign handouts. Her population is still illiterate and increasing at a high rate, and her industrial and manufacture sectors have remained small, inefficient and rent seeker. The surpluses created through monopoly profits have not been re-invested in the country but have flown out. Her primary sector has remained dependent on favourable weather conditions and the management of natural resources including water resources have remained neglected. Her income and wealth inequality has increased over time. Pakistan has become a nuclear power but because of her poverty has remained vulnerable to attacks from external and internal enemies. Her low capital formation with high population growth rate has ensured that the country remains in a poverty trap.

The 30 years of Army rule provided some political and economic stability, which encouraged capital formation and economic growth. But the army generals did not have a long-term vision for the country. Pakistan Army leadership made major blunders under their watch and ended up serving the interests of the USA rather than their country. Maybe they did not have the intelligence or did not care to see through the proclaimed friendship of the Americans. The USA aid and loans increased during the Army rule because Pakistan willingly acted as an instrument to be used to further American interests. The gross growth rate for these years averaged about 7% which is quite remarkable. The 38 years of the civilian rule did not provide any truly national leadership. The institutionalised corruption, economic instability, and regional disparity plagued these years. The state turned ineffective, and its institutions have turned dysfunctional. The political and economic uncertainty discouraged investment and efforts during civilian rule and resulted in some cases reversing growth progress of stable years.

The country has suffered from regular boom and bust conditions resulting from the changing Army and civilian rule. Each Army regime folded when Army head tried to legitimise it by popular mandate and each civilian regime folded when corruption and mismanagement reached the stage where ordinary people found it difficult to survive.

11

GALLOPING HORSE: SOUTH KOREA

Colonial Era

Japan ruled Korea from 1905 to 1945 and like any other colonial power aimed to extract maximum benefit from the colony. In order to protect and prolong rule, she established an effective administrative structure to suppress working classes, introduced land reforms to destroy old established powers and increased agriculture productivity to release labour force for work in urban areas. Japan introduced a western style private property legal system in Korea which secured the control of Korean landowners over their land in perpetuity, but the process also enabled Japanese to take over 40% of all land and take control of an effective tax collection system. Japan did not allow any industrialisation or foreign trade in Korea and protected markets for her manufactured goods during the first decade of their rule. In 1923, all trade barriers between Japan and Korea were removed to integrate Korean agrarian economy. But Japan imposed heavy tariffs on imports from other countries into Korea.

Japan made a limited public investment in infrastructure development and some private investment in food–processing industries during 1910-20 periods. After WWI, some industrial control restrictions were relaxed for the Japanese capitalist to invest abroad including Korea and Japanese businesses invested in textile, raw material processing and mining. After 1919 uprising, some agriculture processing units were established in Korea to take advantage of higher returns and at the same time, Koreans were allowed to participate in industrial development as joint partners. Korean were also allowed to set up small-scale household industries employing less than ten workers. Later on, Koreans were permitted to invest in industries such as metals, dyeing, ceramics, and rubber shoes and knitted cotton socks. According to Eckert (29), Koreans were excluded from any meaning-full participation in their country's governance.

During WWII Japanese established a large hydropower station in the north of the country to provide cheap energy and promoted import substitution industries in Korea. The increased Korean production helped Japan to fight against the West. This made it easy for some large Korean business houses to emerge with Japanese support. Korean first university was established in 1924.

In summary, Japan exploited Korea's natural resources and labour force to gain maximum economic benefits. She introduced land reforms to destroy old power base and introduced limited industrial base to fight western powers. Kohli (64) seems to suggest that Japan had laid down the foundations for a cohesive state by implementing land reforms and building industrial sector for the Korean later day successful transformation of the economy. But Kohli ignores the fact that Korean economy got destroyed during the WWII and the following civil war which divided Korea into two independent countries i.e. North and South Korea. The West defeated Japan in WWII and Korea ended up as a possession of USA and USSR in 1945 and then partitioned into two countries i.e. North and South Koreas on a temporary basis. The following civil war destroyed economy decimated population and left both countries in a permanent state of war.

South Korea inherited uprooted population, very little capital or natural resources, and a minuscule domestic market. Her young people had lost lives in the war and most of the industrial plants left were in the North. After the general election in 1948; South Korea emerged as an independent state but a protectorate of the USA. She had scarce and mountainous land, harsh climate, and widespread poverty with one of the lowest per capita income in the world. A Japanese report, at the time, stated that South Korea was overcrowded, lacked natural resources, and had low saving, investment and poor administration.

South Korean Political Economy

South Korean economic performance since 1948 is quite remarkable by any standard. Within this time, poverty struck, aid receiving country has turned into an industrialised rich nation which competes against the richest and most advanced countries of the world. By 2011, South Korean per capita income based on a purchasing power parity had exceeded $33000. She was ranked 12th in human development index among all nations. Her saving rate had risen to 31%, and capital formation rate 27% of GDP. Her exports were 56% of GDP and rising at the rate of 12% per annum. She had eradicated poverty without creating extreme income inequality, and her average life expectancy has reached 81 years with 100% literacy rate. South Korea joined the 'rich man's club' (i.e. OECD) in 1996, but in 1948, she was dirt poor.

South Korea had adopted a presidential form of political regime which turned authoritarian to create 44 years of political stability from 1946 to 1990. The quality and single-minded nationalism of leadership created an effective state and a favourable environment for a long-term sustained economic development. The State, directly and indirectly, initiated, guided and supported economic development with determination, speed and vision and took measures to avoid sharp inequality of income distribution at the same time.

Syngman Rhee Regime

Rhee had a privileged background, went to the USA for studies and obtained a PhD from Princeton. He was a right-wing nationalist who won the first Presidential election with a vast majority. Once in power, he used every mean to consolidate and prolong his rule. In early years, he focused on acquiring financial aid and unification of the country. He created an elite ruling class through social reforms. The new ruling elites helped him to prolong his rule. The USA financed land reform and universal education programme which encouraged mass employment, higher output, universal literacy and skilled manpower for the future. The material success will ward off the socialist ideology of North Korea and Russia.

Dr Rhee presidency (1946-1960) was authoritarian, marked with corruption, ineptitude and he changed election procedures to keep him in power. But he was forced to resign under mass protests in 1960. By that time, South Korean economy and society had gone through changes of epic proportions through land reforms, universal education, and import-substitution industrial development. The land reform and education both created an equality based society, a pool of qualified scientist, managers and technical experts to meet demand from the expanded investment in the physical capital. The land reforms of 1946, had turned 1 million sharecroppers (i.e. 40% of total farm households) into small landowner and completed, the Japanese started to decline, of the landlord class that had been the backbone of traditional Korean society for centuries. The movement of large armies enforced intermingling of the population, increased rural to urban migration and provided a labour force for expanding industries in urban areas. The agriculture price control policy forced further migration to urban cities. Cuming (20) has stated that wars in Korea destroyed the old social structure and created a new one which brought Schumpeterian entrepreneurs to the front and created a commerce-oriented society. The new entrepreneurs helped in building up auxiliary warfare industrial base and started to grow into some of the later day chaebols (large business houses) in a war-torn economy.

The other post-war government policies had included heavy investment in energy sector, trade protection, import substitution, ease of entry and exit, industrial concentration and creation of capitalist groups, which had contributed to the acceleration of industrialisation and urbanisation process in the country. The large-scale reconstruction projects also helped in transforming the South Korean urban landscape and social-political nature of the society. The establishment of the large urban industrialised hub with increasing returns to scale activities created increasing demand for raw materials and rural labour force. The agriculture prices were subject to a control which encouraged labour movement from rural to urban centres to satisfy increasing labour demand. The produce of rural areas had ready markets in the urban centres. The GDP per capita increased by 5.5 % during the initial years but the industrial sector was growing by 14 to 16% per annum which supported Agriculture growth at the rate of 2.4% per annum. Most of the industrial growth was in mining and manufacturing. Some of the revived manufacturing and mining units were sold to private businesses to lay down the base for Korean capitalistic development.

Rhee period was mainly a recovery period, but 'import-substitution industrial' model along with land and education reforms laid down the foundation for a new social structure and an industrial base for future development. His rule provided political stability and cohesiveness which in turn promoted economic development.

In 1960, a new democratic government headed by Yun Bo Sun took office but folded up under new protests. A five-year development plan was approved but remained uncompleted.

Park Chung Hee era (1960-79)

General Park Chung Hee staged a coup in 1961 and overthrew the elected government. He declared that he wants to eradicate corruption and poverty and then hand over the government to the elected representatives. He ruled South Korea from 1961-1979, kerbed most political activities and built a self-reliant economy. At the time of his takeover, the country was still a relatively poor with per capita income of less than 100 US dollars, per capita export of $1.3 and she exported mainly raw materials such as agar, Pollack, raw silk and tungsten.

Gen. Hee embarked on an anti-corruption drive, jailed heads of all major conglomerates, fired all corrupt employees above bureau chief in rank and disposed of others to two-week re-education camps. He released heads of the conglomerates from jail on the condition that, henceforth, they would put the national interest ahead of the personal interests. The bureaucrats were regularly rotated among jobs and locations to discourage them from developing any ties with the corporate sector. These measures significantly reduce the corruption level and put national interests over and above the individual's interests in the country. Kang (53) states that during Hee rule there was a remarkable progression in the economic powers of Chaebols, a group of companies that exercise monopolistic or oligopolistic control in production lines and industries. In 1991, the top 10 'Chaebols' produced 77% of the GDP.

Gen. Hee established a planning board in 1961 with an objective to achieve rapid industrialisation of the country. He had a deep understanding of the reconstruction of Japan and decided to follow Japanese model of economic growth and invested heavily in developing human and physical capital capabilities. The American Economists helped in formulating development plans. An input-output model with varying coefficients was used to calculate investment needs and sector-wise employment opportunities. Gen Hee presided over four of five-year economic development plans during his time in office. The first plan put top priority on self-sufficiency in grains, reduction in unemployment, and improvement in the balance of payment. The food self-sufficiency was achieved through multiple cropping and increased agriculture productivity. The employment rose by using labour-intensive methods in the construction of infrastructure projects such as roads, dams, and irrigation projects. For the balance of payment improvement, two policies were adopted. One policy helped to develop light labour-intensive industries to increase exports and second helped to develop import substitution and capital-intensive industries that would provide inputs for other industries such as cement, fertiliser, refined petroleum, iron and steel and synthetic fibre. The infant industries were protected with high tariffs and total import bans. Over 600 products were banned from import list. The other policy measures such as managed exchange rates (exchange premiums and cash subsidies) helped to achieve import substitution goals. The rate of protection was highest for consumer goods and lowest on raw materials or intermediate goods. GDP rose by 7% per annum, and the industrial production increased by 50% during the first plan period.

The second plan put top priority on industrial diversification and shifted industrial strategy from 'import substitution' to 'export led' growth. The domestic markets were quite narrow and did not provide enough scope for diversification. A labour-intensive export-oriented industrialisation development plan was adopted to deal with narrow markets and to meet the set targets of the second five-year plan. The industrial development which included the development of heavy and chemical industries brought increasing returns activities and higher productivity which are the main ingredients of economic growth and prosperity. The plan was financed through the USA generous aid of about

$12 billion to utilise South Korea's large skilled labour force. The State took aggressive measures to achieve export-oriented industrialisation. The new industries got protection from external competition and low-interest credit to keep the cost down. The others protection measures included foreign loan guarantees, tax reduction, subsidised foreign exchange for the purchase of machinery, duty-free raw material imports, wastage allowance, and price controls on critical inputs and wages.

The government established institutions for trade promotion and set export targets for individual firms. The President conducted monthly meetings with the exporters expressing his appreciation and encouragement to achieve set targets. Soth Korea adopted export promotion measures at the time when WTO had banned all export promotion schemes. GDP grew at the annual rate of 9.6%, export expanded by 46% per annum, and the industrial production rose by 60 to 70 % for the plan period.

The next development plan put top priority on the heavy industry (including chemical) development. Again, the President was the instigator. The development of heavy industries started in 1973 and consisting of manufacturing of steel, non-ferrous metals, automobiles, machine tools, shipbuilding, electronics, and chemicals. The country's steel production and oil refining capabilities rose most notably. Refineries for zinc, copper, shipbuilding facilities, weapon industries and automobile manufacturing got constructed.

The next five-year plan established a framework to prepare the country for foreign competition in the world markets. Some private firms were ordered to undertake specific highly competitive industrial projects and were protected from competition with low-interest loans, preferential tax treatment and direct access to the President to remove any deadlocks. Many problems arose which got resolved. The winning of infrastructure contracts in the Middle East helped in dealing with oil price shock. The country's foreign reserves provided support to deal with the foreign indebtedness. The government invested heavily in rural infrastructure projects, and a suitable pricing policy was adopted to increase domestic agriculture output.

By the end of Hee presidency, the country had industrialised, human capital had developed, per capita income had increased considerably, and poverty had been moderated. The society had transformed and gained high knowledge base and political maturity. Gen Hee coup was a byproduct of widespread corruption, poverty, and administration inefficiencies. He established central planning, re-enforced institutions to make state authority more cohesive and crushed all political dissent. The State took control of corporate labour force and encouraged economic concentration in the hands of big chaebols.

The USA had facilitated reconciliation between Korea and Japan to build an alliance against the socialist threat. Gen. Hee was invited to pay an official visit to Japan. He accepted the invitation, went to Japan, and formed a close understanding with the Japanese Prime Minister. Japan compensated Korea for the war losses and agreed to help in economic development. In 1965, South Korea got financial assistance, aid, and investment, amounting to almost one billion US dollars as well as Japanese steel technology to develop steel industry. Besides this financial help, Japan offered trade opportunities and the trade between two countries increased to $300 million in 1965. Japanese investment started to flow in South Korea which proved helpful in the industrialisation of the country.

Gen. Hee also agreed to the USA request to send his army to fight in Vietnam. He sent 300000 Korean soldiers to take part in the American war. In return for this favour, the USA provided South Korea with a package of civil and military aid which amounted to billions of USA dollars and decided to acquire essential supplies from S Korea, which helped S Korea to expand steel and transportation equipment industries with secondary expansion in the primary and intermediate industries. According to one estimate, Korean GDP increased by 7% as a result of USA procurement.

Gen. Hee had a clear vision for his country. The economy was transformed from an agrarian to an industrial base. To achieve this end, he eliminated all opposition, created an effective and cohesive state and encouraged concentration of economic power in few big business houses. He was fortunate to inherit a post-land reform agriculture sector, a reasonable industrial base, an entrepreneurial stratum and an educated population. He used his total authority with vengeance to push for industrialisation under protection and reconciled difference with Japan to obtain technology and capital. He engineered an alliance between state and businesses, using nationalism, to push for economic prosperity and formed a partnership with the USA by going to war as an ally and in return got help to develop steel, transport and labour-intensive export-oriented industries. The Vietnam War also provided opportunities for the Korean heavy industries to get established. The industry and exports sectors grew rapidly contributing to rapid economic growth.

In late 70's South Korea suffered few hiccups such as oil price hike, large debts and high service charges resulting in stagnation. The regime used both fiscal and monetary policies to achieve comprehensive industrialisation of his country. The inflationary situation and high debt levels got dealt by orthodox deflationary measures of restrictive income policy and withdrawal of incentives, which reduced effective demand to control inflation and large revenue to pay up the national debt. The economic stagnation led to political unrest in the country which led to Gen Park Hee death. But his legacy of state-led growth model survived and remained in operation throughout the 80's.

Gen. Chun Doo Hawn (1979-87)

After Gen Park Hee death, his Prime Minister Choi Kyu Ha was elected as caretaker president in 1979. He released some political detainees and promised to adopt a new constitution and hold new elections. Meanwhile, Gen. Hawn staged a coup within the armed services to take control of the army high command. In 1980, there was students' unrest again, and the caretaker President's authority got undermined. Gen Hawn declared martial law in the country and promised to create trust and justice in the society. He dismissed about 7000 corrupt state functionaries, arrested opposition politicians and closed down all educational institutions. The USA supported army takeover of the country and helped to establish his authority and stability.

In 1980, the world economies suffered from stagflation and the South Korean economy suffered from weaker exports, high oil prices, and anaemic economic growth. Gen. Hawn adopted policies to achieve economic stability which included a $4 billion loan from Japan on low-interest rates, diverted investment to light labour-intensive export-oriented industries, relaxed import restrictions and labour control laws and allowed increased incomes in the agriculture sector. The economy picked up as a result of expansionary policies and grew at the rate of 8% per annum. In 1983, the annual exports value stood at $23.8 billion. A new 5th five-year plan was approved which relaxed the restriction on labour markets and imports. The economy grew at the rate of 12.5% per annum during 1985-87. The current account went into surplus and the national debt was reduced from $47 billion to $35 billion in 1987. The top Chaebols made a remarkable contribution of almost 70 % to the GDP.

Gen. Hawn was a nationalist who believed South Korea needed political stability to achieve economic prosperity. He faced up to North Korea and kept close ties with the USA and Japan but also initiated and established normal relations with the socialist regimes of China and Russia. This policy paid off and trade with China increased rapidly. In 1987 Gen. Hawn's in-laws were involved in two financial scandals which damaged his reputation as a clean man. There was further students' unrest as one of them was killed by the State security services. Hawn resigned, and a new election took place ending in a political stalemate. The government party defeated oppositions with a thin majority and a new President, an ex-army man, got elected as a President.

Roh Tae Woo Regime (1987-91)

Roh Tae Woo had come to power with the slightly changed state constitution, but the army kept a veto over opposition parties. The 6th five years social and economic development plan was approved which maintained economic relaxation programme. The labour and trade restrictions were further relaxed. GDP grew at the rate of 8% per annum, and South Korean per capita income reached $6498 in 1991, a remarkable achievement by any standard. South Korea successfully controlled inflation and gradually opened domestic markets to face foreign competition. A liberal trade and capital movement policy boosted trade and increased the inflow of capital to raise economic growth and turned a trade deficit into a surplus. It is worth recalling that Fredrick List of Germany had proclaimed in the 18th century that once a country has industrialised than the opening of its markets and international trade will bring riches to that nation

Roh Tae Woo greatest achievement rested with the holding of successful Seoul Olympics of 1988, which proved a great success both politically and economically. The games led to a reduction in military tension between the two neighbours and provided Korea with an opportunity to host sports persons from all over the world.

As 1992 election approached, South Korea politicians got engaged in political horse-trading and new alliances were formed.

Roh joined Kim Young Sam to form a new political party based on the political ideology of Japanese LDP party. This alliance was a marriage of convenience for both politicians and a way to get Kim Young Sam elected as President.

Kim Young Sam 1992-97

Kim Young Sam won the election to become President in 1992. He maintained reformist stand by restoring civil rights and replacing army appointed personals with liberal and politically clean people to various state positions. He arrested two former Presidents and put them on trial for corruption. His economic reforms included removal of all controls on labour markets and banning of fictitious bank accounts which were being used to hide income and wealth from tax authorities. The labour force turned more vocal and demanded welfare safety provisions for the workers and implementation of the pension programme.

South Korea joined OECD in 1996 and accepted entry conditions including the opening of markets, removal of all trade restrictions, free movement of capital and free exchange rates. These conditions hit South Korea hard. The higher labour wages, higher welfare spending, and debt service charges led to current account deficits. The interest rate rose to 30% per annum; labour wages remained inflexible, and unemployment rose to 9%. All economic activities declined, and the country ended up with a negative growth rate of 5.8% per annum. The greater competition from abroad had cut down effective demand for home products and the economy turned recessionary. All major industries including electronics, automobiles, and garments faced declining demand at home and in the overseas markets. The eight conglomerates went bust which made banking sector venerable. The stock market lost 50% of its value. There was a run on the currency which lost value and reached an all-time low of 1640 Won to a dollar. The financial crisis made a complete meltdown a strong possibility. The foreigners bought some financial and industrials units at the knockdown prices. The near bankruptcy of the South Korean economy was a direct result of joining the rich countries club i.e. OECD with the attached conditions.

Kim Dee Jung 1998-2003

As South Korea was going through changing economic conditions, Kim Dee Jung won election to become President in 1998 with 39.7% of the votes and a very narrow majority. He was a left-wing politician, but he had to discard most of the welfare programmes with worsening economic conditions. The country had to go to IMF for loans to stabilise the economy. IMF approved a $7 billion loan with attached conditions i.e. fiscal discipline, privatisation, and financial liberation. The implementation of these conditions added to the deflationary pressures. The conglomerate became insolvent, currency crashed, exports declined, and the banking sector reached insolvency stage. There were 23000 small and medium size firms which went bankrupt. GNP per capita declined by 34%, unemployment quadrupled, and real wage rates declined by 9%.

South Korea took decisions to ignore IMF conditions, adopted Keynesian policies to deal with deflation and within two years its economy recovered. The recovery in the global economy also helped and by 1999 GNP had recovered to pre-crisis level, and the rate of economic growth rebounded to 10% as it resumed its historical growth path.

The South Korean growth story is very similar to the European growth stories of industrialisation (and having reached a solid base) and the promotion of free trade. South Korea had 44 years of political stability and visionary leadership. During this period, it had achieved comprehensive industrialisation by allowing the creation of monopolies or semi-monopolies, created new comparative advantages, prepared for foreign competition and gradually opened up its markets to the world.

The critical factors in growth process are both tangible and intangible. Foremost among them is leadership commitment to development which turns a state into an effective agent of change to industrialise the country. The other important factors are physical and human capital development. The physical capital development is reflected in machines, factories and machines embedded technology and human capital development in education, skills, health, social cohesion, social trust and unity of purpose to promote social good. South Korean had the vision and ability to combine effective state with physical and human capital development to achieve an unrivalled economic and social transformation.

Its financial crisis of 1997-1999, re-enforced the importance of the State role in the development process and provides a clear evidence that no country (unless its currency acts as an international currency) can allow a totally free movement of capital or foreign involvement in policy formulation.

12

CHINA:
A SUPER POWER IN THE MAKING

Pre-Independence Era

China had been a prosperous country from the early 16th century to the early 19th century. Her GDP was almost 25% of the total world output. The rise of West led to the decline of China as a subjugated and plundered country. By the middle of the 19th century, China had become a dirt poor and playing field for the colonial powers. At the end of opium war in 1842, Britain forcefully imposed an unfavourable treaty on China to relinquish her custom control powers from 1863 to 1908.

The WWII ended with Japanese defeat in 1945. By that time Soviet had dismantled and shipped home every type of machine in China that they could lay their hands. There was hardly any transport or communication system left in the country. The power system had been either destroyed or rotted away. The disruption in the agriculture sector caused food shortages. China had a population of about a billion and inflation at virulent level. The economy was mainly agrarian, and exports consisted of some raw materials. There was no effective administration or any other functioning institutions. The Communist Party of China led by Mao Zedong took control of the country in 1949, but the peace and normality took some time to arrive. The normal conditions prevailed after a bloody civil struggle in 1951 when Taiwan, Hong Kong, and Macao got separated from the mainland China. The decades of war had destroyed industries, mines and agriculture. China's per capita income was about $615 in 1950 which was lower than Pakistan's per capita income of $650 at the time.

Political Economy of China

China emerged as an independent country in 1949, adopted a socialist economic ideology and a single party-political system. The unity and social norms of the country had been destroyed in the civil war but she had a committed leadership to guide the nation. The central planning authority was set up given the responsibility for national resource allocation and for creating an equal socialist society in 1952.

After 65 odds years of independence, China has a population of about 1.3 billion and her economy has gone through a total transformation from an agrarian to manufacturing and services base and has become the second-largest in the world. China is now the largest exporter of goods and services and one of the most powerful nations in the world. In 2014, her GNP (in current US dollar) was estimated at $634367.3 billion, gross capital formation at $283017.6 billion, and balance of payment $616.4 billion. China's story of rag to riches is unique in the economic history of nations. The transformation of an agrarian into an advanced industrial society with a fair distribution of income in such a short time is unmatched in human history.

Mao Zedong (1949-76)

Mao was elected chairman of the Communist Party and head of the government in 1949. **Chinese leadership in taking power declared their long run goal as: 'to transform China into an industrialised, powerful nation with greater equality and improved living'. The political leadership had differences. Some of them thought** political consciousness took priority over material progress whereas others believed that industrialisation and economic prosperity were prerequisites for the attainment of a socialist order and material equality. These priority differences would play a major role in changing economic policies and economic growth models in the future years.

The new administration moved quickly to restore the economy. The steps were taken to repair and rebuild industries, transport and communication systems under the State control. The State trading companies were set up and the private traders were helped and encouraged early on. The coal mining and dual-purpose hydropower projects were given top priority to achieve low-cost energy and irrigation water for agriculture development. The development of heavy industries (i.e. steel, mining, transport and chemicals) and human capital (i.e. education and training) started in 1950. The land reforms reshaped the agriculture and rural communities. The landless families got 45% of arable land under lease for up to 30 years and were encouraged to form co-op farming. Each family was allotted 0.2 hectares and encouraged to join co-operative schemes to promote efficiency in production. The People's Bank of China was established and private banking was nationalised to unify the monetary system. The nationalisation of banking sector got completed in a very short time. The State adopted a protectionist foreign trade policy to protect infant industries. Russia supplied most of the required technology to establish a domestic technological base.

The agriculture reforms, centralised annual budgets, and tight credit restored the currency value and price stability. The traditional education system got challenged, overhauled and reorganised to serve new national ambitions. The population control policies got implemented to reduce population pressure and to allow female labour force to participate in the production processes. All policies aimed to ensure that the economy moves away from the diminishing returns activities of agriculture to the increasing returns activities of the industrial sector. It took three years for the economy to start functioning in some normal way. The damaged transportation and communication system got restored to a functional one. The commerce was partially controlled and regulated by the state trading companies. The industry came under gradual state control. By 1952, price stability had been established; commerce restored, and agriculture and industry had regained some normality.

The Central Planning Authority adopted a Soviet-style economic growth model to formulate China's first five-year plan (1953-57), which contained economic development guidelines for the regions and state ownership of non-agriculture sectors as well as large collective units in the agriculture sector. *The first plan main objective was stated as rapid economic growth through industrialisation with particular concentration on heavy industry and capital-intensive technology. The targets were set to complete* 694 large and medium size industrial projects within the five years. The 156 of 694 projects would get the Soviet aid. The agriculture sector was to get organised in co-op schemes during the plan period.

The USSR provided technical knowledge, physical plants and financial support in developing and installing new heavy industries, including many complete plants. About 595 industrial projects got completed within the plan period, and accumulated investment for the plan reached 55 billion yuan. The steel production rose to 5.35 million metric tonnes; the coal production reached 131 million tonnes in 1957. The agriculture and industry contributed 56.5% of gross output in 1957, and food and cotton production exceeded set target figures. The State control was increased over the industry as private owners were encouraged or coerced to sell industrial plants or convert them into joint public-private partnerships. By 1956, about 67.5% of all modern industrial enterprises were state owned, and 32.5% were under joint public-private ownership. The State helped the handicraft industries to develop as cooperatives.

The agriculture sector was encouraged successfully to organise into large collective units and by 1957 about 93.5% of all farms households had joined producer's cooperatives. The amount of labour input determined the income of each family of the cooperative, but each family was allowed to retain a small private plot to grow vegetables, fruits and livestock for personal use. The universal education and health programmes were implemented to transform health and literacy of the mass population.

The first five-year plan succeeded in laying down a solid foundation for heavy industries. Key industries including iron and steel, coal mining, cement production, electricity generation, and machine building were developed and greatly expanded. Industrial output increased by an annual rate of 19% and national income grew at the rate of 9% per annum. The agriculture output increased at 4% per annum, which was a direct result of increased efficiency in production processes.

The second five-year development plan (1958-62), stressed the importance of heavy industries, defence, and scientific knowledge, and put a priority on better quality of life for Chinese people, acquisition of property into state ownership, development of agriculture, handicrafts, and commerce. The Great Leap Forward years (1958-60) weakened powers of the Central Planning Authority. The provinces, county, and local levels bodies were made responsible for allocation decisions. But heavy industry remained under the control of the Central Authority. The dissolved planning bodies achieved most of the industrial development targets successfully, but the agriculture sector lost millions of workers to industry and failed to meet its set targets. The Leadership had believed that spontaneous heroic efforts by the entire population would produce a great leap in the production of all goods and services. But it only created confusion and resulted in a severe economic crisis. The weather conditions turned difficult during 1959-1961 and impacted agriculture output adversely which declined by 13.5 % per annum and created famine conditions, especially in rural areas. The death rate rose to 2.5% from 1.2% per annum. One estimate put the death toll at 14 million during 1958 to 1961. The political differences between Russian and Chinese leadership led to the withdrawal of the Soviet financial and technical assistance in 1961. In consequence, the industrial output plummeted by 38% in 1961 and a further 16% in 1962.

The 'Great Leap Forward' disaster changed the government economic policies directions, and the new growth model combined elements of the centralised industrial system with decentralisation of ownership and decision making. The agriculture development and balanced growth of the economy carried higher priority in the plan. In consequence, some industries were returned to central control, but the rest remained with the provincial and local authorities. Industrial operations were reorganized to use material incentives to increase production. China started to import technically advanced machines from Japan and Western Europe. Once again, the economic stability was restored by 1965. The Central Planning and economic coordination were revived to restore order and direction.

The Central Planning Authority formulated a 3rd five-year plan (1966-70) with priority on agriculture development to solve food shortages and other basic needs but also put a priority on defence, technology, and improvement in the quality of production and education. The economy moved toward greater self-reliance in transport and commerce. The resources got diverted to agriculture, light industry and heavy industry in that order. The agriculture sector was re-organized and allocated new resources in the form of tractors, water pumps, and fertilisers which transformed agriculture production from basic labour-intensive methods to mechanised one which led to higher productivity. The agriculture growth targets were exceeded by 2.2%. The manufacturing grew at an average rate of 9.6% per annum, and industrial output grew at an average rate of 10.65% per annum. Coal mining, electricity generation, petroleum, iron and steel, ammonia, fertilisers, cement, plastic, and chemical; all exceeded the growth rate of 10%, and industrial gross output value grew at the rate of 21.1% per annum.

The health and education programmes made rapid progress in improving people's health and literacy. Within 15 years of revolution, China had eradicated most of the infectious diseases that had plagued its population for centuries, including cholera, diphtheria, tuberculosis, schistosomiasis, typhoid fever, smallpox, and many others.

The 4th five-year plan (1971-75) put a priority on industrial and construction development. An additional investment of 130 billion yuan got allocated to develop infrastructure projects. The plan completed its set targets by the end of 1973.

The late 60's and early 70's also turned into a period of Cultural Revolution, which caused political upheaval but did not change economic policies or the underlying economic model of growth in any major way. The urban society went through a values revolution. The social unrest and civil conflict badly affected the modern sectors of the economy. In consequence, the national output declined, transport and raw materials supplies got disrupted, management got worse, and the imports of foreign technology got hampered. All these factors resulted in reducing the industrial output by 14%. The Army restored some order in 1976, and the industrial output started to increase as a consequence.

Mao Zedong died in 1976. By that time, in spite of Leap Forward and Cultural Revolution difficulties, China had been able to achieve some balanced growth between industry and agriculture and had improved living standards of people in both urban and rural areas. The State policies of first two decades had resulted in creating infrastructure, highly trained and educated human resources and physical resources such as factories and machines with embedded technology. Both human and physical productive capabilities had helped in faster economic growth. The restrictive trade policies promoted industrialisation. Some western economists have described this period of Chinese history as a disaster, but such remarks are based on short-term considerations. Some policy mistakes had happened, and no country in the world can avoid such mistakes. The western policies of war making have killed millions and millions of people and pushed millions of citizens including their own into poverty. Thomas G. Rawski (119) stated in 1979 *'China's entire population has benefited from adequate food, shelter, healthcare, and other necessities of life. China has mastered the old and new technology. The spread of rural electrification, local industry, technical training, and publishing has brought modern science and technology to the doorstep of most of China's households. Nearly universal participation by Chinese youth in primary education and rapid expansion of secondary education ensures that the dissemination of knowledge will continue to broaden and deepen'*. Rawski work endorses the remarkable achievements of the poverty-stricken nation which transformed its people and economy within a very short period.

Deng Xiaoping (1978-92), Jiang Zemin (1992-2002) and Hu Jin tao (2002-2012) eras

Mao died in 1976 and a new generation of leadership rose in the country. An industrial base was already in place, knowledge base society was emerging and infrastructure had become functional. The gross national product had reached 301 billion yuan in 1978.

In July 1977, Deng Xiaoping took control of the communist party and the country and declared **'socialism does not mean that you have to remain poor.'** A battery of new economic policies including autonomy and incentives, support for research and education, relaxation of trade restrictions, foreign investment and technology import from Japan and the west. In addition, a new policy of export-led growth was set in motion. These policies started a new phase of economic development and led to readjustment, decentralisation and rectification of the economy. In a way, the new phase was a natural next step where the economy had existing foundations but still had to face foreign competition which would lead to greater efficiency through specialisation based on newly created comparative advantages.

The ten -year plan (1976-85) got split into two five-years plans i.e. the 6th five-year plan (1981-85) and 7th five-year plan (1986-90). *The 6th plan put a priority on the high rate of growth in export-oriented industries, agriculture, imports of foreign technology and identified and set a target for 120 major construction projects.* The industry and agriculture were to grow at least at the rate of 5% per annum. The resources were diverted to achieve new priorities. The supplies of agriculture and other consumer goods started to improve because of agriculture sector reforms such as land plots for profit and free farmer markets. The import of the technology and capital improved domestic technology and research base. wThe domestic commerce was encouraged through internal markets freedom. These measures resulted in greater efficiency in resource allocation and positive returns on new investment. The management new autonomy and monetary incentives changed work practices which increased productivity, reinvestment, and state-owned and operated industrial and services enterprises. China declared four coastal areas as special zones to benefits from the relaxed foreign trade, foreign investments, and international cooperation. The industrial production in 1978 rose by 13.5% per annum.

The relaxation of trade controls and incentive-based policies resulted in increasing trade, industrial growth, food supplies, consumer goods and per capita income. By 1985, the economic structure had changed; industrial sector now employed 17% of the workforce and produced 46% of GDP, agriculture sector employed 63% of labour and produced 23% of GDP, and foreign trade had increased to 20% of GNP.

The 6th five-year plan proved a great success and exceeded all set targets. The profit maximising production, market-based allocation and foreign trade are basic features of a capitalistic society, and these were creeping in. As a result, some serious issues such as incomes disparity, corruption, and a threat to the party's authority started to emerge which led to a serious debate on how to balance the needs for economic efficiency and market incentives with the need for the State guidance and control.

The 7th five-year plan followed the 6th Plan's principles and embarked on further relaxation of trade and market operations to balance social demand and supply, efficiency and quality of production. The science education development got higher priority in the plan. The industrial production during this period expanded at the rate of 6.7%, agriculture at the rate of 4% and GDP at the rate of 7.5% per annum.

The 8th five-year plan (1991-95) was approved in 1991, and it marked a new phase in China's development. China adopted a new accounting system and adopted a new policy to control population growth. China replaced the Soviet system of accounts (MPS) with the Western system by using exchange values of goods determined by the market forces. GDP data from 1952 up to 1995 was re-estimated and updated. One child policy checked population growth and 374 technical innovation projects and 845 infrastructure projects were undertaken. The capital formation reached 3.89 trillion yuan. China opened 1100 cities to the outside world and created 13 bonded zones. Foreign trade expanded at an unbelievable rate of 19.5% per annum and reached the US $1.0145 trillion which accounted for 3% of the world's commodity trade and China ranked 11th in the world on import and export volume. Foreign exchange reserves reached US$73.6 billion and per capita, income rose to 1578 yuan.

The 9th five-year plan (1996-2000) maintained modernization of economy and control of population as national objectives. The 10th five-year plan (2001-05) put a higher priority on the improvement of medical and health services in both rural and urban areas. The decentralise was greatly enhanced with a delegation of decision making to the provincial and municipal administrations. The civic authorities encouraged and engaged locals in developing productive ventures through granting of licenses, incentives, and other favours. Numerous entrepreneurial ventures mushroomed all over the country and by 2003, small and medium size companies accounted almost half of the country's GDP. The financial institutions remained under state-ownership. The internal movement of capital was controlled. The economy regained momentum and grew at the rate of 9% per annum. Some public companies were privatised and the private property protection act was passed in 2003. The Asian financial crisis affected China only at the margins mainly through declining foreign investment and exports.

A new phase of development became operational at the start of 21st century. A new strategy was adopted to deal with the problems of coordination, information, property rights and operational issues of financial institutions. The central planning authority's operations were halted and the personal incentives and pricing mechanism sorted out the shortages and surpluses in the markets. The efficient producers were allowed freedom to sell their surplus output to the other efficient producers. The non-efficient units remained operational to provide stability and greater incentive to create a surplus. The market was allowed to operate at the margin of operation which provided a framework for equating marginal costs and marginal revenues to ensure efficiency of production. The efficient firms grew rapidly and inefficient firms became less and less important. It is important to note that the inefficient firms were not killed off as these provided jobs and output. The flexible internal trade and land policies resolved outstanding trade and land renting problems. The increased private and public savings were invested into existing and new opportunities in the economy. The agriculture output expanded by 50% and the average real income of farmers doubled within 5 years. China had established partial property rights in the urban areas of the country in 2003 but not in the rural areas. The foreign capital movement was controlled and channelled to develop advanced technological capabilities. The internal competition, incentives, capital formation, and technical knowledge speeded up economic growth.

China declared it was open for foreign direct investment and put out a welcome mat for the foreign investors and they came in drove with ever increasing funds, talent, and knowledge. It was too good an opportunity to miss. China had become the leading investment destinations in the world. The foreign investment brought foreign technology, complete plants, equipment and significant minority stakes in the domestic firms. Wei (145 a) has stated that in spite of shaky legal protection and endemic corruption foreign investment was pouring in 2001. The speed and size of foreign direct investment added to the capital stock, new technologies, skills and made a huge contribution to the 'productive capabilities' and political stability. The financial sector had remained protected from foreign investment. It is only in 2014 that it was partially opened to the outsiders.

In 2005, the 11th five-year plan declared its objectives as balanced wealth distribution, improved education, medical care and social security. It aimed to achieve 45% increase in GDP and 20% energy efficiency. In consequence, the resources were diverted into the development of affordable housing, and infrastructures such as railway network, roads, and ports. The services sector share in GDP went up as national employment and urbanisation increased. In 2009, 40% of the total world foreign investment went to China, which brought latest production technology and organisation skills with it. This investment in electronics and transport sectors turned China into a high technology manufacturer. China allowed foreign direct investment to those sectors where domestic technology and knowledge was inadequate. This policy helped in the development of effective imports substitution and some exports facilities.

The autonomous regions such as Hong Kong, Macao, and free zones had helped in bridging the gap between the mainland and the regions. The creation of special zones for foreign direct investment had restricted the foreign influence spreading to the whole country and avoided the foreign influence and destructive ideas. The successful policies from each zone were copied and applied everywhere. These zones became the hub of increasing returns activities which drew diminishing returns surrounding areas along and opened the way for their development. China's economic progress has been remarkable. Since 1980, her GDP has grown at an average growth rate of 9.9% and foreign trade at the annual rate of about 16.3%. In 1990, China was a minor country in international trade. Germany was the largest trading nation in the world. In 2009, China became the largest exporter in the world. And in 2014, it had become the largest economy on purchasing power parity basis.

Xi Jinping era (2012--)

The Communist Party of China appointed Xi Jinping as a new chairperson and head of state. The 12th five-year plan (2011-15) addresses the problems of increasing inequality, sustainable growth, social safety nets and social infrastructure. The expansionary policies were applied to increase effective demand and economic growth. There was a shift from investment to consumption and from urban and coastal areas to rural and inland areas. The plan recognised environmental issues and established

Hong Kong as a financial centre in international finance and set a 7% increase in GDP as a growth target.

Assessment

China grew at a reasonable rate up to 1980 and then her growth rate rocketed. Why? The answer is not a difficult one. China journey had started in 1949. Her leadership was committed to the socialist economy and did not face any opposition to make any compromises to extend their period in office. This made China as an effective State to implement her policies successfully. Heavy industry had to be developed to lay down the foundations for future economic and military strength. The manpower had to be trained and educated to meet the demand of industrialisation. This process of physical and human development is time and resource consuming. Hence the early years were slow growth years. In addition, China's policy of self-reliance on domestic finance in early years enforced extraction of capital from the agriculture and that created imbalance and slowing down of the economy. The balancing growth of agriculture, heavy and light industries required regular changes in the allocation of resources which ended up slowing the growth process. A series of five years' plans were developed and implemented to accelerate the building of advance industries under protection from foreign competition. China knew she did not have a comparative advantage in industries. Her comparative advantage rested with her large labour force, agriculture and natural resources. But she also knew that the comparative advantage would change with industrialisation and the reliance on agriculture was a mug's game as diminishing return activities would never allow her to become a rich or military strong economy. Once the industrial and technological base had been developed then export-led growth strategy led to faster growth rates. China's industrialisation and trade policy was a copy of the Western countries policies that had made them rich. It is the same policy that South Korea had adopted and implemented through the market system. A similar policy had been proposed by Dr Sun Yet-Sen (135 a), the father of modern China, in his plan for China's industrialisation in 1919. Fredrick List, a German economist, had proposed the same policy in the 18th century and had concluded that a country could only get rich through higher factors productivity from the industrialisation. China adopted Dr Yet-Sen (154) and Frederick List's ideas to achieve economic prosperity and military strength.

Mr Yifu Lin (175), an employee of the World Bank, in his paper entitled *'Perspective on Chinese Economic Growth'* states that the slow growth of China before 1980, was a result of wrong economic development strategy. China did not use comparative advantage of cheap labour to develop. The industrial sector developed under protection was a monopolist and inefficient. Secondly, China's per capita GDP was relatively low compared with the western countries per capita GDP at the time of their industrialisation. Hense, China's was not able to make the best use of advance technology which is a source of productivity and growth. This is a silly argument. If China had not developed heavy industries, technological base or human capital she would still be producing agriculture goods to export, her labour force would still be idle or busy in basic survival activities and her comparative advantage to produce technically advanced goods would have remained a pipe dream. The industrial structure of most rich countries is monopolistic rather than competitive in the 21st century. Does that mean all advanced countries are inefficient? The argument that domestic markets were narrow to support industrial development makes no sense as markets expand with prosperity and the international markets provide unbounded scope for industrial output to export.

I think a better way to explain slow growth in early years is to point out that resources went into the development of heavy industries which affected the productivity and growth of nonindustrial sectors. The investment in the heavy industries and manpower development shows results after a long period. China relied more on self-financing and building its system of technology. This self-reliance on domestic finance and technology slowed down economic growth but had greatly benefited China in avoiding the dependency on international financial institutions and their conditionality's of structural reforms. China had moulded advance technology to its conditions, and this process had allowed her to update indigenous technology and in doing so, she did not discard old machines which were still producing output and keeping people employed even if the production was less efficient. This was an intentional policy and not ignorance.

The agriculture's performance from the land reform policy had created economic difficulties and the leadership differences compounded these difficulties. The culture revolution and accompanying strikes and demonstration also contributed to the slowdown of the economy. Once the leadership resolved their differences the economy resumed its growth path and the country managed to lay down an impressive industrial base. Once the industrial base and human capital had developed, it was time for the economy to change its strategy, use its cheap labour advantage with the most advanced technology and to be opened up to the world competition in a gradual way to benefit from the international specialisation. The new export-led growth policy time had come in 1980, and the change in the political leadership had put a priority on the rapid economic prosperity.

China started to produce at a lower cost what rest of the world wanted. The export trade expanded rapidly and financed the import of new and most advanced technology from the rest of the world. At the same time, China put a priority on higher education and research to have the comparable human capital available to benefit from technological advances. The development of internal markers, gradual opening of foreign trade, import substitution, and export led strategy turned China into a workshop of the world. By 2009, more than 95% of China's export was of manufactured goods. The composition of the manufactured exported goods had also changed from cheap goods such as toys and textiles in 1980 to high value and technologically sophisticated machinery, information and communication technology products. The rate of export was higher than the rate of import during 2001 to 2008 resulting in $1.202 trillion of foreign exchange reserves in 2007 and $ 2 trillion at the end of 2008. Most of these reserves are in foreign currencies (mostly US $) and sit as IOU reserves in the Central Bank. By the end of 2005, China had become a net capital exporter with $570 billion in foreign capital investment (capital import) and $769 billion in foreign exchange reserves (capital export). In a way, these huge foreign reserves or IOU make China vulnerable as her foreign exchange reserves are in fiat currencies. China's industrialisation along with its human capital development has allowed her to buy and exploit the latest and the most advanced technology to achieve higher productivity and extraordinary economic growth. Her technological based has led to a reduction in the costs of renovation, industrial upgrading and social and economic transformation but her domestic technology is still not as good as the Western technology. The utilisation of machine making capacity had remained at 50% of capacity on average which reflects on structural imbalance and increasing dependency on imports.

The change in national objective from equality to prosperity had a trade-off. The greater prosperity comes at the cost of increased inequality. An unequal society creates opportunities for the corrupt official and politicians to get rich through the privatisation programme. According to Pao-yu Ching (108), the reforms introduced since 1979, have fundamentally changed the economic and social structure of the Chinese society. This deconstruction of the economy has: (1) dissolve the communes by breaking up the alliance between workers and peasants. The State has withdrawn workers right to strike and the basic rights of mass protest and demonstration. (2) Dismantled collective ownership of the means of production and turned them into profit making institutions. This policy has deprived tens of millions of workers of their necessities of life including food, clean water, clean environment, medical care and education; and (3) labour reforms have turned labour power into commodity and workers into wage labour, who could be hired and fired at will by new factory managers. Also, favourable terms have been offered to attract foreign investment capital which has increased China's development dependency on foreign capital, technology, and external markets. China now faces huge disparity in income and opportunities available to the Chinese people.

Beijing Consensus or Chinese Development Model

The Chinese success story which has transformed the lives of billions of its people has created a remarkable interest among economists and politicians all over the world. The academic economists have started to mention a new strategy of development, coined as *'Beijing Consensus.' that has become an alternative to the Washington Consensus.* Chinese strategy does not prescribe rigid recommendations (like Washington Consensus) for the economic problems of the developing nations; it is pragmatic-much like China in the post-1979 period- and recognises the need for flexibility in solving multifarious problems. It is less intrusive and has flexible features which make it an appealing strategy and in consequence, it is rapidly gaining popularity in the developing world as a possible model to follow.

The Beijing Consensus contains three main ideas to promote economic development.

1. The pursuit of Dynamic Goals and rejection of per Capital Income as a measure of human welfare. The rejection of per Capita

GDP as a sole measure of human welfare is in a way a rejection of the western thinking and policies which relate per capita income to human welfare under unrealistic assumptions. China has focused on quality of life and equity as the main objective of the development process. The per capita income and human development index (HDI) show different levels of achievements for most countries. In 2007, China was ranked 102nd out of 182 countries of the world in term of per capita GDP, whereas it was ranked 56th in the measurement of adult literacy, 72nd on life expectancy, and 92nd according to HDI value. China claims that her development strategy seeks five balances: balancing urban and rural development, balancing regional development, balancing economic and social development, balancing development between man and nature, and balancing domestic development with the outside world. The multiple goals recognise that just an increase in GDP is not sufficient to deal with the poverty as it leaves other problems unsolved.

2. Innovation: In a changing dynamic situation where policy measures create frictions and losses, the state must actively innovate to address the challenges introduced by the changing economic and social environment. In other words, the changing situation requires constant tinkering and constant change and need different strategies to deal with the different conditions. China introduced export-led strategy in 1979, developed internal markets, and adopted one child policy; all examples of changing policies to deal with changing situations. The Chinese state commissioning of public opinion surveys to find out public attitude toward itself and policies provides feedback to gauge the impact and popularity of policies. The state plays a dominant role in the development process.

3. Self-Determination: This element seeks independence from 'foreign powers' such as the US and the West European countries. The idea that some countries or people are superior compared with

other is rejected. The desire to set up and pursue one's priorities and to rely on one's abilities and capabilities take priority.

Each nation should be able to plan their development without having to accept the unfavourable terms of others such as IMF and the World Bank. The Asian and African countries have a long history of incursion and exploitation, for them the idea of self-reliance is attractive. Which is one reason why China's help is appreciated and welcomed in most Asian and African nations? Chinese strategy does not impose priorities on others; it simply tries to help others to implement their priorities. Such help without conditions is in complete contrast to the Washington Consensus, which forces the recipients of the financial help to adopt the recommended policies.

All three elements of the Beijing Consensus are interesting and appealing. Could other developing nations copy these or is one seeing too much without realising the difficulties of implementing these measures? Inventions and innovations require a sound productive capabilities base, the process of re-engineering require highly trained, and competent engineers and further improvement of advanced technology are money and time-consuming. China laid down heavy industries base, adopted universal education and health care programmes, tried to achieve a balance between agriculture and industry, spread technology to all regions during Mao Zedong times. The balancing policy measures are component elements of the Beijing Consensus, however, within China, there are voices that claim that the post-1980 China's policies have put these elements on the back burner, and new pragmatic policies have serious implications for the stated objectives. Pao-yu Ching (108) in his paper 'China: Socialist Development and Capitalist restoration' states that post-1979 reforms have fundamentally changed the relations of production in China and has reversed the course of development from socialist to the capitalist system. He claims that the reforms have robbed the working people of their rights and have deprived them of necessities of life including food, clean water, clean environment, medical care and education, balanced regional growth, equality of opportunities and economic equality. China has lost her autonomy to develop technology, does not rely on domestic resources especially capital and has become dependent on western countries for economic development. This criticism does reflect on the current state of play where pragmatism has taken a central place, and political ideas have become secondary concerns.

13

INDIA: TORTOISE MARCH

Pre-independence Era

India was not always a poor country. It was her wealth that had attracted invaders time and again. She had plentiful arable land and her agriculture was productive and even a marginal peasant on marginal land got decent returns. She was first among nations to produce fine cotton yarn and had become a leading manufacturer of cotton and silk goods. She had a large skilled labour force, artisans, functioning internal markets, banking (money lending class) and credit system. The internal trade and basic infrastructure were well established; technology was primitive but the economy had sustained more than 100 million prosperous people. Her culture and arts were well advanced in the 16th century. Some recent studies suggest that real wages of Indian labour and artisans were higher compared with European wages of the time. Adam Smith had noted that India was *'one of the most prosperous countries'* in the world and had explained this prosperity in term of India's flourishing system of trade, river navigation and long- established trading connections within the land and beyond.

European had fought each other and lost thousands of lives to win trade concessions and establish a physical presence in sub-continent. Britain, France, Portugal, Netherland, Demark and Prussia established minor trading centres to conduct commerce, mostly exporting quality Indian manufactured goods to Europe and elsewhere. The trade with India was so profitable that it became a catalyst for the formation of Joint Stock Companies such as British East India Companies.

The kingdom of Bengal fell to the East India Company in 1757 which had been supported by organised armed and civil service. The company main objective was to raise maximum revenue from the colony. It imposed heavy tariff duties on non-British goods, exported mainly raw materials and imported manufactured goods from the mother country. The economy remained agrarian without any change in production methods or increase in productivity. Adam Smith attributed the beginning of India's economic decline to '*some injudicious restraints imposed by the servants of the East India Company*'.

India became a British colony in 1858. The colonial rulers implemented various policy measures to extend area under their control and to stabilise their rule. The Crown centralised authority was backed by armed forces, civil service and a monopoly over coercion. A national postal and telegraphs system for effective administration became operational. The British banned Indian textiles from home market and forbade people to wear Indian textile or its luxury goods. But they flooded Indian markets with the British Manufactured goods. India had turned into a source of money extraction and an instrument for British global power. The extracted money from India financed military operation in establishing an unrivalled Empire. The per capita income in India, however, declined to a bare survival level in early years of 20thcentury while the British industrialisation flourished on cheap raw materials and export of high price manufactured goods to India. India made Britain rich, and Britain turned India into one of the poorest countries in the world.

The British invested, a part of locally extracted revenue, in the development of irrigation, railways, and education. The investment increased raw material output, reduced transport cost and cheap educated labour to work in Indian civil administration. The institutions such as civil service, army, judiciary and law enforcement agencies were headed by the British and low ranks were recruited from educated Indian. These services were established to subjugate and control natives.

In recent times, some western historians have claimed that British rule in India was of great benefit to the Indian. Their arguments are based on mostly indirect consequences and manipulated conclusions. The fact is that the British colonial rule was autocratic and despotic and any good that happened such as '*India as a single country*' was an indirect consequence of the desire to subjugate the largest area of the earth. Moreover, any investment or development, which took place, was financed by Indian revenues, which increased raw materials output for export and at the cast of liberty and foreign rule. The benefits of investment went to British and resulted in greater prosperity. The visible poverty of India at the end of colonial rule is a sufficient proof of the exploitative nature of the foreign rule.

During WWI and WWII the colonial industrial policy was relaxed due to internal instability. The WWI had disrupted maritime trade, and Britain had imposed heavy tariffs on imports, to raise revenue and to protect Indian markets from the Japanese competition. These conditions provided protection for industrial development, and Indian capitalist took advantage by investing heavily in textile, steel manufacturing, sugar, cement, and paper industries. WWII had provided further opportunities and numerous industries including engineering products, clothes, food, timber, and woollen industries grew rapidly. Indian business houses grew under protection and were ready to take advantage of the new opportunities that became available after independence. The Indian Businesses took advantage of the situation. Tata family established steel industry in 1907 and new industries such as shipping were established by Indian industrialists. Ray (115) has suggested that at the time of independence, India possessed a large and fairly sophisticated modern industrial complex owned by a strong indigenous capitalist class.

British business had invested in export-oriented industries such as jute, tea, and coal and Indian businesses avoided investment in British owned industries and channelled their resources to the development of textiles for domestic consumption. This Indian investment was mainly around Bombay area. The mining and manufacturing grew at 15% per annum during 1900 and 1946. The share of mining and manufacturing in the economy was about 14% in 1900, and it had remained steady ending at about 17% in 1946. The share of factory production in the national product at was about 7 % in 1946. India's industrialisation took place under protection which increased the political importance of Indian capitalist. Later on, The Indian businesses, which had formed a chamber of commerce, provided financial help and support to the Indian National Congress in the freedom movement. The same chamber produced an economic plan known as Bombay plan to develop independent India in 1943. Rothermund (127) states that the key features of this plan included planning, mixed economy, protection and public investment in heavy industries. In recent time, the business houses such as Tata, Birla, and others have become global business organisations. India compared with Pakistan was more politically matured, had sizable capitalist class and a relatively large industrial sector at the time of independence. Sivasubramonian (141) has estimated that growth rate of Indian agriculture sector from 1891 to 1946 stood at 0.4 per cent, whereas its economic growth rate in real term and food grain output was almost stagnant. It is, however, reasonable to assume, that there was probably significant regional variation in growth rates of food production.

Indian National Planning

On 15th August 1947, JL Nehru, new Prime Minister of India, declared that '*the task ahead included the ending of poverty, ignorance, disease and inequality of opportunity.*' This policy statement charted out the future path of the new country.

India adopted a mixed market economic system and multi-party parliamentary political system for the country. The State was to play an active role in the industrial development of the country through its central planning authority. The Indian industrial policy statement of 1948 had made a case for the State participation in economic activity. Indian planning commission was set up in 1950 to formulate and implement future national economic development plans and it developed its first five-year plan (1951-56) with the stated objective to increase domestic saving for growth and to help economy resurrect itself from colonial rule. It placed priority on economic development and investment in physical capital capabilities but assumed that equality and human capital development would happen as a by-product of economic development. The public sector was to invest in heavy industries and higher education. The plan discouraged the opening of new primary schools on the ground that the children should learn from self-financing handicraft. Such thinking was clearly against the socialist thinking and ideology on universal literacy.

The Second Five Year Plan (1955-60) again put a priority on the development of heavy industries in the public sector to increase national self-reliance, reduce foreign dependency, encourage small scale industries and build indigenous industrial capabilities. The plan also aimed for regionally balanced growth, prevention of economic power, and reduction of income and wealth inequalities with state investment and regulatory controls. Mahalanobis (82) linear optimisation model provided a theoretical basis for the plan. once again, universal education was ignored which is in complete contrast to Nehru's promise of ending ignorance. Sen

(121 a) considers this neglect as 'home grown folly, to a great extent reflecting on an upper-class, upper-caste bias against the education of the masses.'

Mahalanobis had divided the economy into four sectors: heavy industries, consumer industries, small scale- industries and agriculture and services including education and health. The capital and labour inputs for each sector were determined and used to maximise output subject to availability of resources. The industrial sector was allocated one-third of all resources. The model had some obvious problems, but it suited the Soviet-style industrial development framework without the State ownership of means of production. The model had ignored the demand side, factors prices, and had used a constant input production function. The emphasis was on heavy industries, and public ownership (i.e. direct investor and guide for private investment).

The third and fourth Five Year plans had continued with priority on industrialisation. There was an underlying assumption that once the growth process got established; there would be trickle-down of prosperity. Such a trickle down did not materialise because public sector failed to generate a surplus for capital accumulation and agriculture output remained stagnated.

The 5th five-year plan (1974-79) saw a policy shift from mere growth to growth with redistribution. A significant amount of resources got transferred to the development of agriculture sector. But the industries Act of 1956 remained intact and got extended beyond its original timescale. Its scope was enlarged to add additional sectors. Such inclusion was previously reserved for small scale industries and protected by an array of protectionist tariff and none tariff barriers.

The 6th five-year plan (1979-83) continued with the previous economic policy. The investment in agriculture sector increased and went into new technology, irrigation, seeds, fertilisers and rural infrastructure development. The new procurement pricing policy reduced uncertainty and encouraged the growth of food production.

The 7th five-year plan (1984-89) saw a mild shift in the trade policy and introduced a mild version of economic liberation. The licensing activity was modified to exempt Thirty-two groups of industries from any investment limit. All industries except for 26 industries were exempted from licensing requirements. These measured helped in easing the entry to the industrial sector in 1988. A very large public investment went into the development of telecommunication sector.

The 8th, 9th, and 10th five-year plans all have seen meaningful progress on structural reforms and liberalisation such as simplification of investment rules, devaluation of the currency, relaxation of restrictions on capital markets, and liberation of trade. However, the privatisation has not been undertaken, subsidies maintained, and labour laws remained untouched. Some of the Washington Consensus policies were accepted and implemented under duress, but the others rejected, and IMF and the World Bank loans refused. The trade relaxation and heavy investment in telecommunication sector helped to create the conditions for the IT boom, increased productivity and facilitated a substantial reduction in real interest rates.

The central planning in India had dual objectives: economic growth through industrialisation and reduction of poverty. The performance has been mixed so far. The first five of five years plans were successful in establishing a strong heavy industries base but failed to reduce poverty. During the 70's it was realised that trickle down has not worked. In consequence, some resources were diverted to the agriculture sector, and this helped in gaining food self -sufficiency and increasing prosperity for the rural population. During the 80's there was a slight shift in planning strategy and industrial deregulation was introduced but the main objective was still growth through industrialisation. A very significant public investment went in the development of telecommunication sector which later on paid off. Thus, Indian central planning did deliver industrialisation of the country, but investment in the heavy industries resulted in a slowdown of economic growth up to 1990. This result was inevitable as the heavy industry takes the time to mature. India growth rate up to 1990 was about 4% per annum.

The problem of poverty and inequality had remained a secondary concern during the industrial development phase. I do not share the view that this was a failure of the planning on two grounds. First, I believe Indian planners intentionally ignored the equality issue on the ground that given the immensity of poverty, the potential of simple distribution was negligible in its immediate impact and of little-sustained value. Thus, accelerated growth was an instrument to reduce poverty. Secondly, the slow growth rate was a direct result of investment in the heavy industries to build India's productive capabilities.

India's public saving has remained low because the economy grew at a slow rate and did not generate large public revenues and large savings to support public investment in industries. Secondly, the agriculture did not generate a surplus for industrial development. Indian planning may have under-estimated the importance of investment in human capital which plays an equally important role in building productive capabilities, economic development and quality of life. According to Sen, it is the quality of life which is the main objective of pursuing economic growth and if it is ignored then that must count as a failure. Sen thinks that India's failure to invest in basic education and health has been a factor in India's slow growth rate and lower quality of life compared with China or South Korea.

Political Economy of India

Nehru Family Era (1947-90)

Nehru was elected as a prime minister and remained in power from 1947 to 1964 and when he died, his daughter Indira Gandhi became prime minister from 1966 to 1984 and on her death, her son Rajiv Gandhi became prime minister during 1985 to 1989. Nehru's family and Congress party rule of 40 years, with minor interventions, provided political stability, continuity of economic policies and allowed democratic institutions to take roots.

Nehru enjoyed the universal public support and had the comprehensive authority to rule which proved immensely important in safeguarding the country from fragmentation and subdivision. The inherited institutions like the judiciary, civil and military services played their part in keeping India as a unitary state. The democracy requires political compromises for retaining power and Nehru had to agree to a federal-state framework based on languages and reduced central power. Nehru was a nationalist with leaning towards socialism, but India was mainly a private enterprise economy. The socialist ideas clashed with the free market economy and created a mismatch i.e. a mixed market economic system. Nehru's leftist ideas attracted Soviet Union attention which provided technical assistance in developing heavy industries. The economic growth model had implied a large public-sector role in developing industries and the public-sector direct investment and guidance has remained the driver of industrialisation since 1950. The foreign investment and free trade were restricted. Protectionism was justified on two grounds. First, it was argued that India did not produce enough quality products which could be exported and secondly the infant industries could only grow if there were protection for them. Both public and private sectors benefited from the restriction on imports and the industrial sector grew rapidly. Table 5 shows the industrial growth rates since independence.

Table 5: India's industrial sector growth in constant prices.

1947 -1960	6.1
1960-1970	5.4
1970-1980	4.2
1980-1990	5.5
1990-2000	6.2
2000-2010	8.5

Source Government of India

During Nehru period in office, the industrial output and in particular import substitution grew at the rate of around 6% which helped in self-reliance. The quality of technology imports from the Soviet Union was questionable standards. The infant industries were protected with high tariffs or total import ban. The restrictive trade policy remained in force till 1990. The overall average industrial growth rate was 3.8%, but it had varied from decade to decade.

The government policies of direct public investment, industrial regulation and trade protection created semi-monopoly conditions to benefit private investment in import substitution industries with large monopoly surpluses. The over-valued currency, subsidies and cheap credit reduced cost of industrial and technology imports. The industrial licensing policy controlled and guided private investment. The industrial growth increased its relative contribution to the GDP. The foreign trade policy also provided shelter to agriculture, mining and financial sector. The overall economic growth helped in the development of the financial markets and in controlling capital movement. The domestic saving rates remained low and there was no significant transfer of resources from the agriculture to the industry. The land reform programme remained ineffective because of the provincial opposition and the agriculture sector performance remained sluggish. In consequences, India's had to depend heavily on foreign aid to support current account and balance of payment deficits. The balance of payment crisis in 1965/66 was so serious that it required borrowing from the IMF.

JL Nehru left a sound industrial base to build on. The public-sector investment and promotion of import substitution policy in the private sector had rapidly developed electricity, railways, textiles, machinery, steel, and telecommunication infrastructure. A group of Indian entrepreneurs had matured, banking and other financial institutions had become strong and functional, and a limited manpower had been technically trained. But he failed in land redistribution which could have helped reducing poverty and to change the social structure. Nehru was lucky that strong nationalism and post-independence honeymoon period allowed him to carry out difficult policies without much bickering. The State remained effective to carry out difficult policies. But the increasing diversion of resources to the industrialisation led to greater urban-rural inequality, marginalised welfare policies and impacted human capital development in an adverse manner. Moore (86) has dubbed it as a betrayal of masses. Could it be that the Indian caste system played a role in the neglect of poor? Sen seems to think so.

After Nehru death in 1964, Shastri was elected Prime Minister, but he died suddenly in 1966. The political scene was going through a change. The differing interests created factions in the Congress party. The old guard of the party took a pro-business stand to insert business influence. Other political parties like BJP representing different interests started to make inroads in people minds.

Indira Gandhi became Prime Minister of India in 1967. She faced a difficult political struggle within the party and with the opposition. The country faced huge economic problems such as food shortages, unemployment, and overvalued currency. She decided to use nationalism, economic favours, and economic policies to win political victories. She opposed big business and urban interests to win rural opinion and invaded East Pakistan and created Bangladesh as a client country to show her nationalism. She passed 'Monopolies and Restrictive Trade Practices Act in 1969 to safeguard the consumers' interests from monopoly power but used it selectively. She nationalised commercial banks to curtail powers of private banks, allotted import quotas, and industrial licences to win favours. India's political system turned personalist and she used every possible means legal or illegal to establish her authority which encouraged corruption and created political instability and probably undermined authority and democracy. Preservation of power became an objective in itself which shifted attention from national interest to self-interest. The civil service and other state institutions got politicised, less efficient and more protective of their powers. The State turned ineffective. Nehru model of state-directed industrialisation, however, remained intact, but special attention was given to the agriculture sector. Some say that focus on agriculture was a direct result of the USA PL480 agreement to support agriculture in poor countries. Whatever the reason Indira Gandhi adopted a new agriculture policy to improve agriculture productivity using tractors, adoption of high-yield seeds, water pump irrigation, chemical fertilisers, and pesticides. The State set up agriculture credit institutions, price support, and subsidies on fertilisers and electricity. New policy measures boosted agriculture sector output which grew at the rate of 2.4% per annum. This significantly increased the income of top 10% and marginally for the rest of the rural population. The increase in rural per capita income provided some relief from the prevailing poverty. The welfare spending increased through poverty alleviation programs such as Integrated Rural Development programme and subsidies.

Agriculture sector growth in the 1980's helped the overall rate of growth which increased to 5% per annum. Land reform policy remained ineffective, but the Indian Princes privileges came to an end.

As a direct result of agriculture investment, the industrial growth rate declined and heavy industries such as machines, transport equipment, chemical, and rubber stalled which cut down sector growth rate to 4.7% per annum. Both public and corporate sectors capital formation declined during 1965-72. The capital formation in the household sector increased but it did not fully compensate the decline elsewhere in the economy. In consequence, GDP growth rate dropped to 3.5% per annum. The invasion of Pakistan, oil price shocks and successive years of drought put a considerable burden on public revenue and slowed down economic development.

Indira regime increased regulation of domestic and foreign enterprises by Foreign Exchange Regulation Act 1973 and Monopolies and Restrictive Trade Practice Act 1969. Banks were nationalised, and foreign companies such as Coke and IBM had to close their operations in India. The strong regulatory policy helped to regulate both domestic and foreign capital flows that had created an uncertain environment.

To sum up, Indira's ruling period was a period of political instability, agriculture growth, and invasion of Pakistan. The oil price shock and disruption of remittance from the Middle East created a balance of payment difficulties and current account deficits which reached a crisis point in 1976. A partial liberation of foreign trade encouraged imports and discouraged exports, resulting in current account deficit which soars to 3% of GDP and led to huge commercial borrowing, increasing debt servicing and economic instability. The commercial borrowing financed fiscal deficits which increased national debt and service charges. India borrowed $5.2 billion from IMF and agreed to implement some structural reforms. Public investment had declined which impacted both demand and supply side of industrial growth adversely. The steel production declined and lower investment reduced demand for some industrial outputs, thereby reducing production. Private investment also declined because of the anti-business lobby, declining profits, steep corporate taxes, and higher wages. Indira Gandhi's remained true to her father legacy of state-directed growth and nationalism; a member of minority Singh community killed her.

Rajiv Gandhi, Indira's son, became new Prime Minister (1984-91) and continued with the policy of State directed industrial development with some relaxation of welfare spending. He relaxed regulatory controls on industrial sector expansion and dismantled 'license Raj' within 18 months of his taking office. A new industrial policy was put into practice easing controls over banking and financial sector. The relaxation of controls increased profitability and industrial investment. The industrial sector grew at more than 8 % on average for the period 1985-90.

The change in public policy reduced public sector role supported large business groups and new businesses in new areas such as information technology and generic pharmaceuticals. Rajiv chaired planning commission and allocated large investment funds to develop telecommunication sector. He continued with his grandfather state-direct economic growth model and financial subsidies of his mother time which put pressure on current account and balance of payment. The increase in private investment did not fully compensate the reduction in public sector investment. Oil price rise put pressure on current account deficit and economic growth rate declined significantly to just 1% per annum. The monetary policy of printing money to finance current account deficits led to domestic inflation. The twin deficits of the balance of payment and current account eventually led to a financial crisis in 1991. Some extremist killed Rajiv Gandhi in 1989. His period in office was successful in term of higher investment in primary and secondary production, especially in the telecommunication sector. He relaxed foreign trade restrictions to boost exports. However, he neglected the development of social infrastructure and tertiary industries.

Post-Nehru Family Era (1991-2012)

Indian economy in early 90's faced macro instability. Both current account and balance of payment went into huge deficits. Her international credit rating turned risky. The financial crisis of 1991 became acute and proved a turning point in Indian political economy. The next two decades would see structural reforms and different shades of political regimes. A new coalition government, headed by Nassimha Rao came to power with an agenda of liberal reforms. Dr Manmohan Singh, an employee of the World Bank, was appointed as a finance minister. India's foreign exchange reserves had dropped to $1.2 billion, barely sufficient to support two weeks of imports. The new regime borrowed from IMF, liberalised capital flows, cut down public investment and welfare spending and tightened import restriction to deal with deficits, declining foreign exchange and industrial output. The IMF loan had structural reforms conditions attached. Dr Singh also relaxed direct economic controls and physical planning to meet fiscal discipline conditions. There was a shift in the development process from being state directed to market directed. The structural reforms had included fiscal austerity, liberalisation of trade, freedom of capital markets, freedom of investment, and free exchange rates. India implemented only some of these conditions and refused a follow-up loan as it infringed national sovereignty.

India's economic growth has been marked by two distinct phases since 1991. The first phase (1991-2002) witnessed fiscal discipline, uneven investment, unfavourable foreign trade, and moderate growth rate of about 6%. Agriculture sector remained stagnant. The impact of reforms was mildly positive for the Indian economy but with nasty effects on the social fabric of the society. The second phase (2003-2012) saw high average growth rate (8.5%) resulting from favourable foreign trade, high domestic and slightly increased foreign direct investment in the development of infrastructure and public services.

It is worth noting that investment in heavy industries and human capital usually takes a long time to show positive returns and India had benefited in the 90's from the earlier public investment in heavy and telecommunication industries which had provided input to intermediate and final goods industries. The industrialisation had improved the overall productivity and efficiency in the country. The favourable weather conditions and overseas Indian financial and managerial skills helped in agriculture and overall growth. The services sector was the main driver of overall growth, but it did not contribute much to higher employment or higher wages because of selective skills requirements. The austerity measures had helped to stabilise the fiscal deficit at the cost of public investment. The relaxation of controls had led to rapid growth in private luxury consumption, private investment, exports, large and small businesses, and benefited managerial classes. The real focus of growth had shifted to less regulated service sector especially exports of software. The credit for this success must go to Nehru family, who had ensured heavy public investment in the industrial sector including telecommunication

The talented Indian, who had gone to the USA and other foreign countries for higher education, training, and work, had returned to establish computer software companies, data processing, and call- centre businesses. Bangalore, Mumbai, Hyderabad and New Delhi turned into hub cities of IT industry, and some of the related industries mushroomed. The rapid rise of the internet and the availability of highly trained Indian engineers and scientist opened up vast opportunities to exploit internet based businesses. Srinivasan (132) estimated in 2005 that the Indian IT sector would be contributing up to 25% of GDP by the year 2020. Indian expatriates have played a dominant role in establishing high tech, information and trading houses. Several Indians have become leaders of the Silicon Valley venture capital industries and in recent years, they have been active in launching similar ventures in India. It was a welcome policy for the NRI, which resulted in bringing capital and know-how to India from the USA and other countries. The new technology, organisation, and management methods allowed substitution of imports and created products for exports to the advanced countries. With this success, the Indian trade policy has been relaxed for certain sectors, but it is still highly protective of others. A new basic education programme has been in play that has achieved remarkable success in some of the Indian states where the literacy rate is almost hundred percent. A new policy for industry and agriculture with subsidies and tax concessions is also in play providing incentives for hard work and growth.

The global financial crisis of 2008 had marginally increased fiscal instability. The increasing imports are a heavy burden on the balance of payment. The real estate and stock market bubbles have increased the sense of instability. There has been an increase in income and wealth inequality. Nehru dream of creating a just society through economic growth with self-reliance is in tatters. The rising suicide levels in the rural India and the highest number of undernourished Indian children provide enough evidence to belittle all claims of glory. The wages of rural and urban unskilled workers have not improved a great deal. Kotwal et al. (58 a) in a recent paper has shown that the improvement in poverty level has been minimal.

One may sum up India's economic development history as follows. The Indian state had played a guiding and dominant role when the economy was closed to the outside and inside competition. The State, however, failed in introducing effective land reforms. Dr Singh leadership introduced certain structural reforms in the post-90 period. The development strategy turned market directed. India borrowed from the international lending agencies to support current account and balance of payment deficits. The public-sector investment declined, but India resisted the sale of its national enterprises. Fiscal discipline put more restrictions on its growth. Liberalisation of trade and the opening of markets increased foreign and domestic trade and new technology imports helped in the growth of services sector.

The early public-sector investment in infrastructure and public services had created a more favourable environment for private investment in new export oriented products and sectors to increase productive capabilities. The foreign direct investment has increased to take advantage of new opportunities. The exports have grown at the rate of 10% with a large contribution from the services sector. The globalisation policy and large public investment helped the service sector growth during the 90's. The increased capital formation and use of more efficient technology have resulted in higher rate of economic growth, but it has also increased inequality.

India's per capita GDP growth rate in constant prices was about 3.5 % per annum till 1980; it declined to 3.3% during 1980-90 and improved to 3.6% during 1990-2000. But since 2000, the rate of growth has increased to 5.5 % per annum and has been ranked second highest amongst the world's largest economies. Indian life expectancy at birth has also doubled to 66 years since 1947. The living standards of the top 20% of the population have improved beyond all the expectations. But there has been hardly any reduction in poverty and especially rural poverty since 1947.

At the time of writing, India is ruled by a right-wing religious nationalist party (BJP), which has encouraged and exploited

Hindu nationalism. The party is fascist by nature as its popularity depends on politically convenient enemies both within the country namely Muslim and beyond borders Pakistan. India's regions have also gained national political significance with the promotion of ethnic politics.

In some way, the change in the political power had provided a way to adopt a different model of economic growth. The liberalisation trend suited business class interests to support ties with the USA. After the fall of Berlin wall, it was very difficult for any country to take a stand against the USA and argue against the dominant paradigm of free market system. Under the new world order, Indian growth model got revised, but its public-sector enterprises have remained very significant, capital movement restricted, and the foreign direct investment is only allowed in certain selected sectors. The labour laws are still intact and in force.

The increasing prosperity of last two decades has come at a cost. According to Sen, the old class and cast structure have got a new face and new consolidation and entrenchment. These classes have captured all important organs of the state. The old rural elites have migrated to urban areas and have become constituents of urban capitalist classes. The landless poor are committing suicide in increasing numbers as they have no voice. Corruption is rampant, and there is a lack of accountability in administrative, judicial and legislative processes. The regional and urban-rural inequality has increased. The dependence on exports, foreign capital and technology have increased, and the dreams of a just society and self-reliance have blown away. An urban rich class has emerged to rub shoulders with rich people of the world, but more than 800 million Indian do not have access to clean water, basic health or education. Sen has called it an uncertain glory.

India has achieved a substantial and diversified industrial base. At the start, the State was effective and played a dominant role in developing industrial sector. The State protected industrial base by providing protection from foreign completion, by directly investing and supporting and guiding private investment. Later on, it turned less effective because of political horse trading, conflict of interests, and compromises. The political participation with its compromises and conflicting interests produced a mismatch between the State ambitions related to industrialisation and economic growth and its capability to achieve its ambitions. The industrialisation rate under Indian democracy differed under changing political stability, but it has remained steady. The political compromises might have impacted on the growth rate of industrialisation.

Besides slower industrialisation and economic growth, India has failed to deal with poverty and inequality of wealth and income in the country. Why has Indian economic growth failed to touch the lives of millions of its citizen? One possible explanation lies in the fact that its growth has been in services sectors such as software, financial services, and generic pharmaceuticals, where production process is less labour intensive, and wages in these specialised activities have increased without having any impact on the mass unemployment level or wage levels. An ordinary Indian's wage rate has not improved in the face of surplus supply of labour. India had failed to redistribute land and did not invest enough in human capital and failed in providing adequate public services such as education and health, which could have opened up greater opportunities for the population. Another reason may be that India pursued growth ignoring inequality as a national objective in the belief that once the country becomes prosper there would be a trickle- down effect that would take care of poverty. Unfortunately, that trickle-down did not happen. Acemoglu et al. (4), in their book called '*Why Nations Fail*' has provided another possible explanation for India's failure. They suggest that Indian caste system, Mughals absolutism of power and colonial institutions which have remained intact in India, has created a barrier to opportunities and have failed to develop inclusive economic institutions. But India was not unique in experiencing colonialism, almost all Asian countries except for Japan, were subjected to the western colonialism. Glaeser et al. (42) are sceptical about the institution's role and seem to suggest that human development probably plays a much more important role in the development process. Trebilcock (157) seem to be unsure which particular institutions and specific characteristics of these institutions matter most for development. I believe the quality of leadership after Nehru, colonial institutions, parliamentary democracy, ineffective state, lack of human capital, and Indian caste system might have played a negative role in the economic development.

14

PAKISTAN RELATIVE POVERTY

The last four chapters have provided growth narrative of four Asian countries. All of them started their independence at a similar time, with similar poverty levels and economic structures. Two of them have been more successful in alleviating the poverty of their people compared with the other two. At the start, all four countries had some common and some divergent features which distinguish them from each other. This chapter seeks an answer to their differing performance.

India and Pakistan had 90 years of common colonial past and achieved freedom in 1947. Both had multiple ethnicities, low capital formation, many regions and languages, parliamentary democracy, colonial institutions of civil, armed and judiciary, rudimentary transport and communications systems and mainly agrarian economies but differed in level of industrialisation, quality of leadership, education levels, political maturity, nationalism, religion, culture and national heroes. Pakistan and South Korea had some common features such as both came under the USA influence, faced external insecurity, periods of Army rule and very similar economic structures. But there were major differences such as quality of leadership, political system, population size and homogeneity, religion, ethnicity, language, and culture. Pakistan and China had multiple regions, large and diverse population, languages, religions, agrarian economies, basic transport and communication systems but differed in the quality of leadership, political ideology and form of political system, religion, and culture.

China became a single-party socialist economy which sets her apart from others. The central planning authority took the responsibility for resource allocation. The national objective consisted of the creation of an effective state, transformation of economic structure, economic growth and equality. India turned into a multi-party parliamentary democracy and a mixed economy. The planning authority allocated public resources to achieve economic growth but made no attempt to create equality of opportunities. South Korea adopted a Presidential form of democratic political system which was high-jacked by the Army frequently. She adopted a free market economic system with imperfect markets. The State guided national economic growth and created equal opportunities through universal education, land reforms and welfare spending. Pakistan adopted a multiparty parliamentary democracy which was frequently high-jacked by the Army or feudal elites. She adopted a free market system with imperfections. The national objective was declared as growth and equality. China, South Korea and India put a priority on industrialisation for growth whereas Pakistan has relied on her comparative advantage in agriculture to achieve growth and poverty reduction.

In chapter 6, I have described how industrialisation transform economies to increase productivity and economic growth. In chapter 7, I have provided historical evidence on the economic transformation of rich countries. In each case, it was industrial, trade and technology policies which acted as instruments of increased productivity and growth. The creation of productive capabilities is a pre-condition for economic growth. Thus, physical and human capital formation is time-consuming and requires diversion of national resources from consumption. Given this understanding of the growth process, it is important to identify those factors which have been at play in four selected Asian countries to create a different economic performance.

Comparison of Economic Performance

The economic growth rates and human development indicators (quality of life) could provide an insight into the development process and how each country's leadership, state effectiveness, policies and strategies have shaped her destiny.

With their similarities and differences, the march of history has observed four different poverty alleviation stories in four Asian countries. South Korea has become a rich country. China has become the second-largest economy and a world power. India has shown steady growth and is growing with respect. Pakistan has lagged behind the other three in economic performance. She has become a nuclear power but still has not found its place among the comity of nations. Tables 6-9 provide economic indicators of each country performance.

Table 6: Economic Indicators of Four Asian Countries.

Indicator:	South Korea.	China.	India.	Pakistan.
Population (million 2011)	50	1344	1241	177
GDP per capita 2011 (constant 2000 US $)	16684	2640	838	672
GDP per capita 2011 (ppp int. $ 2005)	27541	7418	3203	2424
GDP per capita average annual Growth rates % 1961-2011	5.4	6.8	3.1	2.6

Source: World Development Indicators. UN report 2013.

The four countries have grown at different average rates over 1961-2011 periods. China and South Korea grew at an average rate of 6.8% and 5.4% per annum. India grew at an average growth rate of 3.1% per annum and Pakistan has lagged behind with an average growth rate of 2.6% per annum. These growth rates differences are reflected in per capita income levels. GDP per capita measured at constant prices and purchasing power parity basis points to the stark differences in their historical economic performance. South Korea has become a rich country. China with the world largest population has achieved per capita which is almost three times the size of India's per capita GDP. Pakistan once again lags behind everyone and her per capita income of $650 is not very different compared with per capita GDP in 1950. China and India are large countries with a large population. Pakistan population is relatively large for its size. South Korea has moderate population size. Population size indicates the magnitude of poverty problem which each of these countries had to deal with and its growth rate has two-way relationships with economic growth. A moderately increasing population can increase effective demand and economic growth, but if the population growth rate exceeds GDP growth rate it leads to an increase in poverty level. Pakistan population has grown at 3% per annum for long periods of time and has exceeded the population growth rate of other three countries, which reflects on it being a factor in checking its per capita income growth level and ability to alleviate poverty. The differences in GDP are quite remarkable by any standard and reflect on their level of industrialisation. Leadership quality and ambitions, national objectivity and effectiveness of state to implement correct strategies and policies. **Schumpeter had said that history is a narrative of change and development but history itself is a story of the impact of Leadership on people and societies. It is the driving force of Leadership which makes the difference. The destiny of each nation rests with them.**

Table 7 shows per capita GDP growth rates for different decades, which should help in identifying the periods, when economic management policies, political regimes, capital formation, international trade figures, and structural changes created differences in economic performance.

The changes in per capita GDP growth rates over different decades provide a slightly different picture compared with the

Table 7: Economic Indicators: GDP (per capita average annual Growth rates (%)) of Selected Countries

Period/ Countries	South Korea-	China	India	Pakistan
1961-70	5.7	2.4	1.8	4.5
1970-80	5.5	5.4	0.9	2.2
1980-90	6.5	7.6	3.3	3.2
1990-2000	5.5	8.6	3.6	1.3
2000-11	3.9	9.6	5.6	2.5
Savings: GDS as % of GDP	31	53	31	22
Gross Fixed Capital Formation				
As a proportion of GDP (%)	27	46	30	11
Foreign Net Investment, net				
Inflows as a proportion of GDP (%)	0.4	3.0	1.7	0.6
Exports of Goods and services as a				
Proportion of GDP (%)	56	31	25	14
Average Annual Growth Rate of				
Value of Exports (%)				
1961-90	20.6	---	6.1	6.8
1990-2011	12.0	16.5	13.6	6.0

Source: World Development Indicators see 2013 Report. Savings, investment and export figures are for the year 2011.

overall average figures given in the last table. South Korea per capita growth rate is very similar over each decade except for the last decade when it had fallen to 3.9% per annum. The similar growth rates over time, indicate that the economic transformation was balanced due to physical and human capital development. The drive of nationalistic leadership and effective state carried out policies of land distribution, physical and human capital development with the consistent allocation of resources and protected foreign trade. The investment was comprehensive to cover heavy, intermediate and final goods industries. The last decade figures reflect slacking world economies and the meltdown of the South Korean economy under international competition.

China's relatively moderate per capita growth rate up to 1980 indicates the committed leadership and effective state stress on heavy industries and unbalanced investment in different sectors, unfavourable weather, periodic political instability and balanced approach to growth and equality. The State invested in heavy industries, technology, and manpower development at the cost of consumer and export industries. The diversion of resources from agriculture to the industrial sector harmed agriculture growth and rural population. The protective trade policy protected domestic industries and technology base and the investment in heavy industries and manpower took a long time to bear results. The land reforms and universal education and health policies helped in creating an equal society. China changed growth strategy to export-led growth, invested in consumer goods, import substitution, and export-oriented goods around 1980. The allocation followed new directions of the policy and the growth rates reflect on the combined effect of earlier and later industrial development.

India's per capita growth rate for all decades is much lower compared with China and South Korea. This reflects on lower physical and human capital formation, slow growth of industries and technology, varying quality of leadership and effectiveness of State, ineffective land reforms, protective trade policy, political compromises, internal instability and external wars, unbalanced industrial growth and low priority on universal education and equality. India had reached a reasonable level of industrialisation by 1990 when foreign trade and capital movements' restrictions were relaxed and in consequence growth rates started to improve.

Pakistan's growth rate was second largest in the 60's but since then it has declined steadily. The decline indicates quality of leadership, political instability and uncertainty, low physical and human capital formation, lack of long -term vision, ineffective land reforms, involvement in the USA wars in Afghanistan, oil price shocks, implementation of IMF enforced structural reforms, heavy investment in agriculture sector and neglect of heavy and intermediate industries.

South Korea, China and India gross domestic savings and capital formation as a percentage of GDP are much higher compared with Pakistan savings and capital formation rates of 8% and 11%. Pakistan's foreign direct investment is only 0.6 % of GDP whereas India foreign direct investment stands at 1.5% of GDP and in China more than 3% of GDP. The differences in domestic savings, capital formation, and foreign direct investment can partially explain the differences in the growth rates of these countries. Pakistan lower capital formation can be explained in term of prevailing poverty, macro instability, visionless leadership and ineffective state. Poor don't have enough to save or invest. Visionless leadership and ineffective state lead to macro instability and uncertain future. Individuals are unable to predict future events or returns on investment.

Pakistan export of goods and services is much smaller compared with other three countries. In 2011, it exported only 14% of its GDP, and its rate of export since 1961 has remained at 6% whereas all others have increased their exports levels substantially. India exports 25% of GDP, China 31% of GDP and South Korea 56% of GDP. Low exports indicate a low level of industrialisation and specialisation. Pakistan's exports are narrow and consist of mainly raw materials and semi-finished products and therefore even when the exports volume increases, the adverse terms of trade kick in, and the overall value of exports more or less stays as constant. A country's economic growth is dependent on its productive capabilities of physical and human capital, and Pakistan has failed to match the productive capabilities of other three. Table 8 below provides information on human development index and quality of life indicators.

Table 8: Human Development Indicators of Four Countries 2011

Social indicators.	South Korea	China	India	Pakistan
HDI:_index	0.891	0.719	0.586	0.536
Inequality adjusted Index.	0.736	n.a.	0.418	0.375
Rank	15	91	135	146
Income/command over				
Per capita GNI 2011 PPP$	30345.35	11477.15	5149.81	4651.64
Poverty. Population in				
Multidimensional poverty %	n.a	5.98	55.28	45.59
Below int. Poverty line	n.a.	29.8	68.70	60.2
Life Expectancy at birth.	81	73	65	65
Female	84	75	67	66
Male	77	72	64	64
Infant Mortality rate	4	13	47	59
(as per 1000 births)				
Fertility rate	1.2	1.6	2.6	3.4
Education: literacy rates (%)				
Female	95	91	51	40
Male	99	97	75	69
Youth Literacy rates (%)				
Female	n.a.	99	74	61
Male	n.a.	99	88	79
Gender: female-male				
Ratio in population				
(Female per 1000 of males)	1006	926	937	968
Female labour participation				
Rate over age 15 (%)	49	68	29	22

Source: UN Development Reports.

The HDI ranking of countries shows that South Korea is ranked 15, China 91, India 135 and Pakistan ranked at 146 positions. These ranks also reflect on per capita income levels. South Korea gross national per capita income is almost three times of China, six times of India and about seven times of Pakistan. South Korea and China have done much better in improving the quality of life of their people. South Korea life expectancy of 84 years is like most rich countries; China's life expectancy of 75 years' lags behind

South Korea but is much higher compared with life expectancy in India or Pakistan. All other social indicators show that South Korea and China are far ahead of both India and Pakistan and have achieved universal or near-universal youth literacy. India and Pakistan have a long way to go to merit any credit; however, India is ahead of Pakistan in literacy and especially in female youth literacy. Pakistan and India are both far behind South Korea and China in female participation in the labour force. South Korea and China have universal child immunisation but Pakistan and India both have low immunisation rates and also stand out as having mass undernourishment among children. The infant mortality rate stands at 59% in Pakistan, 47% in India, 13% in China and 4% in South Korea. These results are reflective of the fact that both China and South Korea declared equality as long term objective and diverted resources to achieve it. India and Pakistan have neglected equality.

China is growing at the rate of 9.6% per annum in 2011. India takes the second position with a growth rate of 5.5% per annum. South Korea takes the third position with a growth rate of 3.9% per annum and Pakistan's takes a bottom position with a growth rate of 2.5% per annum. South Korea is presently ranked 30, China 78, India 142, and Pakistan 146 with per capita GDP of $28101, $7589, $1627, and $1343. South Korea has moved to a rich country's status whereas China has moved up among middle-ranking countries. India and Pakistan are still poor nations. Pakistan performance reflects on poor allocation, neglect of productive capabilities, selfish leadership, ineffective state and wrong industrial trade and technology policies. The poor quality of leadership, ineffective state and agrarian economic structure exposes the real poverty of Pakistan.

Pakistan compared with other low-income countries, does not fare any better. Table 9 compares economic and social indicators for Pakistan and average of 16 poorest countries.

Table 9: Pakistan and 15 Poorest Countries

Indicators.	Pakistan.	Average for 16 poorest countries.
GDP Per Capita (PPP constant $).	2424	2112
Life Expectancy at birth.	65	67
Infant Mortality Rate.	59	47
Total Fertility Rate.	3.4	2.9
Literacy Rate (age 15-24 years, 2011)		
Female	40	79
Male	69	85
Child Immunisation rates % 2011		
DPT	56	88
Measles	55	87

Source: World Bank World Development Indicators. 16 poor countries are Afghanistan, Bangladesh, Burma, Cambodia, Haiti, Kyrgyzstan, Laos, Moldova, Nepal, Papua New Guinea, Tajikistan, Vietnam, Cambodia, and Yemen.

Pakistan per capita GDP in constant prices and on purchasing power parity basis is slightly higher than the average of 16 poor countries, but her infant mortality rate is also higher. Some of the countries included in the average, when taken individually, such as Vietnam ($3013), Moldova ($2975), Uzbekistan ($2903) and Laos ($2464), have higher per capita GDP levels compared with Pakistan.

Pakistan population growth rate is higher compared with the average growth rate of the sixteen poor countries but her literacy rate, life expectancy, and immunisation programme lag behind the poorest of the poor.

The living conditions in Pakistan are slightly better, but the rural poverty is much like the poverty faced in sub-Saharan African countries. Pakistan's per capita income and life expectancy are higher compared with the per capita income of sub-Saharan countries, but when it comes to other social indicators such as mass literacy and female literacy, there is hardly any difference.

The African countries, however, perform better on mass nutrition and children nutrition compared with Pakistan.

Causes of Divergent Growth and Why Pakistan has remained Poor?

The economic transformation of an economy from agrarian to an industrial base is the only way to eradicate poverty. But there are many factors which contribute to the economic transformation process. The quality and political philosophy of national leadership determine the long-term vision, the effectiveness of state, formulate and implement policies such as trade, industry, technology, land reforms, universal education and health to achieve long- term vision. An effective state creates incentives, macro stability and external security. The economy and social structure have deep rooted two-way relationships. The State role in economic management involves allocation of national resources. Frederic List had suggested that at early stages of economic development, a state must develop and protect industries, invest in human capital and ensure adequate supplies of raw materials for growing industrial sector. Only a committed nationalist leadership could take difficult decisions to transform an economy.

After independence, each of our selected four countries inherited varying quality of leadership, political systems and international alliances. China had gone through a socialist revolution, inherited a committed leadership which turned the State into an effective organ to allocate resources to achieve long-term goals of growth and equality. USSR became an effective friend and partner to promote a common ideology. India adopted a neutral political stand but leant towards socialist ideas which determined its political and economic framework and formed external relations. South Korea and Pakistan's defence and economic vulnerabilities forced them to side with the USA and adopt markets directed allocation and a democratic framework.

South Korea opted for a Presidential form and Pakistan a parliamentary form of democracy. The political leadership and their political ideas, allocation systems, state effectiveness and role and international relations have played a part in the relative performance of our four countries

Three countries (i.e. South Korea, China and India), were fortunate to have visionary leadership and effective states. India's first prime minister had public support, vision and commitment to transform Indian economy. After Nehru death, the State effectiveness weakened due to political compromises. All Three states vigorously diverted resources to pursue industrialisation policy. Pakistan lost her visionary founder and the State was high-jacked and turned ineffective by feudal leadership who put self-interest over and above the national interest. In consequence, the economy has remained primarily an agrarian with diminishing returns and low productivity. The neoliberals do not challenge the role of industrialisation in economic development but argue that the State intervention in the economy distorts allocation and economic growth. This argument is plagued by empirical and logical problems and has no evidence to support it. The poor economies lack savings, technology and knowledge. The individuals' decisions do not comply with the national interests. The State extraction of resources carries a cost but it is more than compensated with larger output in future. Only an effective State can pursue long-term national interests, allocate resources to develop physical and human capital capabilities to achieve economic growth.

Political systems and regimes

Our selected countries have different political systems, rules to elect or select political leaders, allocate resources, manage economies and preserve the security of the State. All political systems (i.e. authoritarian or non-authoritarian) tend to claim that they have public support and work for national prosperity and equality. There are, however, differences in the processes of election or selection, decision making, and time framework of leaders' tenure and visions. The political regimes set a pattern of state authority, size and objectivity of resource allocation, accountability of institutions and reflect on the power structure of various classes. Democracy evolved through industrial transformation and has taken a long time to establish itself. The political differences, class interests, regional differences and compromises can slow down decision-making process and distort resource allocation in a democratic framework. The other forms of political regimes have different power structures. The authoritarian regimes have complete authority over allocation, make quick decisions in the national interest and can avoid compromises.

Would a poor man starving of hunger and facing death, choose to fulfil his material needs or political participation? It is argued that in a poverty struck country where humans take a risk with life in the course of earning a livelihood. Economic rights take priority above all others and an individual will invariably save his life over political participation. In making this choice he would have a reason to prefer the fulfilment of his material needs above all other needs and he would prefer elimination of economic deprivation and misery. The political rights of individuals in a society are a direct by-product of its political and productive systems. But political participation in poor countries can be highjacked and exploited by the political elite who can use state power to enrich themselves. A strong view prevails that economic development process is a complex and difficult process which requires single-minded toughness, whereas a democracy with its political and civil rights creates indecisiveness and uncertainty.

China adopted a single party socialist system with central planning and absolute authority of the leadership and state. South Korea adopted a presidential democratic political structure disrupted by 44 years of authoritarian rule. India adopted a parliamentary form of democracy dominated by a family rule of about 34 years. Nehru enjoyed loyalty and support of the nation but his daughter and grandson periods in office were frequently marred by political compromises and short-term policy measures to remain in power. India became a federal state with regional rivalries and compromises which impacted the state effectiveness and its role in the economic development. Pakistan adopted a parliamentary form of feudal democracy disrupted with fragmented visionless authoritarian Army rule of 30 odd years. Pakistan political regimes got marred by internal infighting, regional disputes, political horse trading, corruption and personal ambitions. Pakistan has turned into an ineffective federal state where individuals' and regional interests take preference over the national interest.

The strong, stable political regimes of China and South Korea were ruthless in their national ambitions and perused narrow national goal of industrialisation without any compromise and were successful in achieving rapid industrialisation and economic growth. South Korea prioritised economic growth, mobilise private capital, and excluded the working class from benefits in the short run to channel industrial surpluses into new investment. The State was able to capture monopoly profits of the private sector for reinvestment to create productive physical capabilities. China's central planning authority directly invested in physical and human capabilities. Both countries had the narrow national objective of industrialisation and their effective leadership have delivered. India and Pakistan both have polarised democracies with political horse trading, conflicts of interests, regionalism, corruption, and short-term decisions which have failed to deliver multiple objectives of industrialisation and equity. Nehru successors were weak and did not have his authority or vision. Political participation in

Pakistan has created instability, corruption, and short-termism. The Army rule created stability but provided no visionary leadership. It is possible to draw an inference from the performance of four countries that India and Pakistan rates of growth diverged from the other two countries because of their political regimes and quality of their leadership.

China and East Asians countries modelled their economic development on the idea of removing poverty and misery through toughness and discipline before implementing democracy or civil rights and have achieved success. India with parliamentary democracy used a development model which does not place priority on the poverty reduction but aimed to develop physical capabilities. Indian model has created greater inequality and concentration of power to serve the interests of few. Pakistan political structure has varied from democracy to authoritarian rule. Each time civilian rule brought political and economic collapse and put country's survival at risk, it was booted out by the Army which failed to provide a long-term vision for the country. Pakistan regimes seem to have no ideology, conviction or clear-cut national objectivity or a growth model.

In the light of the historical economic development of China and East Asian countries, a question becomes obvious to ask whether mass political participation is conducive or essential to the economic development in poor countries. Some studies have been undertaken to establish an empirical relationship between economic growth (GDP) and political systems and a few of these studies have shown a strong positive relationship, but others have found the relationship very weak and in some cases, there is no relationship at all. The historical evidence of GDP growth rates and political participation in Pakistan supports Lee Kuan Yew (long-serving Prime Minister of Singapore) thesis that *the denial of political rights helps to promote economic growth in early stages of development in the developing countries*. Singapore economic development during Lee rule is an obvious evidence of the Lee thesis. The difference in economic growth rates under Army and civilian rules in Pakistan support this hypothesis even more convincingly.

Social Structure Changes

Marx had observed that a change in economic structure or industrialisation changes social structure and each social structure has a unique economic structure. All four countries had started their independence with agrarian economies and sociopolitical structures based on land ownership. Since then the social structures have gone through a change but at different rates and having gone through a change social structures have started to initiate changes in the political and economic systems.

China political revolution handed absolute power to the nationalist-socialist leadership to create an industrial equal opportunity society. The State diverted resources for industrialisation, distributed land on equal terms and provided universal education and health to transform the economy and achieve national objectives of prosperity and equality. The transformation of economy and equality marched simultaneously, but recently social structure has initiated changes in resource allocation. China also used socialist ideology to create social responsibility of hard work, kept national wage rates low to increase productivity and lower unit cost to make industries productive and competitive. South Korean Army controlled political power and its committed leadership transformed society by industrialisation, land reforms, universal education and health care programmes. She suppressed labour wages, encouraged private capital with monopoly profits and ruthlessly directed surpluses to promote industries. The transformation of the economic structure has started to transform the political structure into more democratic. The industrialisation has created new relations and values in both societies.

In India, the landed classes captured political power in provinces and did not allow any meaning-full land distribution, did not introduce universal education system or training programme which kept the Indian society to its traditional caste base structure. India diverted resources to industrialise in early years. The labour force was organised, but it never became a political force to assert a demand for higher wage rates because of large-scale unemployment. India's social structure has changed marginally in urban but not in rural areas. After independence, the landed class in Pakistan hijacked political power, discarded land distribution, did not promote universal education and developed agriculture sector to have a bigger share of the national cake. Some landowning politicians also invested in import substitution industries to become rent seekers. The Pakistan social structure has remained a feudal pre-capitalist in nature.

A social structure which provides equal opportunities is likely to foster economic growth. The market forces cannot bridge inequality on their own. Moore, Jr. (86) had argued that commercialised landed classes can turn agrarian societies into modern industrial one. The land owners with the largest share of income can invest the surplus in new ventures either commercial or industrial and this process over a long period can change the structure of economies. However, the argument breaks down if the surplus is allowed to fly out of the country or is not invested in industrial development. The other aspects of social structure such as ethnic mix, social classes, and mobilisation levels can have an adverse impact on growth but can be moulded by the effective state policies.

Capital Formation: Self-Sufficiency versus Relative Dependency

The source of savings and investment plays an important role in the selection and level of industrialisation and economic development and an effective state can adopt policies to mobilise domestic resources for capital formation and economic growth.

China relied on domestic sources to finance their industrial development. South Korea used both foreign and domestic sources to develop industrial sector. India relied mainly on domestic savings to finance her industrialisation. Pakistan relied mainly on foreign aid and loans as a source of capital formation in the public sector.

South Korea set a narrow goal of comprehensive industrialisation. She mobilised domestic sources to finance it. If she accepted foreign help it was on her terms. The self-sufficiency policy enabled her to pursue national interests without any outside pressures or influences. The policy of buying foreign technology but not foreign capital avoided capital dependency. She paid for the technology imports by fostering exports with subsidies and incentives. The USA provided financial assistance and technology for Korean support during the Vietnam War to develop steel and transport industries. South Korea with almost 54 years of authoritarian rule created a strong, cohesive and an effective state, which allowed semi-monopolistic markets to generate surplus funds for investment and controlled foreign trade to protect infant industries. The other policy measures such as credit controls, subsidies, administrative support, punishment, nationalist exhortations, positive interest rates, and commercial loans were employed to encourage capital formation. The wage rates were controlled to capture productivity gains for reinvestment and nationalism was used to make labour work hard to support industrialisation and national security. The land reforms and universal education improved equal opportunities. The imported western institutions such as property rights, law and order, accountability and transparency were moulded to local conditions to support industrial expansion. The State did not own any assets but provided every feasible incentive, subsidies, monopoly surpluses, and protection to the private sector to expand industrial capability. The positive interest rates policy encouraged domestic saving.

China socialist regime mobilised mass resources, provided universal education and distributed national land to forge relationships with the peasants. She developed industries under protection and human capital for equality and equal opportunities. The central planning authority allocated resources to develop heavy industries, indigenous technology, import substitution industries, and infrastructure projects. The economy was closed to the outside competition. The Soviet Union provided some help in early years but China has relied mainly on domestic sources for physical and human capital formation and technology development and imports. The increased productivity of industries provided resources for further investment in public services and social infrastructure to reduce poverty. China did not borrow from the international agencies, avoided debt trap and did not need to implement any structural reforms or poverty reduction programmes. In 1979, China changed policy direction by allowing limited competition in internal markets, developed export-oriented industries and liberated foreign trade with remarkable results. The economy has become the largest exporting economy as well as the largest economy on a purchasing power parity basis in the world

India pursued an autonomous development strategy of comprehensive industrialisation. She imposed restrictions on foreign trade, banned foreign direct investment and import of foreign capital and technology. She financed industrial programme from the public and private savings and remained independent of external interests. By adopting self -sufficiency policy she avoided debt trap that has plagued some developing countries such as Pakistan. India invested public money in heavy industries and infrastructure and provided incentives for the private sectors to invest in consumer industries. The restriction on foreign trade provided protection to infant industries and banning of foreign capital avoided financial crisis and foreign intervention in internal domestic policies. After Nehru death, the political stability and domestic levels of saving and investment became troublesome and the state role became flexible. India put a low priority on human capital development which has created greater inequality and rural poverty. India's multiple national goals, fragmented political and social structure, neglect of human capital development, and a limited reliance on foreign aids and loans for capital formation have played a role in determining the rate and efficiency of industrialisation and rate of economic growth. A state with multiple goals does not have the capacity or political freedom to mobilise and divert resources for investment compared with a cohesive state. The existence of multiple goals limits the growth ambitions and political and economic conditions influence the rate and efficiency of investment. The decision-making process, conflicting interests, and investment criterion all impede the ability of a fragmented state. The process of economic policy implementation creates additional inefficiencies such as management appointments, industrial policy intervention and channelling of credit. India dependency on foreign loans and aid created dependency, uncertainty and impacted the selection and direction of development. The foreign donations and loans depend on foreign interests, which do not always coincide with the interests of the recipient countries. These factors have distorted India's growth compared with China and South Korea.

Pakistan political leadership corrupted political system and social structure on languages, racial lines, and multiple interests to tighten their hold on power. They use state resources for personal benefits. Pakistan with its vulnerabilities fell in the lap of USA to be guided, controlled and used against the Soviet threat. The USA has changed political regimes in Pakistan at will. Pakistan growth strategy was formulated by the American free market economists, who believed in the market system, comparative cost theory, free trade, and market-directed economic growth. So, the development of agriculture took top priority. The ineffective state had no moral authority to mobilise domestic resources for investment and the foreign masters were generous to provide aid and loans to finance development of water resources. The agriculture sector grew, but it did not do any good. The terms of trade for agriculture goods continued to decline in the international markets. The land reforms could have increased productivity but did not happen. The comparative cost advantage and the development of agriculture diverted attention from the industrialisation of economic structure. When others were industrialising Pakistan was investing in diminishing returns agriculture.

Pakistan has failed to raise domestic saving and investment levels and to adopt an autonomous growth strategy. Her public investment depended on foreign aid and loans which went into the development of agriculture and agriculture-based industrial units. The domestic saving has remained low because of poor investment returns and negative interest rate policy. The State has failed to capture monopoly rents for industrial expansion. The public investment mostly goes into the development of non-productive or low technology projects. The investment in productive projects like steel production faces numerous corrupt practices such as management inefficiencies and over-manning. In consequence, her growth has been a story of boom and bust linked with the preferences and availability of foreign aid and loans which have distorted size and type of industrial growth. The mass mobilisation of resources, nation building and transformation of economy require a strong, effective leadership and state to guide and support. Pakistan nationalism has remained superficial and fragmented along tribal lines and has failed to unite the country. The leadership corruption has seeped through the veins of the society killing incentives to work hard or create wealth through lawful activities. Pakistan has failed to undertake appropriate industry, trade and technology policies to transform economic structure for national prosperity. The foreign dependency for investment funds has created beggar mentality and investment has gone to sectors which serve foreign interests.

The above argument clearly holds for the colonial periods when investment went into developing raw materials and the countries imported industrial products. The present day foreign loans and investment serve the same purpose.

The changes of regimes in Pakistan, from 'make believe democracy' to the authoritarian Army rule and back, has relied on the same corrupt ex-colonial institutions and in consequence, a regime change has not changed the effectiveness of the State or economic transformation. Each time Army leadership was in power it developed concern about legitimacy under pressure from outside, which made them pursue multiple goals and compromises. For a brief period, during the 60's, Pakistan acted as an effective state and developed industries in both public and private sectors, but even then, a large part of investment went into the development of agriculture sector because of foreign dependency. The limited industrial development got protection at times but it was mostly to benefit the political elites or their friends as rent seekers. The country's export base has remained narrow. The balance of payment deficit is a regular occurrence needing borrowing. The twin deficits create macro instability and increase dependency on foreign financial aids and loans. The foreign debt has taken on a new dimension. Pakistan is poor because it has failed to transform its economy from an agrarian to the industrial base.

One may sum up and conclude that China and South Korea relied on domestic resources and appropriate trade, industry and technology policies to transform their economies. India identifies industrialisation as a mean to economic transformation but after Nehru death, she failed to mobile sufficient domestic resources to achieve national prosperity or equality. Pakistan dependency on others for capital formation has affected her growth strategy and she has failed to learn the secret of industrialisation and economic transformation.

Human Capital

The physical and human capital formation increases productive capabilities to absorb new technology. Only a committed nationalist leadership and resulting effective state is capable of mobilising and diverting resources to create and balance both physical and human productive capabilities. The failure of leadership can lead to a mismatch between human and physical capabilities and retard industrialisation process.

South Korea and China both invested heavily in human capital which enabled them to match technical and managerial manpower to the expanding physical industrial capacities. Their educated healthy people were able to meet industrial expansion and seek new opportunities to better themselves. India allocated resources to promote selective higher technical knowledge and skills which have paid off with a time lag but failed to promote universal education because of her caste system. In consequence, her labour force has remained devoid of skills and aspirations, growth has remained anaemic and the quality of life has failed to improve. Pakistan failed to invest in universal education or health care and has failed to create both human and physical capabilities as others. The failure has resulted in low aspiration and low labour productivity and poor quality of life. The corrupt leadership exploitation of national resources for personal benefits has continued without any national protest. More recently, Pakistan has relied on the private sector to provide education and health facilities in compliance with the structural reforms of the international lending agencies. In consequence, the education system has turned fragmented and shambolic. There are so-called imperial colleges and universities located in every second street of every city and even villages. There is no uniform syllabus or valid tests to assess the output of these institutions. Indeed, these are business factories which are awarding useless and worthless degrees and diplomas. Young people attend the universities and remain illiterate and unskilled. There are some good schools which serve the interests of rich and powerful and provide excellent schooling to their children to enable them to get places at the elite universities of the world. The unequal education opportunities have created greater inequality and entrenched social structure. The state education system ends up producing idle young people without discipline or required technical or managerial skills which have distorted the country's development efforts. The private health care provides no health. Life is cheap in Pakistan.

The Washington Consensus Policies

The neoliberal market paradigm of resource allocation has become dominant since the fall of Berlin wall in 1989. The paradigm was sold to loans and aid-receiving poor countries as a default condition for economic growth. The international lending agencies such as IMF, the World Bank and the WTO imposed this paradigm on poor as structural reforms or poverty alleviation policies. South Korea, China and India largely relied on domestic resources to finance their investment and deal with the twin deficits and therefore did not have to abide by the pre-conditions of loans and aid. Pakistan has faced financial crisis regularly over time because of her agrarian economy.

During the 60's and 70's the international lending agencies did not enforce any loan conditions but since the 80's loan receiving countries have been subjected to the structural reforms and poverty alleviation schemes and in consequence, the lenders have taken control of economic management policies of poor countries to promote privatisation, liberalisation and minimum state.

The privatisation has destroyed most of Pakistan privatised industrial units. Public enterprises have been made bankrupt and sold off at knock down prices and few which are still under public control are suffering huge losses due to poor management and energy shortages. Some of the national industrial units are left rotting. The financial markets have become playing fields of foreign fund managers. The capital flies away to foreign bank accounts. The education and health programmes have disappeared from public services. Pakistan's foreign and domestic debts have reached critical limits, and her inflation is at least in double digits. The State is stealing money through indirect taxes and forced low-interest rates. The country still suffers from fiscal and balance of payment deficits, low domestic saving, and limited investment in physical capacity. The imposed policies are opposite of what is required to deal with these problems. The industrialisation has been forgotten and there is no investment in intermediate and capital goods industries. The limited investment focuses on import substitution. The near collapse of the State is a direct result of the bankrupt political leadership and system and the Washington consensus policies are helping in quickening this collapse.

In the 90's South Korea joined the rich nation club with attached conditions of the Washington Consensus policies and as result, the economy went into decline. The foreigners bought a large number of businesses at knock down prices. The high unemployment created political unrest. The South Korean economy had to be bailed out. Some of the structural reform policies were ditched and Keynesian policies were adopted to revive economic fortune of the country. The 90's and early years of this century proved difficult one for the economy. Recently South Korean economy has stabilised with considerable slow growth rate

India was forced to borrow money to avoid an economic crisis in the 70's and 90's. The international lending agencies imposed conditions. India complied and relaxed trade restrictions, cut down public investment, encouraged and supported private investment in industrial development and provide incentives, subsidies, to encourage exports. The mild relaxation of trade restriction boosted Indian imports more than its exports, and she refused a followed-up loan as an infringement of her sovereignty. The Indian markets are still closed to the outside competition, and relaxation of trade has been allowed only in some sectors of the economy.

It is tempting to draw a conclusion that free markets, unrestricted trade, free movements of capital, minimum state and political participation, played no role in China's industrialisation or economic development for the first 30 years of her life. Once the country had achieved a sound industrial base she has the relaxed restriction of foreign investment in sectors of her choosing.

Entrepreneurship

Schumpeter had suggested that the entrepreneurs are the main driver of industrialisation and economic growth in each society as they take the risk to invest in new technology to start a 'destructive creation' process.

Japanese rule in Korea had permitted Korean to establish businesses and industries. As a result, a sizeable group of entrepreneurs was available at the time of her independence. After independence, the State fostered local entrepreneurs with incentives, foreign training and job opportunities and protection. China developed state entrepreneurship and provided managerial education, work ethic, social philosophy and training in the art of enterprise to promising young people. India was fortunate to have a class of indigenous entrepreneurs to establish and promote industries in pre- and after independence and allocated considerable funds to promote selective higher education, technical and managerial skills. Thus, all three countries provided help and support to groom national entrepreneurship that in turn has helped in economic growth. Pakistan did not have any entrepreneurial class at the start, and it took a long time for such a class to appear and was dismantled in the 70's by the socialist regime. Her socio-political structure has been obstructive to the entrepreneurial spirit. Her civil service had no capabilities to manage national enterprises and ended up making them bankrupt. It is possible that the scarcity of entrepreneurship in Pakistan might have played a role in the slowing down of industrial process and economic growth.

Concluding Remarks

The effectiveness of China and South Korea leadership with narrow objectives of industrialisation and equality helped in their rapid transformation. India's semi-effective and Pakistan's ineffective leadership and resulting ineffective states with multiple objectives have failed to match the rapid transformation of other two.

Some economists have claimed that export-oriented strategies of free markets and free international trade have transformed South Korean, Chinese and Indian economies. But a closer look reveals that it was devaluation, direct state investment or numerous support measures including subsidies that helped these countries to industrialise and to become competitive in the international markets. South Korea has not been a 'minimalist state' at any time in its development history and she had already developed a sound industrial base under protection by the time it adopted an export-led strategy. China and India both had already developed their industrial sectors under protection and had reached that level of industrialisation when the opening of trade benefits all trading partners.

The neoliberals claim that free markets, free foreign trade, and less state intervention ensure economic growth in developing countries. Such a claim is hard to sustain. Instead, a central proposition that fits the historical evidence and cannot be refuted is **'that without state intervention industrialisation will be less successful and without industrialisation economic prosperity is an impossible dream'.**

PART 5

UTOPIA: DREAM OF A WELFARE STATE

Up to this point, I have investigated the theory and practice of economic growth and how various countries got rich. I have explained that the poverty can only be eradicated through an industrial transformation. The industrial activities are increasing returns activities, involve division of labour and specialisation that increases productivity and leads to economic growth. The creation of productive capabilities needs investment in new machines with new technology and investment in human capital. The resulting industrial and social structure increase production efficiency and economic growth.

I have explained how an effective leadership and state play an essential role in initiating, promoting industrialisation and why the mainstream economic theory is virtually bankrupt in resolving human poverty.

A positive analysis is bound to have some normative implications. The historical evidence suggests that rich countries have achieved prosperity through industrialisation. If this evidence cannot be refuted then it ought to have some benefit for poor countries like Pakistan.

The previous sections of this book have made certain choices clear which have always existed but not favoured by the corrupt political elites of the poor countries. The founder of Pakistan had visualised that the new country would one day turn into a welfare state. The choices in this chapter can help in realising his dream.

15

PURSUIT OF UTOPIA

Introduction

All shades of economists agree that growth results from increasing productivity but they differ on how to achieve industrial transformation. This study has highlighted these differences in detailing the markets allocation and the State directed economic growth theories. Since 1989 the neoclassical general equilibrium model has dominated the world and the State-directed development theory got forgotten. More recently, however, the East Asian countries economic growth has revived the old debate and this study makes an effort to contribute and by showing a preference for the State role in economic development.

The neoclassical general equilibrium theory of free choice and free markets of goods and factors (within and across borders) does not consider long-term unemployment or poverty as a problem. The price flexibility in the marketplace ensures that there is no surplus or shortage of goods or unemployed factor. **'Get the price right' and hey presto, the poverty will disappear.** The price changes reflect consumers' preferences; producers follow these signals and allocate resources to produce goods and services desired and in exact amount which leads to maximum output and human welfare. The long run equilibrium ensures full employment of resources within and across nations which make poverty disappear. *But unfortunately, things do not work like this in the real world. The beautiful theory cannot face ugly facts of its failures* *like poverty in poor countries and the regular financial meltdown in the capitalist economies.*

The qualitatively different productive activities have been discarded in the supply and demand analysis. The economic structure of poor countries is qualitatively different compared with rich and lacks increasing returns activities and capacities to absorb new investment. The differences in physical and human capabilities lead to differences in economic activities across countries resulting in different economic outcomes. The chip making for computers and shoe polishing are qualitatively different activities and have different dynamic for economic growth, which cannot be assumed away with unrealistic equality of factor-price assumption across borders. The differences in the quality of productive activities provide opportunities for foreign lenders to earn interest usually greater than the rate of returns on investment in new productive capabilities in the poor countries.

The neoclassical theory of development assumes full employment in poor countries where few work and markets are dysfunctional and fail to restore or even move towards any long run equilibrium. Keynes had understood this market failure and had suggested that the State should directly intervene to increase effective demand to cut down unemployment as low-interest rates could not inspire entrepreneurs to invest without profit making opportunities. He had suggested that the State intervention socialises the risk of investment by investing in schools, hospitals, and public goods to create wealth, which increases effective demand, reduces unemployment and increases national output. The foreign economists on their mission to the poor countries do not recognise Keynesian economics or unemployment as a problem and recommend free market system as a default condition for poverty eradication. This study has repeatedly highlighted the inadequacy of the mainstream economics to provide a viable solution to the poverty problem.

The economic history of countries getting rich has provided irrefutable evidence that all of them transformed their economies to an industrial base. The industrial activities are high value-added activities which constitute the key to the process of economic development. The transformation of the economy does not happen naturally or automatically. The 'invisible hand' or 'automatic adjustment' of markets fail because discrepancies exist between social and individual investment returns. The foreign competition from technically advanced countries would destroy infant industries. Mill knew this fact and said so a long time ago. The social and private returns differences make it essential to socialise the risk involved and protect infants' industries from foreign competition. The risk could not be socialised and infant industries cannot be protected without direct or indirect state intervention. In every case, growth has always come from a committed nationalist leadership and resulting effective state which invests and protects (directly or indirectly) productive capabilities for sustained growth.

Over the last three centuries, each country that became rich had a strong, cohesive, and effective state, which used suitable industrial, trade and technologies policies to transform the economy. Friedrick List insight of development process, role 0f effective state, industrialisation under protection, land distribution to change social structure and gradual opening of the markets to take advantage of international specialisation, have turned out to be immensely important to achieve economic prosperity. At the end of WWII, the Marshall Plan was implemented to re-industrialize all countries along the borders of the socialist bloc to avoid the spread of socialism. The fear of socialism played a role, but the realisation that increasing returns activities create higher productivity compared with diminishing returns of agriculture and mining played an even bigger role in aiming for prosperity. The passage from economic ruins to riches was clear in the mind of George Marshall, US Secretary of State and Nobel Peace Prize winner. He knew that higher productivity would lead to higher wages which will result in higher saving, higher investment, and large-scale production with economies of scale. The higher profits will allow the introduction of labour-saving technologies and higher capital-labour ratios in the production processes to generate higher productivity resulting in higher rate of economic growth. The resulting prosperity of labour forces will be the best countermeasure against the spread of socialism in Europe or anywhere else. Keynes had provided the same insight at the end of WWI but no one had listened to him.

All Marshall Plan countries, in time, have become rich, and not a single country had to face the horror of comparative cost advantages and free trade during their development process. In recent times, South Korea and other East Asian countries have followed the Marshall Plan policies to transform their economies. It would be reasonable to think that contrary historical evidence and ugly fact of the recent financial collapse would end the political domination of free trade, free markets, minimum government policies, but the neoliberals continue to ignore the real world and the Listian theory of development to protect capitalist system and market paradigm.

Pakistan Revisited

Pakistan has gone through quite a few political and economic experiments, and each experiment has left nothing but few scars of hopelessness and increasing desperation. The foreign ideas and direct intervention of the international lending agencies in the running of the economy have not done much good to the country. It is therefore high time that the country should start to think for itself, believe in her convictions and take steps to transform its economy and society to provide a decent living for her citizen. It is not an easy job when the odds are against you, but it is not an impossible one as other nations have successfully defeated the odds to achieve prosperity for their citizen.

Pakistan's colonial legacy of subjugation and agrarian economy, social and political structure, corrupt regional minded leadership and dysfunctional institutions have turned it into an ineffective State, where personal interests have taken control of national resources, and national goal of industrialisation for economic prosperity has got lost. She has become a client state of the USA, which uses her and then discards her. The USA changes political regimes in Pakistan at will, and once a regime has served its purpose it is changed with a new regime for a new purpose. Each new regime is aware of its limited life and serves personal and foreign interests at the cost of national interests.

Pakistan in 2016 has no control over its economic management or welfare distributional policies. These are now controlled by the international financing agencies as conditions of providing loans. Her existence is in danger from outside and inside. Her economy is still agrarian with a narrow manufacturing and export base, limited division of labour, and limited knowledge base service sector. The urban economy is unable to exchange requirements of the rural economy. Any increase in agricultural productivity through technology or better input ends up in lower prices in the international markets and does not increase real wages or effective aggregate demand. Pakistan's infrastructure has moderately improved except for energy sector, but her present economic structure has created an unequal distribution of income and wealth and mass unemployment.

Pakistan's human capital has remained underdeveloped, and there is no universal education or a health care programme. Her children either have no school to go or being brainwashed by illiterate religious demagogy. Pakistan's education business factories have no national curriculum or accreditation system and higher education is mostly about liberal arts or social sciences and lacks provisions for the technical and managerial skills. The young people coming out of so-called universities are mostly illiterate, but they have Master degrees obtained by paying hefty fees.

Pakistan's health system has no national plan or assessment of its population needs. There is no effective regulatory regime to monitor the professions or performance. The substandard medications fetch sky-high prices in the market, and poor get robbed of their small savings buying fake drugs. There are probably, one or two good medical schools, but others are simply business factories, and their output is not trustworthy.

Pakistan has a very little technological base, limited basic machine tool industry, dysfunctional heavy industry, narrow industrial base, no tradition of inventions or innovations, and very limited pure or applied research. The private sector is relatively small but operates under imperfect conditions, does not invest in heavy industry or infrastructure sectors, seeks rent and does not pay any taxes. The State is ineffective in all its functions. The present economic structure simply strengthens the existing feudal or semi-feudal interests.

Pakistan has become a heavily indebted nation. Its international debt amount to $80 billion in 2017 and its domestic debt is even of bigger magnitude. The quarterly service charges for the domestic debt amount to Rs 549 billion in 2016 and the service charges for external debts eat up most of the export earning of the country. Her inflation is running in double digit numbers, and her currency is getting worthless. The layman life has become harsh with ever rising prices of essential goods. The increase in energy prices and its non-availability is killing the remaining industries. Above all, her economic management and distributional policies are formulated and dictated by the international loan providing agencies. Pakistan has lost her political and economic sovereignty, and her political elites are mere stooges who serve foreign and personal interests at the cost of national welfare.

Pakistan's past economic policies, except for one decade, were mostly misguided. The foreign economists told Pakistan to invest in comparative cost advantage in agriculture. So, the investment from domestic saving, foreign aid, and loans, went into the development of water resources and agriculture. Any increase in agriculture goods simply ended up in lower international prices and investment in water resources has proved less satisfactory because water flows from Kashmir illegally occupied by hostile India which has been cutting the water supplies on the quiet.

Early on, most of the investment ended up in the development of labour-intensive agriculture processing production with low capital-labour ratio and low productivity. These are diminishing or constant marginal product activities. Such industrialisation did not allow any increase in real wages or aggregate effective demand, and the national product has not grown very much in real term. The small scale industrial units did not raise industrial wages because a large pool of unemployed had existed ready to take up work at any wage rate.

Pakistan is still a poor country, and all economic and social indicators put her among the poorest in the world. She is an ineffective State with limited physical capital, undeveloped human capital, dysfunctional institutions and feudal social structure; these are real causes of her poverty.

The neoliberals of international lending agencies have forcefully argued in Pakistan that industrial development under protection is inefficient, and a waste of national resources and it does not matter if these are state-owned, import substitution or mature technology industries. They claim it is better to sell or close them down because either these are rent seekers or loss maker which cause current account deficit. This argument has forced privatisation in the country which has wiped out most of the country's industrial base. *But the neoliberals' argument is a false one, but no one has challenged it in a serious way in the country.* In most cases, the so-called inefficiencies of national industries are the inefficiency of management and lack of accountability, which can be overcome by installing skilled management and making them accountable for performance. Similarly, the rent seekers surplus could be captured for public or private re-investment. It is important to note that the so-called inefficient industries still produce output and provide jobs with wages, which are higher compared with the rural wages. In such a situation, the closing down of these industries has no justification and amounts to a loss of national capability. The privatisation in Pakistan had destroyed a large number of industrial units in the 90's. Such a destruction of national wealth was a criminal act undertaken to satisfy IMF loans conditions. China did not shut down or destroyed her non-productive industrial plants during her development period.

The 'patents protection' laws can provide a counter-argument to defend the restrictive trade policy for development. The rich justify 'patent protection' laws but not the protection of infant industries when both are rent seeking activities. The infant industries need protection from foreign competition. Once protected these can operating under Schumpeterian-dynamic imperfect competition and generate surpluses for reinvestment. Only an effective state can capture and use the economic surplus for capital formation. It is worth noting that the rich countries produce goods under Schumpeterian imperfect completion which get exported to the world markets. But the Western Economists preach perfect competition to the poor to gain efficiency. It is, however, important to identify industries where long-term protection could result in 'rent-seeking' behaviour. The mature textile, sugar, rice and eating oils industries receive subsidies through subsidised cheap raw materials. If the monopoly rent cannot be captured by these industries then these should face foreign competition which can lead to increased efficiency.

It is interesting to note that when South Korea and China were promoting state-led development and effectively transforming their economies to an industrial base and creating new comparative cost advantages to benefit from trade, Pakistan policies and strategies based on the market led development was taking her to greater dependency and slow national death.

The temporary problems of balance of payment or current account deficit are not the real cause of poverty in Pakistan. These are indeed a symptom of an agrarian economic structure. The poverty is deep rooted in agrarian economies. The narrow industrial and technological base offer few opportunities for inventions or innovations, diversification of professions and division of labour. The limited agriculture specialisation does not contain growth momentum and increasing population is still a problem because agrarian economy suffers from diminishing returns. The slow growth turns negative if the population is growing at the faster rate than the economic growth rate. The domestic saving levels have remained low, and Pakistan relies on foreign handouts of aid and loans to deal with fiscal deficits or public-sector capital formation. The dependency on foreign loans with attached conditions has taken away the control over domestic economic management and distributional policies. The structural changes are needed to take the country out of poverty trap, but IMF and the World Bank imposed policies have already produced negative effects on the economic development in Pakistan and many other poor countries. The history has provided clear evidence that every rich country adopted industrial, trade and technology policies to protect and promote their infant industries. The form and emphases of these policies might have differed, but there is no denying that the industrialisation took place under protection and each state played an effective role in her economic development. Each country emulated and copied the economic structure of wealthy nations. In each case, the Industrial development was matched by human capital and urban development. At the start, each country protected its inefficient industrial sectors and relaxed trade restrictions when higher cost of production got offset by higher wages and increased employment. The European Union has put these ideas into practice in recent times to integrate Spanish and other East European economies.

The trade between the nations on different levels of development destroys the most efficient industries in the least efficient countries. Thus, the timing of relaxation of restrictions on foreign trade can be a factor in success or failure of a nation to benefit from it. An early and rapid opening of markets can de-industrialize and bankrupt countries as it happened in the communist countries and slow late opening can seriously hamper growth as it happened in India. There seems to be a trade-off between freedom to trade and freedom from hunger.

The rich countries mostly exchanged manufactured goods for manufactured goods which have been under dynamic imperfect competition. Their market structures contain large industrial linkages which play a major role in creating new synergies, new institutions, and knowledge intensive services.

Pakistan's pursuit of a welfare state has to start with turning it into an effective state with functional institutions and economic and political sovereignty. The new assertive and effective state would use its authority to direct industry, trade and technology policies to transform economic and social structure to eradicate poverty and find a respectable place among the comity of nations.

Seeking Utopia: Pakistan as a Welfare State

The rich world is still getting richer, safer, and healthier. That is a huge triumph for them. On the other hand, poor are getting poorer, unsafe and unfit. 'Progress is the realisation of Utopias' Oscar Wilde wrote many years ago. The freedom from hunger and healthy life for poor is not an unreasonable utopia. Are these crazy dreams? In my gloom, I tend to think so.

Pakistan must follow rich countries in their historical policies and not dictated one. The 'magic of free markets' is a myth and nothing but a theoretical illusion of human construct. Pakistan faces serious existential issues of corrupt leadership and ineffective state, and unless it can transform its dysfunctional state into an effective one, the poverty reduction would always remain a pipe dream. Pakistan political system of parliamentary democracy polarises the country and provides justification for corruption, macro instability and dysfunctional state institutions. what is the value of political participation or free speech when one has nothing to eat or say? What is the point of freedom of association when there is no affiliation?

The free trade, free market economic paradigm enforcement on poor simply ensures that they have no control over the economic management of their countries. According to JK Galbraith (37,39,40), ' In *rich countries, oligopolistic competitions prevails in the manufacturing industry and power and rent are distributed among the countervailing powers of big business, big labour, and activist government. The poor countries face the reality of perfect competition (agriculture) with no power'*.

Creation of an Effective State

In order to seek utopia, Pakistan needs honest committed nationalist leadership that turn Pakistan into an effective state which would direct appropriate industry, trade, technology and universal education and health policies. The industrialisation and equality of opportunities will create its own dynamic for economic prosperity and improved quality of human life. The appearance of a committed nationalist leadership and resulting effective state would be a miracle to happen.

The poorly constructed Pakistan state got high-jacked by a variety of personalist and sectional forces. British had ruled India as a limited laissez-faire state to keep her as a closed market for the exchange of manufactured goods for raw materials. This necessitated a variety of arrangements with traditional native powers. In the territories, which form present day Pakistan, a feudal class was created to collect revenues and soldiers from the farming families to preserve the colonial rule without any cost. The colonial institutions of civil administration, judiciary, and Army were established to serve colonial interests. These institutions have remained intact in Pakistan being helpful to feudal classes to establish their control over power. The country had not gone through any revolutionary or nationalist movement to gain her freedom and had not produced any nationalist-minded civil or military ruler who might have sought to change the inherited administrative, economic or social structures of society. Pakistan's feudal class and ex-colonial institutions have moulded each other to serve their mutual interests. Pakistan has turned into a federal state and her regions are divided on ethnic and language basis. In consequence, the society and country have been fragmented and polarised. Pakistan Army is the only national force to bind the country together at present.

Pakistan's present economic structure is still mostly agrarian with a minor industrial base consisting of import substitution, basic technology and small industrial units. Such an economic system is consistent with a type of advanced feudal social structure, where ruling Mafia extracts economic surpluses from both countryside and cities but does not give back anything in higher wages or tax revenues to the society. The 'parasitic' political system is called democracy in Pakistan.

Pakistan military has intervened three since 1947 to protect the State from the failures of social and political forces and to create workable economic and political conditions. But each time, it failed to become an agent of change to create an effective State to transcend from its ineffective character. Each army regimes lost organisational cohesion and advantage of being 'above' politics and had to negotiate with opposition to internalise social patronages and cleavages. This failure is a direct result of ex-colonial institutions, USA control over civil and military regimes and lack of radical ideas or political movements. South Korea was more fortunate in this respect that its Army created a more cohesive capitalist state by altering the class basis and organisational character and coerced and cooperated with local entrepreneurs to make them work in national interests.

Pakistan's political parties are personal properties of their corrupt leaders, who have no national aspirations or reasons to bring any change. Over time, no social class such as capitalists or labour force has emerged to push for a change. The old feudal class has turned into pre-industrial capitalist to strengthen their hold on power and has repeatedly appropriated the State for personal enrichment. In consequence, Pakistan suffers from frequent macroeconomic instability, policy inconsistencies, and lack of long run ambitions to build its economic and technological capabilities. The policy implementations process is haphazard and fails to provide clear signals to economic agents for them to undertake investment decisions. The State directed economic activities have channelled public resources into corrupt private interests in the past, and more recently the State role has become marginal. In the introductory chapter of this study, I have stated that the people of Pakistan are aware of the corrupt leadership and ineffective State, which serves personal interests of the political elite at their expense. But they do not know who is going to bring change to the socio-political-economic structure of their country? Are they waiting for Allah to initiate such a change? Cristiana Lamb said that much in her book on Pakistan. In early days of 2017, the people of Pakistan had built up high hopes that the country Prime Minister would be declared corrupt and disqualified from the office by the Supreme Court of the country. The history of Supreme Court ruling does not give me any confidence to believe that would happen. This time the Supreme Court has not obeyed the wishes of the powerful and has disqualified the Prime Minister but his appointee has taken his place and his party still rule the country. There is one political leader, IK, who stand tall among the pigmies. He is honest and has the determination to change things, but he heads a political party which is right of the centre and wishes to reform rather than change. This may be a ploy to stop foreign intervention in the country politics or may be a political conviction. I have no way to know. But if he does become a President or a Prime Minister and keeps the status co, he would fail just like army regimes to bring any fundamental change in the country.

I have now identified the forces that can turn Pakistan into an effective State. These are namely, a nationalist committed leader who would turn dysfunctional institutions into functional and change the political system of parliamentary democracy. A mass nationalist movement to over-through existing power bases. The political parties which would put nation above personal interests and have a narrow objective of industrialisation with equality of opportunities. A centralised power of the Armed Services. Given the history of people, literacy levels, social structure, religious ties and nature of political parties, it is not very likely that a political or social revolution or a mass nationalist movement can take place anytime soon. The change in the objectivity or nature of political parties is not likely to happen as long as these remain personal properties of their leaders. Given low literacy levels, social structure and subjugated nature of people, the absence of any popular and organised nationalist or revolutionary movements or purposeful political parties, who is likely to become an agent of change to mend fragmented society and establish an effective State with functional institutions. There is only one possibility left, the centralised power of the Armed Services, which can become an agent of change to transform social and political structure to make Pakistan an effective and cohesive State. For this to happen, Pakistan military has to produce a General like Park Chung Hee of Korea or Atta-Turk of Turkey, who would have nationalist ideas, be free from foreign dictates and be determined to change the social, political, and economic structure of the country. The military can also back IK who is truly honest and a committed nationalist to serve as a President with a group of talented Pakistanis as a functionary. He would need to follow a systematic, prolong programme to achieve such a transformation. The following steps can prove useful for a committed leader to transform a failing country to revive and march on a road to recovery.

a. Suspension of all political participation for a long enough period to establish a presidential system with absolute power. Ban all present and past politicians and their relatives ever to take part in the running of the country in any shape or form.

b. Confiscation of all land and its free distribution among landless farmers on a long lease to gain their support and improve productivity in the agriculture sector. Such a policy would create an equal social structure and end power base of the feudal class. There should be an upper limit on the allotted land on the East Asian countries experience.

c. Sack all corrupt civil service officials and retrain others to make them capable of serving national interests. There should be accountability for all public employees. The civil servants should be re-trained in entrepreneurship, risk taking and technical and managerial capabilities to manage public businesses.

d. The introduction of universal education and health care programmes under public control with common national curriculum and accreditation system.

e.   Reconstruction of state institutions on Japanese and South Korean model.

f.   Control of media to get rid of anti-state elements and to promote nationalism and state policies on national integration.

g.   Have an industrial, trade and technology programme on Korean lines and enforce it in the public and private sectors. Control and coerce all large business houses to work for national interests by re-investing monopoly profits to expand the industrial sector.

h.   Pay off all foreign debts, refuse all aid and loans in future and kick out all foreign-financed NGOs in the country.

i.   Introduce national service for all 18 years to inculcate national identity and nationalism which should help in dealing with regionalism, race and caste issues. The national service time should train young for army duties as well as professional skills.

j.   Use nationalism and incentives to encourage and promote internal migration from over populated to less populated regions to overcome negative forces of regionalism and multiple interests.

k.   Enter in defence agreements with the regional powers that share interests with Pakistan and develop defence technology and industry to become self-sufficient in the defence needs of the country. This objective takes priority over all other objectives.

These proposals present a tall order but 25 years should provide enough time to establish a strong central authority to pursue long-term development and equity objectives. The process of creating an effective state is difficult, complex and often requires the use of force to impose a preferred design. Incremental changes do not work. The new regime would need to rise above the existing social and political patterns to launch an industrial and social revolution (i.e. land reform, industrialisation, human capital development and functional institutions) to create an effective modern State.

The land redistribution takes priority as it can increase agriculture productivity and lay down the foundation for an equal society. The socio-economic context can be altered by land redistribution, mobilising resources, channelling them into priority areas, and by undertaking direct economic activities, which requires the State power and commitment.

The State can follow either China or South Korea allocation model. If it selects Korean model then it can coerce and cooperate with the entrepreneurial class to make them work in the national interests, control labour wage demands, rebuild public institutions, and set course for rapid industrialisation of the country. The State must be disciplined and disciplining and support cooperating entrepreneurs and silence those who might detract from the narrow goal of industrialisation and rapid growth. It must harness all sources of power in the society and use authoritarian control and ideological mobilisation as a strategy to achieve objectives. The State should mobilise resources and utilise power in a purposeful way. One way to achieve this is to redefine national security as an essential component of rapid industrialisation like it was done in South Korea. Pakistan faces a permanent external threat from India and from other countries which could be used to raise nationalist feeling and unity of purpose. Nationalism has always played an essential role in economic development. The wish for a strong country and security of future generations is a strong motivating force. All European countries had used nationalism to emulate each other. Adam Smith had shown his nationalist feelings when he stated that the USA should not industrialise but remain an agrarian economy because it has a comparative advantage in producing agriculture goods. Frederick List was a European nationalist and was an early proponent of a united Europe. Nationalism requires and promotes industrialisation and it can help in establishing mutually beneficial relations with other nations.

The poverty in Pakistan is a direct result of corrupt leadership and an ineffective State which has failed to transform the economy to an industrial base. the industrialisation can change the socio-political structure and cultural values. Marx had said that much when he stated that it is an economic structure which brings changes to the political and social structure of a country. JJ Meyen (80) had described the same process in 1769 by stating *'that primitive nations do not improve their custom and habits to find useful industries, but the other way around.'* The habits and customs change with the mode of production. What distinguishes the long-term success from the continuing failures is pragmatic national leadership. When programmes fail, an effective state can terminate them and tries something else with ease. Different successful countries (i.e. China and South Korea) both used pragmatism to transform their economic structures resulting in changes in social structures, a large variety of institutions, habits, customs and other values. The sustained investments can create complex networks of interdependencies that can lead to high productivity and high income.

The colonial legacy is highly resilient and influential and difficult to dismantle. South Korea and China, both in their ways, destroyed their political structure to achieve industrialisation and economic development. India failed to change its political and social structure and has paid the price in term of slow growth rate and huge rural poverty. If Park Chung Hee of Korea was able to build an efficacious cohesive capitalist state and put his country on a trajectory of rapid industrialisation and growth, so can the ambitious new regime with will in Pakistan. Such a will should be there, as the survival of Pakistan and armed services are interdependent.

Having described the most difficult task which Pakistan must undertake, the task to turn Pakistan into a welfare State becomes relatively a simple one although new barriers such as patent laws and restrictive trade policies have been enforced by the rich countries to the industrialisation of poor countries. Pakistan needs to emulate industry, trade, and technology policies of rich and strong nations. There are many variations of these policies which can be used to achieve economic prosperity. Here is my take on policies and strategies that can help Pakistan to deal with her persistent poverty.

Industry, Trade and Technology Policies

Pakistan needs to follow Listian ideas and reject the Washington Consensus laissez-faire policies which enrich rich at the expense of poor. The experience of last two decades has shown that the neoliberal economic paradigm has failed to deliver economic development and has ended up increasing poverty and inequality in the poor countries. Weisbrot et al. (146) have described the negative effects of these policies on the growth rates of poor countries. Stiglitz (133,134) has described misery caused in the former socialist economies of East Europe as a result of the Washington Consensus policies.

The WTO agreements on foreign trade are current day version of old colonial 'unequal trade treaties' which had put colonies in a no-win situation by taking away their rights to manage their trade policies. The implementation of the structural reforms and poverty alleviation programmes do the same job and deprive poor of their control over economic management and distribution policies. The good historical policies of rich have become bad policies for the present-day poor.

This study has meshed up enough historical evidence to support Listian development theory of economic development. Which consists of strong, effective state with policies such as public intervention in the economy to initiate, develop and support rapid industrialisation, strong domestic technology base, and a restrictive foreign trade policy to protect infant industries. The other essential Listian policies support human capital development in the public sector, land redistribution and gradual relaxation of trade restriction. These are the policies which have been used time and again to achieve economic prosperity in different countries of the world. The detailed measures related to each policy have varied over time from country to country and have become more complex and effective over time. However, the general pattern has remained intact. Pakistan does not need to reinvent the wheel; it simply needs to follow Listian development model and emulate rich countries to eradicate her poverty.

The main issue is how to transform the economy to increasing returns or higher value- added activities, the magic ingredient of the economic development process. The shift from an agrarian to an industrial economy does not occur automatically because of human sentiments about future, imperfect information, disparities between public and private returns on investment and a number of other reasons. The imaginary long-run adjustment of the mainstream economics does not happen anytime soon and 'we are all dead in the long run'. Keynes had said it in the second half of the last century. The 'infant industry' can be wiped out by the foreign competition if the unrestricted trade was allowed. Pakistan should set a narrow goal of comprehensive industrialisation for her national planning. A central planning authority (current planning commission is useless) should be entrusted with the mobilisation of resources to invest directly and indirectly in physical and human capital development. Land redistribution will increase productivity in agriculture to provide a surplus for industrial development. The State institutions remodelled on Japanese and South Korean institutions will improve their effectiveness and functionality. South Korea transformed its socioeconomic structure and created an effective, cohesive capitalist state. She invoked nationalism, re-distributed land, invested heavily in education, skill training and health care, and coerced entrepreneurs to put nation before self-interest. She developed local supplies chains and created equality of opportunities based on meritocracy. She made a massive investment in comprehensive industrial development, put restrictions on foreign trade, allowed domestic competition based on a dynamic Schumpeterian view of market driven 'creative destruction', and imported cutting edge technology to grow and achieve self-sufficiency in technology. She also allowed the emergence of imperfect markets with large profits and captured them for further investment in industries. South Korea growth model can be emulated in Pakistan.

Industrialisation and Foreign Trade

Pakistan is a large country of about 180 million people. It can sustain comprehensive industrialisation containing heavy, intermediate and final goods industries. The heavy industries and machines and tool making capabilities are essential for developing a technological base. There is also a strong case for establishing and protecting high value-added industries with rapidly changing technology. The heavy industry provides input for other industries, and high value-added industries help to create highest possible productivity, imperfect competition, monopoly profits, large tax revenue and large surpluses for reinvestment and economic growth. The imperfect competition avoids waste of resources and production with economies of scale and division of labour. South Korea intentionally allowed the imperfect market structure to shape its development path and then aligned the vested interests of private sectors with the national interests of the country. Industrialisation under protection may be less efficient, but import duties provide funds for further industrial development and create productive capabilities and diversification in production structure. The sound industrial base widens exports base and enables the country to benefit from the relaxation of foreign trade restrictions. Economic diversification maximises the number of professions in an economy and creates synergies. Diversity in economic structure creates tolerance, choice of selection between products, technologies and management/organisational methods and encourages balanced development.

Pakistan has already established some agriculture-based import substitution and mature technology industries with end-product manufacturing or processing, but her industrial development should be comprehensive. She has failed to establish successful heavy or export-oriented industries with high-income elasticity and low transport cost. The sustained growth depends on heavy and export-oriented industries with forwarding and backwards linkages, specialisation and complementarities. The main arguments against the comprehensive industrialisations policy are the size of the market and the opportunity costs, but these are bogus arguments. Pakistan is a large market compared with South Korea or a number of other countries, and industrialisation creates new comparative costs advantages and new markets. The long-run benefits from the industrialisation wipe out the short-term opportunity costs over time. The export-oriented industries usually lag behind the development of heavy industries but contain activities with high-quality characteristics such as new knowledge, new technology and high market value. These industries have high R&D contents, learning by doing processes and large indivisible investment with economies of scale in branded products. A policy of industrial concentration, product innovation, linkages and synergies can establish these industries successfully.

Pakistan's past development strategy of comparative cost advantage led to heavy investment in the agriculture sector with diminishing returns activities. The policy maker believed that an increase in the output of cotton, rice, and fruits would earn large foreign exchange for the country and will pay for the imports and surplus funds for reinvestment. This strategy has not worked as any increase in the raw materials potential earnings was eaten up by the adverse terms of trade. Pakistan needs a new strategy of growth, based on increasing return activities. For example, taking cotton textile to its value-added end of garments manufacturing can increase productivity that will raise real wages, but this has not happened in Pakistan. The real wages have remained stagnant because of the large unemployed labour force. Pakistan new comprehensive industrial policy should set up new industries, upgrade existing technology and industrial units, and control wage rates. But such controls become impossible task with double digit inflation in the country. There is considerable scope in expanding food processing, pulp, papers, wood, plywood, cement, chemicals, pharmaceuticals, aluminium, energy, materials, biotechnology, plastic and petroleum refining facilities. The new industrial policy should plan development in different phases and each following phase should build on the previous one. Every country has to go through certain stages as no country can directly move from hunting stage to supersonic aircraft production stage. Some industrial units will consist of certain minimum size and diversity which can bridge some of the development phases. Synthetic fibres and plastic represent import substitution aimed at the upstream of export industries. Synthetic include rayon, nylon, plastic including PVC, benzenes, xylene, fertilisers, lubricating oil, naphtha cracker, synthetic rubber, and many other products. The development of these industries might require joint ventures or production under licensing from advanced countries.

The heavy industries must include an efficiently integrated steel mill and mini steel mills to cater for specialised products. The mini steel mills with the latest technology will provide high-quality speciality steels and alloys to avoid their imports. The current steel mill is an integrated one which can be updated and made profitable with the production of flat products and tubes. Just a few years back, this public enterprise was quite successful and was making a reasonable return on investment, so what has gone wrong? In simple word, the ruling elites have appointed incompetent managers to serve their interests. Such practices have to be weeded out.

Other industries such as machine tools, automobiles, electronics, shipbuilding, basic metals, nuclear, weapons, electrical, plastics, and synthetics fibres will provide a reasonable Industrial base. Pakistan has some of these industries, but most of them are final assembly point. The foreign companies should bring technology if they wish to operate in Pakistan. Pakistan's machine tool makers are small in size, with little financial resources and use antiquated machines. This industry must be developed to produce technologically advanced component to meet the country's security needs as well as to sell defence goods in the international markets. Pakistan has already got a couple of automobiles assembly companies, which use a certain percentage of domestic components' in assembling. However, the engines and gearboxes still come from abroad, and there is no export of automobiles or commercial vehicles from the country. Pakistan remains a last stage assembly facility. At Present, the country does not have a coherent plan for this industry and provides no assistance beyond protection to assemblers. Pakistan is a large market; it must establish domestic capacities to produce engines, gear boxes, automobiles, commercial (i.e. trucks and buses), tractors and other agriculture machinery. The production of engines and gearbox is essential for the industry to grow. The assemblers who have made a huge amount of money should have incentives to find a partner to build and operate complete automobile plant in the country to meet domestic and potential foreign demand. A local firm produces tractors under licence but still imports engines from abroad.

The agriculture machines production would help agriculture to develop and increase its productivity. Similarly, shipbuilding capability is crucial for the national defence and future trade. The development of an integrated information industry linking semiconductor, computers, software and telecommunication is essential to building technological competence in electronics to serve national defence needs. The industrialisation requires energy industries to meet its demand. The development of hydro, solar and nuclear power for base load is cost effective. The multi-fuel plants (i.e. coal, gas and oil) can meet the peak demand. See (120 a) for a comprehensive analysis of the Pakistan energy sector.

The successful industrialisation requires parallel investment in human capital. A programme of universal education will greatly enhance human capabilities. The technical skills and professional capabilities take priority. There is a need to establish centres of excellence in engineering, pure sciences, technology, biotechnology, medicines, and managerial and professional skills with highest standards like the LUMS in Lahore. The resources going to liberal arts and social sciences facilities may require reassessment. The expanding industries would require trained and competent manpower to manage them and to compete internationally. The development of schools, hospitals, ports and stations around manufacturing sectors are effective and create real assets as long as the process is a dynamic one. Europe at the end of WWII had adopted such a strategy of development.

Capital Formation

An effective state is always able to mobiles mass resources to transform economy and society. China and South Korea provide strong evidence to support this claim, although they took two different routes to do so.

An effective Pakistan state should be able to use numerous policy measures to transfer resources to initiate, support and establish comprehensive industrialisation. A land redistribution programme can increase agriculture productivity and transfer of resources for industrial sector development. Alfred Marshall had suggested that a nation should tax diminishing returns (raw materials) activities and pay a subsidy to increasing returns (industry) economic activities. Most industrialised nations have used agriculture surplus to finance industrial development. The industries operating under imperfect competition can generate huge surpluses which can provide funds for reinvestment in the country. There are a large number of cartels in Pakistan such as sugar, cement, fertilisers, cooking oils, automobile assemblers, etc., which are making monopoly profits but do not pay any taxes. Their surpluses can be taxed by an effective State to finance other industries. Besides both fiscal and monetary policy measures are available to support investment. The monetary measures like positive interest rates can encourage national saving and the money supply can increase commercial credit to support investment.

Pakistan can use overseas remittances amounting to at least $19 billion per annum by effectively controlling its capital markets, and by preventing the illegal outflow of foreign exchange. In addition, secure investment opportunities to Pakistani settled in rich countries can increase foreign exchange availability. The details of productive projects, secured returns, support with build up factories and security to take profits back can act as incentives for the overseas Pakistani origin entrepreneurs to invest and bring their capital, technology, and management experiences to benefit the country. Such schemes have been successful in India and China, and there is no reason why these could not work in Pakistan.

Pakistan can also allow foreign countries to invest in selected industries to benefit from new technology and managerial experiences. China has already shown willingness to invest in

Pakistan and other Asian countries can be encouraged with suitable incentives to do the same. The industrial policies are not neutral and are difficult to formulate. The R&D policy is helpful for some industries such as pharmaceutical and chemical industries but has no impact on others such as printing industry. The creation of national clusters is helpful and the linkages between urban and rural activities crucial because of their qualitative differences. It is the bonding of these divergent activities that create a successful economy.

Management of the Foreign Trade

An agrarian economy exposed to international free trade has no chance to transform into an industrial one. The tariff duties provide protection as well as generate surplus funds for industrial expansion. Most countries pursuing industrialisation had used a 'cascading' structure of protection, with a total ban on final goods, lower protection on intermediates and complete exemption for the raw materials. Pakistan would need to use intelligence and may be boldness in emulating the protectionist trade policies. A country can use various policy measures to protect its industries. It can completely ban the import of goods, levy heavy tariffs on imports or nontariff barriers, local content requirements, foreign exchange controls and subsidies to domestic industries for export promotions. Tariff controls have the added benefit to raise revenues for further industrial expansion. The trade controls can reduce trade surpluses/deficits with selected countries and sometimes these can act as a substitute for diplomatic relations.

The tariff duties on export can be given back, deferred, or exempted. The raw materials and intermediate goods such as machines can be rebated or exempted. The raw materials imports are exempted from duties to serve domestic or export demand. The machinery and equipment not manufactured within the country can be imported free of import duties. The capital goods for such industries as iron and steel, machines tools, chemicals, electrical engineering, electronics, automobiles, shipbuilding, and petrochemicals and others should have low import duties to reduce the cost of building 'productive capabilities'. Once the country is ready for the international competition, the duties can be relaxed.

In the start of liberalisation process, an integrated trade and industrial policy can impose origin or agency restrictions to avoid real competition. Machinery items, which are possible to manufacture locally, can be subjected to origin or agency restrictions where imports are allowed by the end users but not dealers which ensure that windfalls go to producers in the hope that they will use it more productively than the dealers. The entitlement to import goods for sale can have restrictions imposed. Import licences can be used to restrict trade. The allocation of import licences to exporters can be designed to ensure that those who can get the windfalls from importing scarce commodities contribute to the economic development of the country. The licensing system can be used to promote selected industries. Sometimes product designs or specifications are used to control imports of specific goods. Some countries have used local content requirements to foster backwards linkages in some sectors, including autos, televisions, refrigerators, air conditioners, and diesel engines and it is especially important in direct foreign investment agreements.

The central bank can decide to hold all foreign exchange reserves and not allow commercial banks, private firms or citizen to hold them. The control over foreign currencies reserves provides a mean to ensure that foreign exchange does not get used for disapproved purposes such as currency speculation, unproductive investment abroad and taking foreign exchange out of the country to deposit in foreign banks or imports of restricted items. By controlling foreign currencies reserves, the central bank can channel these into productive investment through various means to safeguard domestic capital markets.

The State can subsidise directly or provide incentives such as tax holidays or concessions to promote export. The methods of export stimulation include export credit, export cartels, quality control, and provision of marketing information, export awards, and export requirements in the fiscal investment incentive schemes.

The management of foreign direct investment is a part of trade controls. The Washington Consensus policies enforce opening of capital markets on the ground that with low savings and investment levels the poor countries should allow inflow of capital. However, things are not that straightforward. Foreign direct investment is made up of 'portfolio equity investment' which seeks highest returns by influencing the management on a regular basis. The direct foreign equity can create asset bubbles which can make downturns worse. The poor must emulate the rich who had always protected their currencies and economies from foreign investment. The USA does it even at present time. The only time one should seek foreign direct investment is, when it meets the requirement of industrialisation programme and brings cutting edge technology. But this does not happen very often. To conclude, a state has a large number of policy measures at its disposal to manage its foreign trade and use trade controls to achieve its narrow objective of industrialisation. The task has become that much difficult as the WTO agreements make it impossible for poor to protect industrialisation programme.

Urban Regeneration and Development

Industrialisation leads to urbanisation of the societies and unplanned urban settlement could lead to nightmare situations. Urban slums could generate resentment and increased unequal societies. The eradication of poverty must aim to provide better living conditions to improve the quality of life.

The central planning authority can support local bodies in large cities and towns to develop local development plans for both services and productive activities. The services such as education, health, clean water and sewerage, old age and orphan care can be assessed and provided by the local bodies which can also help local businesses to expand and the surrounding rural agriculture to mechanise.

The local initiatives can create employment opportunities for all young school leavers. Similarly, urban development and regeneration responsibilities should rest with the local bodies which can cooperate with large real estate groups to regenerate or develop sustainable energy efficient new cities. These bodies can acquire land under compulsory purchase; create city wealth funds to tap local saving, use property and business taxes, and certain types of sales taxes to raise funds to finance local services and projects.

The housing schemes can be undertaken either directly by the local bodies or indirectly and costs could be recovered in instalments. Such local developments will transform these cities into garden cities, and Pakistan would get rid of its slums and shanty towns. Urban developments can support rural activities developments with ready markets for mutual benefits.

Agriculture Sector

In poor countries like Pakistan, the transformation of agriculture sector is as important as the establishment of the industrial sector. The agriculture is the dominant sector. It can provide an economic surplus for the industrial development and can make an important contribution to overall growth and poverty reduction in the country. The transformation of agriculture sector will involve changes in the mode of production, new technology, new economic organisation and new investment to generate a sustained increase in agriculture productivity. The agriculture development history of nations provides the following conditions for the successful transformation of the agriculture sector.

a. An effective State exists with functional local government institutions and a climate of political and macroeconomic stability. This is essential for peaceful enforcement of land distribution policies.

b. The National land has been distributed on a long lease and the farmers have the security of tenancy and can benefit from their hard work and risk taking.

c. An effective technology transfer system has been established which can take new research and messages to the majority of farmers in the country.

d. Access to lucrative expanding national markets which make agriculture a profitable business.

e. Employment creating and expanding industrial sector to absorb increasing surplus agriculture labour result of increased agriculture productivity. The labour wage rate in non-agriculture must be higher than agriculture to provide incentives for labour mobility.

All conditions must hold for the successful transformation. If one or more conditions fail to hold the agriculture development can occur but the rate of development can slow down a great deal. In China and South Korea, all five conditions prevailed to transform their agriculture sectors, which have played a positive and supporting role in the overall economic development and in the reduction of poverty. In India and Pakistan, these conditions failed to happen and in consequence, the agriculture sectors of both countries have not played any role in the economic development or poverty reduction.

The creation of an effective state in Pakistan would ensure that some of the above-given conditions are already satisfied. The industrialisation would ensure that conditions d and e are satisfied. The condition c can be met by changing the existing systems of agriculture colleges and departments. The reorganisation of land ownership can lead to greater productivity, surpluses of food and cash crops, level playing fields, and an efficient support mechanism to improve the quality of life immensely in rural areas. The effective state can immediately embark on land redistribution which should revoke all inherited land rights and transfer national land to landless families on a long lease with an upper ceiling. The existing landed classes should not be allowed to redistribute their land among relatives and family members to keep their power base intact. Such policy will win public support for the regime and smallholding cultivation of foods, and cash crops will lead to greater efficiency to create a surplus to be invested in industrial development. These improvements will transform the country from a 'backwards' and neglected land into a prosperous country, where young would wish to stay and build their future.

In order to achieve successful agriculture transformation, it is crucial that Pakistan's inspects its soil with the greatest possible care to explore and assess all agriculture, and mining possibilities. Every single type of plant should be experimented to see its adaptability to the country. No effort or money expense should be spared to discover mineral resources. All efforts should be made to use raw material and minerals resources for manufacturing development within the country. There is no justification to import raw material that is available locally. But the raw materials which are not available should be imported and used to manufacture final goods. The country must get along with the domestic production to get into the habit of self-sufficiency. The traditional agriculture sector must be transformed from independent dirt- poor farmers eating the food they grew to commercial farmers and farming societies, growing crops primarily for sale. The transformed agricultural will have high specialisation and complex networks of interdependent individuals, schools, businesses, industries, research institutions, and state agencies. The commercial farmers will be much more dependent on finance, other businesses, and the State. The farm co-operative societies and irrigation associations should be encouraged to accelerate the spread of technical knowledge, use of agriculture machinery and promotion of better seeds and use of fertiliser. These societies can also be organised to take advantage of large holding crops where there are sufficient organisational economies of scale to be reaped.

The state should develop transport infrastructure, cheap credit facilities for irrigation schemes, establish agriculture research and teaching institutions for the farmers training. The existing institutions have to be made aware of new development needs to train manpower accordingly. The training programmes could be tailor made to meet short or long- run needs. The targeted research must provide a solution to agriculture diseases and improved seeds for crops yield improvement. The basic and advanced agriculture-related research is essential to avoid becoming slaves to GM seed suppliers like Monsanto of USA. Given the climate changes of recent times which are going to impact Pakistan greatly, it is crucial that water management should become a top priority which would require the building of numerous large and small dams to store excessive rains and floodwater.

Some policy measures such as price controls on agriculture input and output and fixed exchange rate policy can be employed to extract agriculture surplus to invest in agriculture-based industries. The State support and incentives can help in developing agriculture-based industries such as food processing, textiles, pulp and paper, sugar, chemical fertilisers and tobacco industries.

The rural education and housing development with sanitation, clean water, and solar energy will bring the rural population to 21st-century living and would stop the huge migration to urban areas or foreign countries. The surplus farm labour can provide labour and national financial institutions cheap credit payable in easy instalments, to rebuild rural Pakistan. The rural housing development will reduce rural unemployment to a large extent and slow down rural migration.

Concluding Remarks

The current pre-capitalist economic structure in Pakistan can be transformed by the simultaneous implementation of land distribution, universal education, and industrialisation. The new nationalist leadership and the effective state can formulate and implement policies to eradicate poverty. The mindsets and institutions change rapidly with a change in economic structure. The mode of production changes the century-old habits and customs of societies within a short period. Again, one can look at the new China and South Korea and the habits and custom of their citizens and how quickly the old ways has given way to the new way of living.

The heavy investment in infrastructure and industrialisation under protection will increase employment. The internal migration, housing development and free trade within national borders would bring about unity among the regional ethnic forces. Free movement of people and goods will promote harmony, and cut down disparity between urban-rural areas. The critical mass of industries with new technology can increase productivity and open a way for economic expansion. The consumers could turn into self-employed producers and help in reducing unemployment. Keynes had suggested 'deficit financing' to deal with ineffective demand, and Schumpeter had provided a solution in term of a cluster of innovations in time. The process of economic transformation usually creates Schumpeterian imperfect competitive markets for new industries. Labour wages in these markets should rise provided a share of higher productivity gets allocated to them. The higher industrial wages will increase effective demand, but it should not be allowed to suck in imports. The higher effective demand for domestic products will encourage further economic activities in the economy. The rich nation's economic history provides many lessons for the poor countries. The US had used a policy of economic boycott of foreign goods around 1812 and her industrial development mushroomed to create a critical mass to establish a vast system of manufacturing. Such a policy can be a 'blueprint' for economic development.

I have almost reached my destination. I have laid bare the process of economic development with three hundred years of economic thinking, historical evidence on the practice of economic development and how rich countries got rich. This insight, I have used to suggest what Pakistan needs to do if she wishes to become strong and prosper nation. Such a transformation is a complex task and given the present socio-political and economic conditions prevailing in the country; I have turned gloomy about her prospects to ever eradicating poverty or to gain respect among the comity of nations. I am not sure that Pakistan judiciary could act as an agent of change when its history is laced with compromises and subservient nature. Moreover, the replacement of a corrupt leader with another corrupt incompetent does not bring a real change.

I see very little chance of Pakistan becoming an effective State. She requires a revolution to transform her social, political, and economic structure as well as reconstruction of her institutions. There is no revolutionary or nationalist movement in the country which could bring about the desired revolution. The nature of the political parties and the quality of their Leadership is only capable of serving their personal interests. In future, they may tinker with the system, but they would never replace it as it serves their interests. There is no universal education or health care and no land distribution to create an equal society or productive capability. I have expressed my hope that one day, Pakistan Army may produce a leader like Park Chung Hee or Atta-Turk to take Pakistan to its destination. They can back IK but I do not think they will do that. A truly great Leader comes only once in generations. Pakistan's previous experience of Army rule and the Army's current involvement in political and economic affairs does not give me any confidence to build any hope for the near future, and yet I must hope that Army or by luck a political party would produce such a leader because giving up, simply makes existence difficult. Land distribution, restriction on foreign trade, universal education and health systems, complicated industrial development and reliance on domestic resources and sacrifice of present consumption to have more in future are difficult policies and that elusive leadership where will it come from? I must not accept defeat and lose sight that people of Pakistan can bring a change and yet I don't see how that change will come.

The formation of suitable industrial and trade policies is difficult, and long-term management of economy requires sharp minds, selfless commitment, and abundance of enterprise, and disciplined skilled labour force. The adaptation of trade protection policies, when you are dependent on foreign aid and loans and part of WTO agreements, is virtually impossible, and yet it has been done by others. The State has to be bold and strong to defy international pressures to industrialise under protection. Single most important policy to get out of poverty is to build productive capabilities in manufacturing because these activities are higher productivity activities which generate economic growth. The long run national objectives conflict with short-term personal objectives of the ruling elites which require the sacrifice of present needs to improve the future national prosperity. The industrialisation is time-consuming and can take quite a long time to bear fruit. It is worth pointing out that the Toyota took almost 30 years to become competitive and profitable in the international markets. Pakistan is in short supply of main ingredients required for industrialisation, and her macro policy decisions reflect on the short-term self-interest of the corrupt political elite who are happy to accept conditional international loans from the international agencies which provide opportunities to lace their pockets.

The selection of correct industries for development and management of imperfect markets 'need intelligence and commitment. Pakistani people are intelligent and hardworking and are no worse than others, who has established and managed industrialisation successfully. Forget the free market, free trade, the comparative cost advantage of agriculture, discounting of future and the post-industrial economy touts or who preach development of services. Manufacturing is the most important and proven way to create wealth and eradicate poverty. The services sector development can only play a limited role in the economic development of poor countries. The knowledge-based services like finance management, pharmaceutical and IT are highly productive but high salaries in these services do not spread to the rest of the economy or increase overall effective demand to increase economic development. whereas most other services are low productivity activities. India provides a prime example of this fact where large salaries in software and pharmaceutical have failed to make any impression on the mass poverty of Indian people. The new technology induced higher productivity has led to higher profits and not higher wages and increasing inequality in the advanced countries.

The policy of high-interest rates raises the cost of investment for the poor to discourage them from the manufacturing route. The imperialists of yesterday are back in new clothes. They have the power to change regimes to safeguard their economic interests. They have international agencies such as IMF, the World Bank, the WTO, and the regional financial institutions, which impose their policies on the poor, to take away their economic sovereignty and exploit their markets. They have their aid budgets, bilateral free trade agreements, and investment agreements to block poor from industrialisation. They have created loyal classes within poor countries to side with their interests. They have WTO agreements to enslave poor, and they have new international copyrights and universal patent laws, which have made reverse engineering impossible and have increased the percentage of share of royalties in the world trade and widen the gap between the rich and poor nations. They have already extended pharmaceutical patents rights for almost 28 years through data protection as a part of free trade agreements. They force poor to open their capital markets for their speculations and financial crises prone. The enforcement of free markets, free trade and free movement of capital, imprisons poor in their current production activities as markets are very good at preserving the status quo. They have money to finance NGO's to fragment societies and demand that poor should not be allowed to use extra policy tools for protection such as subsidies and regulation, as this constitutes unfair competition. They say get rid of all protective barriers and make everyone compete on an equal footing, but they do not look at the difference in the players' capabilities and do not allow access to their cutting-edge technologies in the name of national security. Why are they otherwise enforcing their patent laws?

Also, technological landscape is changing. The 'factor biased' technologies are more suited to the scale and can make development uneven. Similarly, some technological breakthrough may be impossible to copy or replicate. The mass scale manufacturing by robots may not allow wages to increase to increase effective demand and economic growth. These conditions are already appearing in some industrialised countries where wages have become stagnant and where increasing automation in manufacturing and decentralised franchising has weakened the labour bargaining power in the marketplace. The new information technologies have changed innovation processes and these are applied in poor countries to lower prices and wages. The collapse of Soviet Union in 1989, waning labour power, and China's rapid upgrading of technology have put downward pressures on wages in the international markets with implications for labour wages in the poor countries. If the poor cannot increase wages to increase effective demand, the economic development becomes that much more difficult to achieve. The decline in transport costs has made matter worse for the poor. The neoliberals reject Keynesian solution of increasing effective demand to deal with the stagnant economy and promote monetary policy and automatic market adjustment mechanism to the forefront of economic policy. The financial crisis of 2007 has exposed the failure of the monetary policies in no uncertain term. The high wages strategy under new international labour market conditions cannot be sustained. These are some of the added difficulties facing poor with ambitions to eradicate poverty. Pakistan will have to face up and overcome these difficulties if she is to deal with her poverty problem.

I have reached the end of my story and the story of rich and poor nations. I feel empty, sad and not so hopeful and yet I must hope that one day, Pakistan will have a new Leader and an effective state, which will adopt rapid industrialisation under protection as a narrow objective and the nation will go along with that to attain international respect and economic prosperity. I do not think I would still be alive to see that day but I have paid my debt to my birth country.

REFERENCES

1. Abramovitz, Moses, 'resources and Output Trends in the United States since 1870' in AER, Vol 46. No2, 1956.

2. Abramovitz, Moses, 'The Search for the Sources of Growth: Areas of Ignorance, Old and New' in Journal of Economic History, Vol. 53, No.2, 1993.

3. Aghion, P, et al., 'Industrial Policy and Competition' Harvard University Press, Cambridge, 2012.

4. Acemoglu, D, and Robinson, J.A. 'Why Nation Fail' Books 2014.

5. Armentano, Dominick, 'Antitrust: The Case for Repeal' Cato Institute, Washington, 2001.

6. Arrow, J. K, 'An extension of Basic Theorems of Classical Welfare Economics' in Proceedings of the Second Berkeley Symposiums of Mathematical Statistics, edited by J Nayman, Berkeley.calif: 1951.

7. Ayres, C.E. 'The Theory of Economic Progress' University of North Carolina Press, Chapel Hill, 1944

8. Barro, Robert, 'Inflation and Growth' Review of Federal Reserve Bank of St Louis, vol 78, 1996

9. Baumol, W.J. et al., 'Good Capitalism, Bad Capitalism, And the Economics of Growth and Prosperity' Yale University Press, New Haven & London.

10. Bentham, Jeremy, 'An Introduction to the Principles of Morals and Legislation' Claredon Press, Oxford, 1907.

11. Bhagwati, Jagdish, 'Free Trade Today' Princeton University Press, Princeton. 2002

12. Bruno, M and Easterly, W, 'Inflation crises and Long Run Economic Growth' NBER, Working Paper No: 5209, Cambridge, 1995

13. Botero, Giovanni, 'The Reason of State', Yale University Press, New Haven, 1956

14. Buchanan, James, 'What Should Economists Do?' Liberty Press, Indianapolis, 1970

15. Carey, Mathew, 'Essays on Political Economy; or, The Most Certain Means of Promoting the Wealth, Power, Resources and Happiness of Nations: Applied particularly to the United States, H.C. Carey & I. Lea, Philadelphia, 1822.

16. Chang, Ha-Joon, 'Rethinking East Asian Industrial policy-past Records and prospects' in 'industrial policy, innovation, and Economic Growth; The experience of Japan and The Asian NIEs' ed. Wong et al., Singapore University Press, Singapore, 2001.

17. Chang, Ha-Joon, 'Bad Samaritans' Rh Business Books, London, 2007.

18. Chang, Ha-Joon, Kicking Away the Ladder: Development Strategy in Historical Perspective' anthem, London, 2002

19. Chang, Ha-Joon, 'Rethinking Development Economics' Anthem, London, 2003

20. Cuming, Bruce, 'Korea place in the Sun: A Modern History' W.W Norton, London, 2005.

21. Dani, R, 'Growth Strategies' Harvard University Press, Cambridge, 2003.

22. Davis, R, 'The Rise of Protection in England, 1689-1786' Economic History Review, vol. 19, 1966.

23. Debreu, G, 'A Theory of Value' Wiley, New York. 1959.

24. Dennison, Edward, 'Why Growth Rates Differ' Brooking Institution Press, Washington D.C. 1967

25. Dennison, Edward, 'Accounting for Economic Growth' Brooking Institution Press, Washington D.C. 1974.

26. Easterly, William, 'the Elusive Quest for Growth: Economists' Adventure and Misadventure in the Tropics', MIT Press, and Cambridge, Mass. 2001

27. Easterly, William, and Levine, Ross, 'It's Not Factor Accumulation: Stylised Facts and Growth Models, 'World Bank Economic Review 15 (2) 2001

28. Easterly, William, 'The White Man's Burden: Why the West Efforts to aid the rest have done so much Ill and so Little Good' Penguin, New York, 2006

29. Eckert, Carter, 'Korea Old and New: A History' IIchokak, Soaul, 1990.

30. Edwards, Sebastian, 'Openness, Trade Liberalization, and Growth in Developing Countries' Journal of Economic Literature, 31, no.3, 1993.

31. Ferguson, N, 'Empire: The Rise and Demise of the British World Order and Lessons for Global Powers' Penguin Books, 2003.

32. Fisher, Stanley, 'Globalization and Its Challenges' AER Vol.93, No.2, 1993.

33. Friedman, Milton, 'Essays in Positive Economics' Chicago University Press, Chicago. 1953

34. Fukuyama, Francis, 'The end of History and the Last Man' Free Press. New York, 1992.

35. Fukuyama, Francis, 'State Building: Governance and World Order in the 21st Century' New York, 2004.

36. Fukuyama, Francis, 'After the Neocons: America at the Crossroads', Profile Books, London, 2006.

37. Galbraith, James, 'Development's Discontents: How to Explain the Link between economics and Democracy and how not to' in Democracy. A Journal of Ideas, Issue 2, Fall 2006.

38. Galbraith, John Kenneth, 'American Capitalism: The Concept of Countervailing power' Houghton Mifflin, Boston, 1952.

39. Galbraith, John Kenneth, 'The New Industrial State' Houghton Miff. Boston. 1967.

40. Galbraith, John Kenneth, 'The World Economy since the wars' Mandarin, London, 1995.

41. Geertz, Clifford, 'Myrdal', Mythology' No: 1, Encounter 33.

42. Glaeser, L, 'Do Institutions Cause Growth.'

43. Gras, N S B, 'Stages in Economic History' Journal of Economic and Business History, II, 1930

44. Gulick, S, 'Evolution of the Japanese' Fleming House, New York, 1903

45. Graham, Frank, 'some aspects of Protection further considered' in QJE, Vol.37, 1923.

46. Hamilton, Alexander, 'Report on the Subject of Manufactures' (1791), the Library of America, reprinted in 1893.

47. Hansen, Lars & Heckman, 'The Empirical Foundations of Calibration' (1996), Journal of Economic Perspectives' vol.10

48. Hasan, P, 'Learning from the Past: A Fifty Years Perspective on Pakistan's Development' The Pakistan Development Review 36, Winter 1997

49. Hasan, A. 'Pakistan Report: Asia Study Group2020' Islamabad, May 2012

50. Hobbes, D, 'Leviathan' London, 1651

51. Hobson, John M, 'The Eastern Origins of Western Civilization' Cambridge University Press, Cambridge. 2004

52. Hecksher, Eli, 'Mercantilism' Allen & Unwin, London. 1935.

53. Heilbroner, Robert, 'Is Economic Relevant: A Reader in Political Economics' Goodyear Publishing Company, Pacific Palisades, 1971.

54. Heilbroner, Robert, 'The Worldly Philosophers' Simon & Schuster, New York, 1999.

55. Hoffman, W G, 'The Growth of Industrial Production in Great Britain: A Quantitative Study' Economic History Review, II, No.2, 1949

56. Hume, D, 'A Treatise of Human Nature' Clarendon Press, Oxford, 1896.

57. Huntington, S, and Harrison, 'Culture Matters-How Values Shape Human Progress' Basic Books, New York, 2000.

58. Juhasz, Reka, 'Temporary protection and Technology Adoption: Evidence from the Napoleonic Blockade' LSE, 2014.

59. Kang, David, 'Crony capitalism, corruption, and development in South Korea and Philippines' Cambridge University Press, Cambridge, 2005.

59a. Khaldun, Ibn. 'The Muqaddimah: An Introduction to History. Translated by Rosenthal,F. Online Version.

60. Kemal et al. 'Sources of Growth in Pakistan' in Parikh, K, 'Explaining Growth: a South Asian Perspective' Oxford University Press, New Delhi. 2006.

61. Keynes, John Maynard, 'The General Theory of Employment, Interest and Money' Macmillan, London, 1935.

62. Keynes, John Maynard, 'The End of Laissez-faire' The Hogarth Press, London, 1926.

63. Khan, S, 'Macro-determinants of Total Factor Productivity in Pakistan' State Bank of Pakistan, working paper 10. Karachi. 2006.

64. Kohli, Atul, 'State-directed Development' Cambridge University Press, Cambridge, 2004.

65. Kotwal et al., 'Why Poverty persists in India: A Framework for Understanding Indian Economy' Oxford University Press, 1994

66. Kregel, Jan, 'External Financing for Development and International Financial Stability' G-24 Discussion Paper Series, No: 32, UNCTAD, Geneva, and October 2004.

67. Kregel, Jan et al. 'Banking and Financing of Development: A Schumpeterian and Minskyan Perspective' in Silvana de Paula and Gary Dymski (Eds) 'Reimaging Growth' Zed, London, 2005

68. Krueger, A. O. And Tuncer, B. 'An Empirical Test of the Infant Industry Argument' American Economic Review, 72, 1982.

69. Krugman, Paul, 'Rethinking International Trade' MIT Press, Cambridge, Mass, 1990.

70. Krugman, Paul, (Ed) 'Strategic Trade Policy and new International Economics' Cambridge.1986

71. Krugman, Paul, 'Ricardo's Difficult Idea, why Intellectuals Don't Understand Comparative Advantage' in Gary Cook (Eds) 'The Economics and Politics of International Trade, Freedom and Trade' Vol, II, Rutledge, London, 1998.

72. Kuhn, Thomas, 'The Structure of Scientific Revolution' Chicago University Press, 1962.

73. Kuznets, Simon, 'Shares of Upper-Income Groups in Income and Savings' National Bureau of Economic Research' Cambridge, MA. 1953.

74. Kuznets, Simon, 'Economic Growth and Structure' Heinemann, London, 1965

75. Kuznets, Simon, 'Population, Capital, and Growth' Heinemann, London, 1973

76. Lawrence, BB & Karim, A, 'on violence: A Reader' Duke University Press, Duke. 2007.

77. Lendes, David, 'The Wealth and Poverty of Nations' Norton, New York, 1998.

78. Lendes, David, 'Culture Makes Almost All the Difference' In L Harrison & S Huntington 'Culture Matters-How Values Shape Human Progress' Basic Books, New York, 2000.

79. Leontief, Wassily, 'Input-Output Economics' Oxford University Press, 1966.

80. List, Friedrick, 'the System of political economy' Longman, London, 1885.

81. Lucas, Robert e, 'On the Mechanics of Economic Development' in JME, Vol, 22, 1988.

82. Mahalanobis, P, 'Some Observations on the Process of Growth of National Income' Sankhya, 1953

83. Malthus, Thomas Robert, 'Essay on Population' Macmillan, New York, 1966.

84. Marshall, Alfred, 'Principles of Economics' Macmillan, London, 1890.

85. Marx, Karl & Engels, Friedrich, 'The Manifesto of the Communist Party, Collected Works, Progress Publishers, Moscow. 1976.

86. Matthews, R.C.O, et al., 'Slower Growth in the Western World' Heinemann, London. 1982

87. Meek, Ronald, 'The Economics of Physiocracy' Harvard University Press, Cambridge, Mass. 1935.

88. Meyen, J, J, is quoted in Reinert, E S, 'How Rich Countries Got Rich...' Constable, London, 2007.

89. Mill, James, 'Elements of political economy' Kelley, New York, 1963 (reprint)

90. Mill, John Stuart, 'Principles of political economy' Longmans, London, 1909.

91. Mitchell, Wesley Claire, 'Types of Economic Theory, From Mercantilism to Institutionalism' Kelley, New York, 1967.

92. Milward, A and Saul, S, 'The Economic Development of Continental Europe, 1780-1870' Allen and Unwin, London. 1979.

93. Misra, B. B. 'The Bureaucracy in India: An Historical Analysis of Development up to 1947' Oxford University Press, New Delhi, 1977.

94. Moore, Barrington, 'Serial Origins of Dictatorship and Democracy: Land and Peasant in the Making of the Modern world' Beacon Press, Boston, 1966.

95. Morgenthau, Henry Jr, 'Germany is Our Problem: A Plan for Germany' Harper, New York, 1945.

96. Myrdal, Gunnar, 'Asian Drama' Pantheon Books, New York, 1971.

97. Naqvi, S.N.H, and Kemal, A. R. 'Privatisation, Efficiency and Employment in Pakistan' Pakistan Development Review,

98. Nield, Robert, 'Public Corruption- the Dark side of social Evolution' Anthem Press, London, 2002.

99. Nagaraj, R, 'Growth Inequality and Social Development in India: Is Inclusive Growth Possible?' Palgrave Macmillan, New York, 2012.

100. Nordhaus, William D, & Tobin, James, 'Is Growth Obsolete?' In National Bureau of Economic Research, Economic Growth Series, Vol. 96, Columbia University Press, New York, 1972.

101. North, Douglass C, 'Structure and Change in Economic History' WW Norton, New York, 1981.

102. North, Douglass C, 'Institutions, Institutional Change, and Economic Performance' Cambridge University Press, Cambridge. 1990.

103. North, Douglass C, 'Understanding the Process of Economic Change' Princeton University Press, Princeton. 2005.

104. Nozick, Robert, 'Anarchy, State and Utopia' Basic Books, New York, 1974.

105. Nye, J, 'the Myth of Free Trade Britain and Fortress France: Tariffs and Trades in the Nineteen Century' Journal of Economic History, Vol. 51. 1991

106. Okun, Arthur, 'Equality and Efficiency: The Big Trade-offs' The Brooking Institution, Washington, D.C (1975)

106a. Olah, Daniel. 'The Amazing Arab Scholar Who Beat Adam Smith by Half a Millennium' Online Version. 2017

107. Pareto, V, 'the Mind and Society' Translated by A. Bongiorno & A. Livingstone. Harcourt, Brace and Co, New York, 1935

108. Pao-Yu Ching, 'China: Socialist Development and Capitalist Restoration.'

109. Pigou, A C, 'The economics of welfare' Macmillan, London, 1920.

110. Piketty, Thomas, 'Capital: in the Twenty-First Century' Harvard University Press, Cambridge, USA, 2014

111. Porter, Michael, 'the competitive advantage of Nations' Free Press, New York, 1990.

112. Quesnay, Francois, 'Traite des effects et de l' Usage de la saignee' d'Houry, Paris, 1750

113. Quesnay, Francois, 'Circulation of Blood' in Meek, Ronald

114. Rahul & Vakulabharanam, 'Growth and Distribution Regimes in India' December 2012

115. Ray, Rajat, 'Industrialization in India: Growth and Conflict in the Private Corporate Sector, 1914- 47' Oxford University Press, New Delhi, 1979.

116. Ramsay, G D, 'The English Woollen Industry, 1500-1750' Macmillan, London. 1982

117. Raymond, D, 'Thoughts on Political Economy' Fielding Lucas, Baltimore, 1920

118. Rawls, John, 'Theory of Justice' Columbia University Press, New York, 1971

119. Rawski, T.G. 'Economic Growth and Employment in China' The World Bank, 1979

120. Reinert, Erik, 'How Rich Countries Got Rich...and Why Poor Countries Stay Poor' Constable, London, 2008.

120 a. Riaz, T. 'Pakistan Energy Sector: A Study in Sector Planning' Feroz Sons, Pakistan, 1984.

121. Ricardo, David, 'The Principles of Political Economy and Taxation' John Murray, London, 1917.

122. Ridgeway, William, 'The Political Writings of Richard Cobden, 1868' London.

123. Robbins, Lionel, 'The Theory of Economic Policy in English Classical economics' Macmillan, London, 1952.

124. Rodriguez, F and Dani, R, 'Trade Policy and Economic Growth: A Sceptic's Guide to the Cross-national Evidence' in Ben Bernanke and Rogoff, K, S (Eds) Macroeconomics Annual 2000, MIT Press, 2001.

125. Rodrik, Dani, 'Has Globalization Gone too far?' Institute of Economic Affairs, 1997

126. Roemer, John, 'Theories of Distributive Justice' Harvard University Press, 1996

127. Rothermund, Dietmar, 'An Economic History of India: from pre-colonial time to 1986' Groom Helm, London, 1986.

128. Romer, Paul M, 'Increasing Returns and Long-run Growth' Journal of Political Economy, Vol. 94. No: 5. 1986.

129. Romer, Paul M, 'The Origins of Endogenous Growth' Journal of Economic Perspectives. Vol 8. No: 1. 1994.

129a. Romer, Paul M, 'The Trouble with Macroeconomics, Update'. Paul Romer Blog, 2016.

130. Rostow, WW, 'The Stages of Economic Growth' Cambridge University Press, Cambridge, 1960

131. Sachs, Jeffrey, 'The End of Poverty: Economic Possibilities for Our Time' Penguin Press, New York, 2005.

132. Samuelson, Paul, 'International Trade and the equalisation of Factor Prices' in EJ Vol. 58, 1948.

133. Schmoller, Gustav, 'The Mercantile system and its Historical Significance' Macmillan Kelley, New York 1967.

134. Schumpeter, Joseph Alois, 'Theory of Economic Development' Harvard University Press, Mass, 1934.

135. Schumpeter, Joseph Alois, 'History of Economic Analysis' Oxford University Press, New York, 1954.

136. Schumpeter, Joseph Alois, 'Capitalism, Socialism and Democracy' Harper, New York, 1942

137. Scot, M, 'Pay or Delay' Competition Policy International, Vol. 4, No.2. 2013

138. Sen, Amartya, 'Development as Freedom' Oxford University Press, Oxford, 2001 Jean,

139. Sen, Amartya, and Dreze, 'An Uncertain Glory India...'Penguin Books, 2013.

140. Shelly, M, 'Rambles in Germany and Italy' Edward Monkton, London, 1843.

141. Sivasubramonian, S, 'The National Income of India in the twentieth century' Oxford University Press, New Delhi, 2000.

142. Spencer, Herbert, 'Man versus the State.'

143. Serra, Antonio, 'Breve trattato delle cause che possono far abbondare l'ore e l'argento dove nonsono miniere' Lazzaro Scorriggio, Naples, 1613.

144. Smith, Adam, 'The Theory of Moral Sentiments' in collect works. Cadell & Davies, London, 1812.

145. Smith, Adam, 'The Wealth of Nations' Chicago University Press, Chicago, 1976.

146. Sombart, W, 'Der Moderne Kapitalismus' Duncker and Humblot. Leipzig, 1916

147. Solow, Robert, 'A Contribution to the Theory of Economic Growth' QJE, Vol.70, 1956.

148. Solow, Robert, 'Technical Change and the Aggregate Production Function' RE&S vol, 39. 1957.

149. Solow, Robert, 'Perspectives on Growth Theory' JEP vol, 8. No: 1, 1994.

150. Srinivasan, T. N. 'Information-technology Enabled services and India's Growth Prospects' Brooking Trade Forum, 203-31, 2005.

151. Stieglitz, Joseph, 'Whiter Reform- Ten years of Transition' in H –J Chang, 2001, ed. 'The Rebel within Joseph Stieglitz at the World Bank' Anthem Press, London.

152. Stieglitz, Joseph, 'Globalization and Its Discontents' Norton, New York, 2002.

153. Stiglitz, J.E. and Greenwald, B.C, 'Creating A Learning Society' Columbia University Press, New York, 2014.

154. Sun Yat-Sen, 'The International Development of China' G.P. Putman, New York. 1929

155. Taylor, M W, 'Men versus the State: Herbert Spencer and Late Victorian Liberalism' Oxford University Press, 1992.

156. Tennyson, GB (Ed) 'A Carlyle Reader: Selections from the Writing of Thomas Carlyle' Cambridge University Press, Cambridge. 1984.

157. Trebilcock, C, 'The industrialisation of the continental powers, 1780-1914' Longman, London. 1981

158. Thunen, JHV, 'Der isolierte Staat in Beziehung auf.........' Penthes, Hamburg, 1826

159. Veblen, Torstein, 'The Instinct of Workmanship' Macmillan Co, New York, 1914

160. Veblen, Torstein, 'The Theory of Leisure Class' Modern Library, New York.1934.

161. Veblen, Torstein, 'Why is Economics not an Evolutionary Science' in QJE, XII, July 1898.

162. Walras, Leon, 'Elements of Economic Pure (1874-77)' Academy of Lausanne, Switzerland, 1878

163. Wade, Robert, 'Governing the Market: Economic Theory and the Role of Government in East Asian Industrialization' Princeton University Press, Princeton, 1990.

164. Warsh, D, 'Knowledge and the Wealth of Nations, A story of economic discovery' Norton, NY, 2006

165. Webb, M, 'The Diary of Beatrice Webb: The power to Alter Things' Virgo/LSE London, 1984.

166. Weber, Max, 'Economy and Society' Bedminster Press, New York, 1968 (original 1904)

167. Weber, Max, 'The Protestant Ethic and the Spirit of Capitalism' Allen and Unwin, London, 1930

168. Wei, Li, 'The Impact of Chinese Reforms on the Performance of Chinese state-owned Enterprises' Journal of Political Economy, No.105, 1997

169. Weisbrot, M, Naiman, R, and Kim, J, 'The Emperor Has No Growth: Declining Growth Rates in the Era of Globalization' Centre for Economic and Policy Research, Washington DC. Briefing Paper, September 2000

170. Williamson, John (Ed), 'The Political Economy of Policy Reform' Inst. For International Economics, Washington D.C. 1994.

171. Williamson, John, 'The Washington Consensus as Policy Prescription for Development' Inst of Int Economics, Washington D.C. 2004.

172. Wolf, Martin, 'The Morality of the Market' in Foreign Policy, Sept/Oct 2003.

173. Wolf, Martin, 'Why Globalization Works' Yale University Press, New Haven, 2004.

174. World Bank, 'The East Asian Miracle: Economic Growth and Public Policy' Oxford University Press, New York, 1993.

175. Yifu-Lin, 'Perspective on Chinese Economic Growth' The World Bank, 2012